D1076652

Quasi-Markets and Social Policy

Biomedical Library
Queen's University Belfast
Tel: 028 9097 2710
E-mail: biomed.info@qub.ac.uk

For due dates and renewals see
'My Account' at
http://qu-prism.qub.ac.uk/TalisPrism/

This book must be returned not later than
its due date, but is subject to recall if in
demand

Fines are imposed on overdue books

Quasi-Markets and Social Policy

Edited by

Julian Le Grand

and

Will Bartlett

MACMILLAN

1 52762

Selection, editorial matter, Chapters 1, 2 and 9 © Julian Le Grand and
Will Bartlett 1993
Individual chapters © Will Bartlett and Lyn Harrison,
Glen Bramley, Lesley Hoyes and Robin Means, Carol Propper 1993

All rights reserved. No reproduction, copy or transmission of
this publication may be made without written permission.

No paragraph of this publication may be reproduced, copied or
transmitted save with written permission or in accordance with
the provisions of the Copyright, Designs and Patents Act 1988,
or under the terms of any licence permitting limited copying
issued by the Copyright Licensing Agency, 90 Tottenham Court
Road, London W1P 9HE.

Any person who does any unauthorised act in relation to this
publication may be liable to criminal prosecution and civil
claims for damages.

First published 1993 by
MACMILLAN PRESS LTD
Houndmills, Basingstoke, Hampshire RG21 6XS
and London
Companies and representatives
throughout the world

ISBN 0–333–56518–5 hardcover
ISBN 0–333–56519–3 paperback

A catalogue record for this book is available
from the British Library.

10   9   8   7   6   5   4
02   01   00   99

Printed in Hong Kong

07 FEB 2001

Contents

Acknowledgements

This book is an outcome of the Quasi-Markets Programme set up by the School for Advanced Urban Studies in 1989. The writing of the book and most of the research reported in it was funded by the Economic and Social Research Council under Grant No. W-102-25-1016, as part of the Functioning of Markets Initiative. Other funders who have contributed to the Quasi-Markets Programme include the Joseph Rowntree Foundation and the King Edward's Hospital Fund for London. We are grateful to all these organisations for their support.

Although each chapter of the book is individually attributed, all have been discussed and commented on by members of the Quasi-Market Programme. The book is thus in large part the product of a collective enterprise, although the contributors vary in their optimism about the ability of quasi-markets to improve the delivery of welfare services. We are grateful to Gervas Huxley and Marilyn Taylor for their contributions to those discussions. There have also been many fruitful debates of the relevant issues with Howard Glennerster and other members of the Welfare State Programme at the LSE. John Cable, Research Co-ordinator of the ESRC's Functioning of Markets Initiative, organised useful workshops as part of the Initiative; he has also contributed directly to the project in several other ways. Much of the material has been presented in other seminars, workshops and lectures throughout Britain and elsewhere; although too numerous to list, we are grateful to the participants of those occasions for stimulating questions and comments.

Lorraine Cantle has helped organise the production of the manuscript with her usual efficiency and good humour. Other members of the SAUS support staff have helped in a number of small but significant ways. And our families have bravely put up with the dislocation to domestic life that inevitably seems to accompany this kind of project. To them all, our deepest thanks.

Julian Le Grand
Will Bartlett

Notes on the Contributors

Julian Le Grand is the Richard Titmuss Professor of Health Policy at the London School of Economics and Professorial Fellow, King's Fund Institute. Previously he was Professor of Public Policy and Director of the School for Advanced Urban Studies, University of Bristol. He is a leading authority on the economics of the welfare state. His recent publications include *The Economics of Social Problems* (with Carol Propper and Ray Robinson) and *Equity and Choice*.

Will Bartlett is a Research Fellow at the School for Advanced Urban Studies, University of Bristol, researching into the role of quasi-markets in the provision of welfare services. He has previously worked at the Universities of Bath and Southampton and at the European University Institute in Florence.

Glen Bramley is a Senior Lecturer in the School for Advanced Urban Studies, University of Bristol, specialising in housing, local government finance and the economic analysis of public policy. He has written extensively on housing finance, needs affordability and supply, on equalisation grants to local government, and on more general policy analysis issues.

Lyn Harrison is a Lecturer in Health Policy at the School for Advanced Urban Studies, University of Bristol. She is working on a range of research and evaluation projects concerned with the implementation of quasi-market reforms in health and social care.

Lesley Hoyes is a Research Fellow at the School for Advanced Urban Studies, University of Bristol. She has undertaken considerable research and consultancy work around her central interest in the development and implementation of community care policies. She is currently joint director (with Robin Means) of a major research project studying the impact of community care reforms on users and carers.

Robin Means is a Lecturer in Social Policy at the School for Advanced Urban Studies, University of Bristol, where he has worked on housing and social care issues. He is currently joint director (with Lesley Hoyes) of a research project studying the impact of community care reforms upon users and carers.

Carol Propper is a Lecturer in the Department of Economics and the School for Advanced Urban Studies, University of Bristol. She specialises in the economic analysis of health care markets. She publishes regularly in economic journals and has recently co-authored *The Economics of Social Problems* (with Julian Le Grand and Ray Robinson).

Introduction

1

Julian Le Grand
and Will Bartlett

When a new Conservative Government came into power in Britain in 1979, the welfare state was the biggest area of non-market activity in the British economy. The vast bulk of social security, education and health care, and a large proportion of housing and social care, were produced, allocated and distributed by bureaucratic mechanisms. Many of these activities dwarfed market activities. The National Health Service, for example, was the largest employer in Western Europe; and the welfare state as a whole consumed almost a quarter of the Gross Domestic Product.

In these areas, how much was produced and who got the fruits of production were not the unintended consequences of self-interested decisions made by individual producers and consumers operating in a competitive market. Rather they were the outcome of conscious decisions of politicians, bureaucrats and professionals operating in a bureaucratic environment and, ostensibly at least, intending to work in such a way as to further the public interest.

Given the market ideology of the 1979 Government and the rhetoric that accompanied its arrival, it might have been expected that the welfare state would be an immediate casualty. However, to the surprise of many commentators, on the whole the first two Thatcher administrations avoided direct confrontation with the welfare system. With the major exception of council house sales,

1

the basic structure of the welfare state in 1987 was much the same as in 1979. The vast majority of the population was still served by state-funded and state-provided systems of education, health care, social services and social security. Even the proportion of national resources going into public welfare did not change significantly; in 1987/88 it was exactly the same percentage of the Gross Domestic Product (23 per cent) as it had been in 1978/79 (Le Grand, 1990b).

Quite why there was this fundamental stability during the period is an interesting question but one that has been extensively discussed elsewhere (see, for example, Le Grand and Winter, 1987, and Le Grand, 1990b). Whatever the reason the calm was not to last. A major offensive against the bureaucratic structures of welfare provision was launched in 1988 and 1989: years that in retrospect will be seen as critical in the history of British social policy. For it was then that the Government began to apply a programme of introducing internal or 'quasi'-markets to the welfare state. It is these quasi-markets in welfare – their development, their impact and their desirability – that are the subject of this book.

'Quasi-market' is not perhaps a term that will be immediately familiar to all potential readers of the book and we explain later in this chapter what we mean by it.* However, to set the context for that discussion, we begin by describing the development of these markets. We conclude the chapter with an outline of the rest of the book.

The Growth of Quasi-Markets

As noted above, a striking feature of the welfare state during the first two Thatcher administrations from 1979 to 1987 was its preservation. This was confirmed in a recent publication by the LSE Welfare State Programme (Hills, 1990). This found that, contrary to popular

---

* Our use of the term derives from an intervention by Glen Bramley in one of the early discussions that led to the setting up of the SAUS Quasi-Market Programme. However, we have subsequently discovered that it was originally used in this kind of context by Oliver Williamson (1975, p. 8).

perception, indicators of welfare inputs, outputs and outcomes in key areas such as education, health care and community care had either remained constant or had actually risen over the period, even when changes in needs were taken into account. There were significant exceptions, notably in housing and in some areas of social security, but the overall picture was one of a possibly surprising degree of resilience.

More importantly from the point of view of this book, the basic form of the welfare state remained intact. Again there were exceptions, of which by far the most significant was the sale of council houses (Hills and Mullings, 1990; Forrest and Murie, 1991). There was also some contracting-out of ancillary services in the Health Service; the development of the Assisted Places Scheme for school education; and a significant growth in the private finance and provision of some areas of welfare, notably pensions, health care, school education and residential care for elderly people (Le Grand, Winter and Woolley, 1990; Glennerster and Low, 1990; Evandrou, Falkingham and Glennerster, 1990). However, apart from these, overall the basic structure of welfare provision and finance was much the same in 1987 as it had been in 1948. The National Health Service, the personal social services, social security benefits, most education and the (sizeable) remaining council house stock were all still largely both paid for and provided by the state at either central or local level.

But all this was to change in 1988 and 1989 (Le Grand, 1991b). In those years, the Government introduced a series of radical reforms in key parts of the welfare state, all with a fundamental similarity. In each case, state finance of the service concerned was to be retained; but the system of service provision was to change, often radically. All the reforms involved a decentralisation of decision-making; most also involved the introduction of competition in provision. In these cases, the state was to become primarily only a purchaser of welfare services, with state provision being systematically replaced by a system of independent providers competing with one another in internal or 'quasi'-markets. The method of finance was also to change. In some cases a centralised state agency would continue to act as the principal purchaser; in others an earmarked budget or voucher would be given directly to potential users, or, more commonly, to agents acting on their behalf, who would then allocate the budget as they chose between competing providers.

The first of these changes was the set of reforms to primary and secondary school education introduced as part of the Education Reform Act of 1988 (discussed by, *inter alia*, Glennerster, 1991). These included provisions for *opting out, open enrolment, formula funding*, and *the local management of schools* (LMS). Under the opting-out provisions, schools could choose whether to be funded by their local education authority or by the central government. Under open enrolment, parents could choose within certain limits the school to which they could send their child. Under formula funding, the amount of resources a school (opted-out or not) received depended in large part on the number of pupils it could attract. Both opted-out and LMS schools were given control over the internal allocation of their resources, becoming in effect semi-independent providers. Together these reforms amounted to a form of education 'voucher', with resources being no longer primarily allocated to schools by bureaucratic decision, but by the choices of parents.

The next major quasi-market developments were the National Health Service reforms detailed in the White Paper *Working for Patients* (Department of Health, 1989b) and implemented in the National Health Service and Community Care Act of 1990 (discussed by, *inter alia*, Barr, Glennerster and Le Grand, 1989; Culyer, Maynard and Posnett, 1990; Klein and Day, 1991; and Maynard, 1991). These involved the splitting of health authorities into *purchaser* and *provider* units and the introduction of *GP fundholders*, who also acted as purchasers. The provider units were of two kinds: *directly managed units* that nominally at least were still to be managed by the health authority and *Trusts* that were essentially independent of direct authority control. The GP fundholding scheme was again a form of voucher, whereby GPs with practices over a certain size held budgets to be spent on a range of secondary care services for each of their patients that they could allocate on behalf of those patients. Although not a voucher scheme in the same sense, the purchasing health authorities and provider units were also intended to operate in a quasi-market environment, with the provider units competing for contracts from the purchasing health authorities and from GP fundholders. By April 1992, the purchaser/provider split was almost complete in all health authorities, and around 160 Trusts and 600 GP fundholding practices had been established.

Another set of quasi-market proposals appeared in the same Act concerned with community care, based on the Griffiths Report

(1988), and the subsequent White Paper (Department of Health, 1989a). Generally, as in the case of health authorities, local social services departments were supposed to reduce their role as providers, becoming instead primarily *purchasing* or *enabling* authorities, buying community care services from independent *provider units*. And, in another parallel with health, this time to the GP fundholder, it was envisaged that eventually budgets for purchasing care would be allocated to *care-managers*, who would be appointed for each client to construct a package of care for the client concerned. In making up the package of care, the care-manager would consider bids from competing organisations, including public, voluntary and private sector agencies. Again, this part of the system can be viewed as essentially a voucher scheme, with care-managers allocating budgets on behalf of clients between competing institutions and with the allocation of resource being determined by client choice (as delegated to care-managers) instead of by bureaucratic decision. The reforms were phased in from 1 April 1991.

Ironically there is one aspect of these changes that could be viewed as moving away from a market system of resource allocation. The budgets that care-managers will have, or should have, will be partly financed by eliminating the residential care allowance element in social security. This allowance was in one respect closer to being a genuine voucher than the new system, since the budget allocation was under the control of the client her- or himself and not, as it will now be, under the control of an agent acting on the client's behalf. However, under the new system, the budget will be available to spend on care other than residential, so in that respect at least it is more market-like than the old system.

Quasi-market developments have also characterised the development of housing. Under the 1988 Housing Act, the state would continue to subsidise local authority tenants (primarily through Housing Benefit); but tenants were now able to choose their landlords from competing suppliers. However, transfers of this kind have not been significant in practice, with perhaps the main role of the legislation being to spur local authorities into a more consumer-responsive style. Instead, there has been a wave of interest among local authorities in *voluntarily* divesting themselves of their housing stock, generally to a specially created housing association akin to a management buyout of a monopoly supplier. Even more significant from the quasi-markets perspective is the gradual but accelerating phenomenon of the expansion of the housing association movement to supplant local authorities as the main new providers of social housing; while the role of the state as a funder is shifting from general 'bricks and mortar' subsidies to individual means-tested subsidy in the form of Housing Benefit. Again, this can be likened to a voucher; indeed its portability extends into the private rented sector.

Although we shall be concentrating in this book primarily on these changes in school education, health care, community care and housing, it should be noted that similar changes have occurred in other areas of welfare, including higher education and social security. In higher education, a bidding process for contracts to teach undergraduates at higher education institutions was set up in the late 1980s. Also, fees for students were raised, student grants frozen and a top-up loans system introduced. The first of these changes again reflected a shift from the state as purchaser and provider to the state as purchaser only, but a centralised one. In partial contrast, the student aid system and the increased reliance on student fees constituted the basic elements of a (partly repayable) voucher scheme with students exercising their choices between independent institutions and with the pattern of resource allocation being partly determined by the pattern of student choice.

An Executive Agency has been set up for social security benefits, with the intention of separating service delivery from policy formulation: essentially a split between purchaser and provider, although as yet with only one provider. There were also significant changes on a more micro level in social security. In particular, the Independent Living Fund, for example, was set up in 1988 to provide cash payments to severely disabled people to enable them to assemble their own package of care (Kestenbaum, 1990; Craig, forthcoming).

Given their radical nature, it is not surprising that many of these measures have been highly controversial with equally passionate critics and proponents. The full impact will take several years to be felt. But it is already clear that, if these changes continue to be implemented in their present form, the provision of welfare in the 1990s will be very different from that of the previous forty years. Under the 'old' system of welfare local governments owned, managed and directly financed nursery, primary and secondary schools, local colleges and polytechnics; they owned and managed large stocks of public housing, letting them out to tenants at subsidised rents; they owned and operated residential homes and provided other facilities for the care of children, elderly people and people with physical or mental handicaps. Similarly, the central government owned and managed hospitals and other medical facilities; it funded and provided a general practitioner service and it financed students and allocated their numbers to higher education institutions.

In the 1990s central government and/or local authorities will still be *paying* for these activities. But they will no longer be *providing* the services concerned (or, if they do, their role will be increasingly that of a residual provider). Instead, welfare services will be supplied primarily by a variety of semi-independent agencies. Schools will be competing for state-financed pupils; higher education institutions will be competing for students, more and more of whom will be privately financed. Independent hospitals of various kinds will be competing with each other for patients; private and voluntary suppliers will be catering for the residential and domiciliary needs of the clients of local authority social services departments; and housing associations, or even private landlords, will be managing most erstwhile council estates.

All of these changes were of course the product of a Conservative Government. Many of them emanated from the right-wing think-tanks that strongly influenced the ideology of that government, such as the Institute for Economic Affairs and the Adam Smith Institute. However, an important aspect of the quasi-market phenomenon is that proposals of this kind are not confined to the Conservative end of the political spectrum. For instance, in the centre-left publication *Samizdat*, Michael Young proposed a voucher system for GPs, to replace the present payment structure based on capitation fees (Young, 1989). As at present, doctors would receive a payment for each patient they had on their list. Unlike the present system, however, every year patients would have to choose their doctor, or confirm the choice they had already made. In Young's view,

> *this would bring it home to patients that it is they, as taxpayers, who are paying the doctors; and likewise to the doctors who would be less likely, when faced by patients who have their doctors' salaries in their pockets, to consider they are being paid by 'the state'.*

Accountability as well as choice would be enhanced.

In the same issue of *Samizdat*, Patricia Hewitt suggested applying the voucher idea to child-care for the under-fives (Hewitt, 1989). The voucher would be given to each parent at the end of the period of parental leave. Parents could then 'spend' the voucher on a range of approved child-care provision. The value of the voucher could be higher for single parents and for children with special needs. The voucher could only be spent on approved facilities.

The voucher idea has also been extended to the other end of the education ladder (Le Grand, 1987; Barr and Barnes, 1988). The suggestion is that all institutions of higher education should charge full-cost fees, and that all students should receive a non-means-tested grant (or voucher) that would cover those fees plus a generous allowance for maintenance. There is an equity issue here, in that many students (indeed most) come from well-off backgrounds; moreover, many will go on to well-paid jobs as a consequence of the education they have received at public expense. But this could be overcome by the introduction of a graduate tax, originally suggested by Glennerster, Merrett and Wilson (1968), discussed by Le Grand (1987) and Barr and Barnes (1988) and currently being implemented in Australia. This would be a tax set as a proportion of income levied on higher education graduates and collected through the income tax, or through the national insurance system (Barr, 1989). The advantages of the graduate tax would be that, unlike the repayment of conventional loans, people on low incomes would pay less than those on high incomes: hence any deterrent effect on graduates of taking up low-paid activities would be reduced.

A quasi-market idea that was actually put into practice in a welfare-related area well before the Conservative Government came to power involved the replacement of public transport concessionary fare schemes by transport vouchers. The problems with concessionary schemes are numerous. They are usually confined to one form of transport (such as buses or trains) thus disadvantaging those who, for one reason or another, cannot use that particular form (such as those in wheelchairs, for instance). They are also usually specific to one area, so that they provide no help for cross-boundary travel or for travel outside the area. Also for the authority operating them they represent an open-ended commitment, with little idea of exactly how much they will be called upon to contribute.

To provide an alternative to such schemes, a consortium of public transport organisations has set up a non-profit-making company, National Transport Tokens Limited. This provides transport vouchers to local authorities or any other authority operating a concessionary fares scheme. The issuing authority buys a quantity of vouchers (in the form of coin-shaped tokens) from the company and then issues the tokens to eligible concessionary travel-users. They use the tokens as full payment for their travel to any participating operator (buses, trains or taxis). Finally, the operator returns the tokens to the company, who redeems them at their face value, plus a handling charge. Any surplus is shared with the operating authorities. The scheme has obvious advantages. To the users the scheme offers far greater flexibility than concessionary fare schemes, for the tokens can be used for any form of public transport, so long as the relevant operator accepts them. And to the issuing authority it offers budgetary certainty: they know exactly when, where and how much they are paying for the service.

It is also worth noting that quasi-markets in welfare were already in place or are being put into place in other countries. In much of the rest of Europe, social housing is already provided by the equivalent of housing associations. A study of recent reforms in health care in seven European countries concluded that there are 'signs of convergence on the public contract model and increased reliance on market and quasi-market relationships that permit governments to regulate at arm's length' (Hurst, 1991, p. 19; see also van de Ven, 1991). Propper in Chapter 3 of this book illustrates how in the United States contracting-out has long been a prominent feature of health and social care services.

Indeed, as Hoggett (1990) points out, changes of this kind are not even confined to the public sector. So-called 'post-Fordist' changes of a similar type are occurring in the private sector, with companies that were previously vertically integrated and tightly controlled from the centre now increasingly contracting out their operations and engaging in other forms of decentralisation. More widely, there is a worldwide disenchantment with the perceived inefficiency and unresponsiveness of large-scale, centrally planned organisations and a greater reliance on decentralisation and markets, quasi- or otherwise; beliefs that have their most obvious expression in Eastern Europe, but are pervasive throughout the West as well.

Characteristics of Quasi-Markets

We must now specify in a little more detail precisely what we mean by quasi-markets. They are 'markets' because they replace monopolistic state providers with competitive independent ones. They are 'quasi' because they differ from conventional markets in a number of key ways. The differences are on both the supply and the demand sides. On the supply side, as with conventional markets, there is competition between productive enterprises or service suppliers. Thus, in all the schemes described, there are independent institutions (schools, universities, hospitals, residential homes, housing associations, private landlords) competing for customers. However, in contrast to conventional markets, all these organisations are not necessarily out to maximise their profits; nor are they necessarily privately owned. Precisely what the non-profit enterprises do have as their objectives is often unclear, as is their ownership structure.

On the demand side, consumer purchasing power is not expressed in money terms in a quasi-market. Instead either it takes the form of an earmarked budget or 'voucher' confined to the purchase of a specific service allocated to users, or it is centralised in a single state purchasing agency. Also, it is important to note that, in most cases, it is not the direct user who exercises the choices concerning purchasing decisions; instead those choices are often delegated to a third party, such as a social services department or care-manager in community care, and a GP or a health authority in health care.

These welfare quasi-markets thus differ from conventional markets in one or more of three ways: non-profit organisations competing for public contracts, sometimes in competition with for-profit organisations; consumer purchasing power either centralised in a single purchasing agency or allocated to users in the form of vouchers rather than cash; and, in some cases, the consumers represented in the market by agents instead of operating by themselves.

The Rest of the Book

The fact that, as noted above, the quasi-market changes appear to be part of a much bigger social phenomenon makes it certain that they are going to be a prominent feature of the British welfare state throughout the 1990s. It is therefore important that they be examined in an impartial, dispassionate fashion to see whether they yield the benefits their proponents hope, or whether they impose the costs their critics fear. Will they reduce the costs of welfare provision and thereby bring about greater efficiency and resource savings? Or will they prevent sensible planning and thereby create other sources of resource waste? Will they make welfare providers more responsive to the needs and wants of their clients, and increase the choices open to those clients? Or will they distort the relationship between welfare provider and welfare user, replacing one based on trust by one distorted by a suspicious commercialism? Will welfare services serve the poor and/or those really in need, or will the changes simply create two-tier services that discriminate against, and perhaps stigmatise, the most vulnerable people in our society? It is to these kinds of questions that this book is addressed.

Chapter 2 sets out the theoretical framework by which the individual case studies are organised. It focuses on the criteria for evaluation of the success of the quasi-market experiment, and proposes a set of conditions which would have to be fulfilled if these criteria are to be met. Chapter 3 reviews evidence from the health and social care sector in the USA. The next four chapters present the results of detailed case studies in the areas of health care, social care, education, and housing. These chapters form the core of the book. They report the research findings from detailed studies of both the problems involved in the introduction of quasi-markets during their inital stages of implementation, and the variously favourable and unfavourable perceptions of key individuals and organisations responsible for the difficult task of institutional transformation. In Chapter 8 the key policy issue of the appropriate degree of regulation of quasi-markets is discussed. It is suggested that further regulation is largely undesirable but that an important area for future policy action is the improvement of the information flows on the quasi-market. Chapter 9 draws together the main results and findings from the research as a whole, and indicates the areas in which policy action is still required to remedy the defects of existing arrangements, and to fulfil the potential of quasi-markets for the decentralised delivery of welfare services.

A final introductory point. The book's authors include economists and social policy analysts. However, the book is aimed at non-specialists as well as specialists, at policy-makers and practitioners as well as academics. Hence we have tried to avoid technical expositions and to use jargon-free language throughout. This has not always been possible: however, where it has been necessary to use technical terms, they have been explained.

The Theory of Quasi-Markets

2

Will Bartlett
and Julian Le Grand

As noted in Chapter 1, the majority of the quasi-market changes are only just being put into place, and it will not be feasible to assess their empirical consequences for several years. However, this does not mean that any kind of evaluation is impossible. It is possible to undertake a theoretical analysis that specifies the conditions quasi-markets will have to meet if they are to succeed, and then to make a preliminary empirical assessment of the extent to which those conditions appear to be met in practice. However, to do this requires development of the theory of quasi-markets; and such is the aim of this chapter.

The first section of the chapter specifies what might be meant by 'success' in this context – or, more generally, the appropriate criteria for the evaluation of policy changes such as those explored in this book. The second considers the conditions that quasi-markets will have to fulfil if they are to succeed according to those criteria. A concluding section summarises the principal arguments.

Criteria for Evaluation

It would be easy to spend a great deal of time discussing possible criteria for policy evaluation. There are issues concerning their scope (what should be included?), their definition (how should they

13

specified?) and their ownership (whose criteria: politicians, civil servants, users, researchers?). The proper treatment of any of these could take a book on its own. Here we short circuit many of these issues by simply proposing a number of criteria against which the reforms may be judged. They concern *efficiency, responsiveness, choice* and *equity*.

Efficiency

The idea that the criterion of efficiency be applied to the provision of welfare services is anathema to many of those working in the area, as indeed for many of those involved in analysing it. For them, it appears to be, at best, a inappropriate application of a business concept to a field where some conception of social care or need, not commercial profit, is the prime concern and, at worst, simply a disguise for cutting back welfare services.

Yet there is nothing caring about wasting resources. And it is the avoidance of such waste that is the prime motivation behind the application of efficiency considerations in any area, including those that form the welfare state. However, it is important that the term be defined both clearly and in a way that displays sensitivity to the charge of inappropriateness.

The literature on efficiency is replete with references to a large number of different interpretations of the concept. There are also a number of other terms that are used in similar fashion, including, most prominently, value for money. Despite the proliferation, there appear to be two basic concepts that underlie most of these different interpretations. The first of these refers simply to the costs of service provision. On this interpretation, an efficient service is one that minimises the *total costs* of service delivery. The total cost is the aggregate expenditure on the service concerned; so, under this definition, a service is more efficient than another if the total cost of the service is lower.

This definition of efficiency, which we might term *crude efficiency*, is perhaps closest to the way in which the term is used in common parlance. It is also the definition that, in some quarters at least, gives efficiency a bad name. For it apparently ignores anything other than costs. In particular, it appears to be unconcerned with either the *quantity* or the *quality* of the service concerned. A low cost service may also be a low quality and/or a low volume service: that is, it may deliver a low level of benefits 'to the people who use it. A drive for efficiency, interpreted in this way, could become simply an excuse for cost-cutting, regardless of the impact on the quantity or quality of the service provided.

A second concept of efficiency, known to economists as *productive efficiency*, does not suffer from this problem. For this explicitly relates the costs of a service to the quantity and quality of service provision. More specifically, a provider unit is said to be efficient if its activities are organised in such a way that the costs of providing any given quality or quantity of a service are minimised. So, in contrast to crude efficiency, a low-cost operation that delivered a low quantity and quality service that was of little value or benefit to its users could well be *less* productively efficient than a system that was extremely expensive, but that delivered a high quantity and quality service to users; for the costs of the latter per 'unit' of service delivered could be much lower.

Productive efficiency can be related to the other phrase that often features in current discussions concerning the objectives of policy: *value for money*. The dubious reputation of the latter in some circles derives in part from the fact that it is often identified with crude efficiency; hence, as with crude efficiency, a drive for value-for-money can be viewed as a euphemism for cost-cutting. A more sympathetic interpretation would be to identify it with productive efficiency. In that sense, providers that give the most value for money are those which provide a given quantity and quality of service for the lowest possible cost. And this is the way that these terms will be used in this book.

Responsiveness

A common criticism of old-style welfare bureaucracies was that they could on occasion be unresponsive to the concerns of their clients. The critics regarded welfare bureaucrats and professionals as more interested in improving the working conditions of themselves and their staff and/or in pursuing the political and budgetary agendas of the politicians (local or national) to whom they were accountable, than in meeting the needs and wants of users. These criticisms were generally supported by more by anecdote than by systematic empirical evidence; nevertheless enough people had encountered at least one apparently insensitive social worker, an arrogant hospital consultant, an unhelpful teacher, or a recalcitrant housing clerk to give the argument a fundamental plausibility in all areas of welfare.

It is perhaps not surprising therefore that much of the motivation for several of the quasi-market reforms appears to derive from a desire to improve welfare provision in these respects. For example, the White Paper outlining the quasi-market reforms for the NHS, *Working for Patients*, gives as the two objectives of the reform programme presented: 'to give patients . . . better health care' and by providing 'greater . . . rewards for those working in the NHS who successfully respond to local needs and preferences' (DoH, 1989b, pp. 3–4). And the White Paper concerned with quasi-markets in community care, *Caring for People*, includes as one of its four 'key components' of community care that services should 'respond flexibly and sensitively to the needs of individuals and their carers'.

Responsiveness could be viewed as part of the quality of the service and hence as a factor determining the level of 'benefits' derived from it; it could therefore be merged with the definition of productive efficiency to produce an omnibus criterion. However, since considerations of responsiveness appear so prominently in the debates concerning the desirability or otherwise of the reforms, it seems useful to treat them separately for the purposes of this book.

Choice

The importance of increasing user choice is underlined at several points in government documents concerning the quasi-market reforms. So, for example, *Caring for People*, states that one of the 'key components' of community care is that services should 'allow a range of options for consumers' (DoH, 1989a, p. 5). More generally, it argues that 'choice and independence underlies all the Government's proposals' (*ibid*, p. 4). And *Working for Patients* gives as one of its two objectives the aim of giving patients 'greater choice of services available' (DoH, 1989b, p.3).

However, there are a number of different aspects to the concept of choice that are not often brought out in the relevant debates. First, there is the question as to whose choice is the focus of concern.

Increasing the choices open to one set of people (by, for example, offering users of residential care services the opportunity to stay at home) may reduce the choices open to others (carers, for example, now under considerable moral pressure to care for users at home).

Second, there is a distinction between the choice of *service* and the choice of *provider*. The choice of service concerns the choice between the kinds of services received by the client: for example, between domiciliary care or residential care or between hospital or GP care. The choice of provider concerns the choice between several providers offering the same service: a choice between home help providers, for example, for someone in domiciliary care, or between homes for someone in residential care.

The choice of service is often seen by the Government and others as of particular importance. However, choice of provider is also a significant motivating factor behind the Government's attitudes towards the reforms, especially with respect to the involvement of the private and not-for-profit sector. So, for example, in a speech concerning the transfer of funds from the social security budget to local authorities to underpin their community care plans, the Secretary of State for Health stated that:

> *The Government is also fully committed to ensuring diversity and choice in community care provision. This must include a full role for the independent and voluntary sectors. For this reason we have decided to issue a binding direction to local authorities which will enshrine the right of individuals to choose the location and character of their residential and nursing home. Furthermore, we will also require that a proportion of the grant be spent in the independent sector.* (Virginia Bottomley, speech to the annual social services conference on the Isle of Wight, 2 October 1992).

A third point to be made with respect to the aim of increasing user choice of both kinds concerns its fundamental rationale. A concern for choice may be justified in two ways: either as an *end in itself*, or as an *instrument* for achieving other ends. Thus it may be considered simply to be desirable in and of itself that people are free to make choices over the services they receive. Alternatively, it may be viewed as important to allow people to make such choices because this may facilitate other policy aims, such as efficiency and responsiveness. So, for example, for people in need of care to be offered a realistic choice between domiciliary care and residential care, or for parents to be offered a choice of schools, might be regarded as part of a set of individual 'rights' and therefore be *ipso facto* desirable. Or it could be viewed as a way of ensuring the system's responsiveness to user requirements, and/or of promoting provider efficiency through the mechanism of competition.

If the principal justification for selecting choice as a criterion by which the quasi-market reforms are to be judged is because of its role as an instrument, it is important to recognise that there may be other ways to achieve the ends concerned. In particular, there are mechanisms that involve 'voice' as an alternative to choice mechanisms such as quasi-markets that use 'exit' as a way of ensuring responsiveness. (see Hirschman, 1970, for an elaboration of the terms 'exit' and 'voice'; and Taylor *et al.*, 1992, for their application in welfare contexts). These include, at the level of the individual, complaints procedures, citizens' charters, etc., and at the level of the collective, community pressure groups or electoral processes. Given the complexity and long-standing nature of much welfare services, voice mechanisms may on occasion be preferable as instruments for achieving, for instance, responsiveness, to exit mechanisms involving extensions of choice.

Equity

Equity is a concept subject to many interpretations in policy contexts, properly to discuss all of which could take a book of its own (see Le Grand, 1991a, for one such book). Moreover, it rarely appears explicitly as one of the policy objectives of the quasi-market reforms, no doubt because they are being driven by a government for which equity considerations are not necessarily a high priority.

However, the chief policy documents concerned do not ignore the issue of equity entirely. For example, *Working for Patients* has several references to the paramountcy of need and openness to all regardless of income (see, for example, the Prime Minister's foreword); and *Caring for People* includes as a third key component that services should 'concentrate on those with greatest needs' (DoH, 1989a, p. 5). Moreover, since the motivation that underlay the creation of the welfare state in the first place was in large part the promotion of greater social justice or equity, no evaluation of the success or otherwise of a particular set of welfare reforms would be complete without reference to equity criteria.

But according to what definition of equity? It is perhaps least controversial for the purposes of this book explicitly to define equity in relation to need. More specifically, we shall consider an equitable service to be one where use is determined primarily by need and not by irrelevant factors such as income, socio-economic status, gender, or ethnic origin. 'Need', of course, is itself far from unproblematic as a term; here we shall regard it as referring to the resource requirements of the individual concerned, with the specific implication that the more care resources an individual requires to bring his or her level of welfare up to some predetermined level, the greater is his or her need. Hence the question to be asked of a quasi-market service with respect to this criterion is whether it improves the correspondence between individuals' resource requirements and their use of a welfare service.

Conditions for Success

Now it is possible to specify a number of conditions that have to be satisfied if these reforms are to achieve the ends of increased efficiency, responsiveness and choice without adverse consequences in terms of increased inequity. They concern *market structure, information, transactions costs* and *uncertainty, motivation* and *cream-skimming*.

Market Structure

For the allocation of a service by a conventional market to be efficient, responsive and to offer genuine choice, the market concerned has to be *competitive*. That is, there should be many providers, each unable to influence the market price by changing their output, and many purchasers, each unable to influence price by changing their purchases. If there are not enough actual providers, and hence not enough competition on the supply side, there should be the potential for competition: that is, there should be an opportunity for new providers to enter the market relatively costlessly. There should also be the possibility of exit from the market: that is, providers should face the risk of bankruptcy, or, more generally, that if they consistently make losses they will cease to be a provider. (There are market structures other than purely competitive ones that can be efficient: for instance, a monopoly provider with the ability 'perfectly' to price discriminate between its purchasers. However, the conditions necessary for such structures to exist are sufficiently unlikely as to make them little more than curiosa). Finally, prices should reflect the interaction of supply and demand for the service concerned, and should be able to move freely in response to changes in supply and demand conditions.

These requirements apply as much to quasi-markets as to markets proper. The problems that a lack of actual or potential competition among *providers* can create for quasi-markets are obvious. A single dominant provider can use its monopoly power to raise prices and to lower the quantity and the quality of the services provided. Without the threat of competition it can afford to be unresponsive to the needs and wants of their consumers. And a monopoly by definition offers no choice.

However, it might be thought that a lack of competition among *purchasers* would present fewer problems for quasi-markets, at least from a user perspective. In the case of health care, for example, the district health authorities should operate on behalf of NHS users (both actual and potential) and therefore should exercise any monopoly power that they have in a way that benefits users. Similarly, social service departments acting as the principal purchasers of community care should operate on behalf of users. Further, planning is facilitated by large purchasers. Only they can properly assess the needs of the community and ensure that all the facilities appropriate to meet those needs are provided. Finally. large purchasers can engage in batch purchasing and thereby lower costs.

Also, in several welfare areas, there are dominant providers, who, if not actual monopolies, are close to being so; again health care provides obvious examples, such as large general hospitals in small cities and towns. In such cases, it could be argued that the presence of these dominant providers makes large purchasers essential; for only then can they exercise a sufficient degree of countervailing power to offset the power of the providers.

However, there are several counter-arguments that in the end load the case against the large purchaser. First, even if those running large purchasing authorities are primarily driven by a concern for user interests and planning to meet those interests, it is far from clear how they will know what they are. The problem increases with the size of the authority; the bigger it is, the more difficult it will find the task of keeping in touch with the individuals and groups with whose interests it is supposed to be concerned.

Second, even if a dominant purchaser does know what the public interest is, it may not always exercise its power so as best to serve that interest in the long-term. A purchaser that exploits its monopoly power to drive a hard bargain may sour relationships with providers, lower their morale and motivation, and perhaps eventually drive them out of the business. People who feel inadequately rewarded do not perform well in the short term; and, in the long term, they find something else to do. More precisely, competition among purchasers is required for efficiency because it ensures that resources are drawn into their highest valued uses. In doing so it provides a buoyant market with plentiful profit-making opportunities to attract new entrants and to prevent the 'exit' of efficient suppliers.

There is more to the argument that monopoly providers need monopoly purchasers to offset their power. But there is a danger here, too: that the relationship between the two sides will be too intimate. There will be a relatively small number of people dealing with each other, a large proportion of whom may well have been erstwhile colleagues under the old system. In the circumstances it will be difficult to construct or maintain the distance that a market or bargaining process requires. Instead, the system could become one simply of decentralised budgets, with a management contract between purchaser and provider, but with no real competition on either side.

The dangers involved are illustrated by some of the experience with the Next Steps agencies, where some of the classic examples of bilateral monopolies can be found. Many of these are still locked into departmental organisation. The Benefits Agency states in the introduction to its Framework Document that 'the Agency works within the DSS as a whole'. The most significant risks of this incorporation are duplication and confusion about real responsibilities or 'ownership' of the Agencies' activities, which may have a direct bearing on the quality of the service the Agency provides' (Davies and Willman, 1991, pp. 29–30). That these dangers are real was confirmed in a Price Waterhouse survey of Next Steps agencies in practice (Price Waterhouse, 1991).

However, there is one area where it may be important to preserve monopoly purchasing power. This concerns the purchase of inputs into the production process that, for one reason, or another are monopolised in their supply. One example is land for housing. Suitable land, available for housing use, in the right place at the right time, is generally scarce enough to command a monopoly rent. If there competition among purchasers is introduced (as, for example, when several housing associations replace one local authority), then the process of bidding against one another for sites may drive the rent higher than the cost of alternative use (for example, private sector development).

Another example concerns different kinds of labour input. Staff in many areas of welfare provision are organised in trade unions or in powerful professional associations which in key respects operate like trade unions. Now the power of a labour supply monopoly can be offset by a monopoly purchaser of labour. However, if there is competition for labour, then the competitors, bidding against one another, will drive up wages. This in turn will put considerable pressure on budgets, leading either to strong political representations for an increase in the budget limit or to reduction in service quality or output – which can then be used as ammunition for a further attempt to raise the budget.

The National Health Service reforms can be used to illustrate the point (Mayston, 1990; Le Grand, 1991b). The NHS is virtually a monopoly employer and is therefore able to bargain more effectively with the relevant professional associations and trade unions. However, under the quasi-market proposals, the NHS as a monopoly employer is to be broken up. Independent trusts are being set up, and these are able to determine pay and conditions for staff. The consequence of setting up these trusts is to convert the NHS from a (virtual) monopoly purchaser of *labour* to a (virtual) monopoly purchaser of *services*. It will now buy services from competitive hospitals, themselves competing for doctors, nurses and ancillary staff. Economic theory would predict that this change will bring about a widening in the dispersion of wages and salaries and probably a rise in their mean levels as well. This prediction has been borne out in the United States, where hospital wage rates have been found to be higher in competitive than in concentrated labour markets (Feldman and Scheffler, 1982; Robinson, 1988; Sloan and Elnicki, 1978).

This is not to imply that if the salaries or wages of people working in welfare provider units do rise it is automatically undesirable. Monopolies of any kind can be exploitative. Wage rises may have a positive impact on morale and productivity. Also there are differences between the relevant labour markets in Britain and the US that suggest a need for caution in making comparisons (for example, in health care, consultants in Britain can already make large sums from private practice). However, overall, it is fair to say that a real danger for the quasi-market developments is that one of the major virtues of a monopsonistic public sector, its ability to control the power of the professions and hence an important part of its overall labour costs, will be lost.

What of the requirement that prices should reflect supply and demand? In a conventional market, the forces of supply and demand establish prices which act as signals for the efficient allocation of resources. Increases in demand for a product will lead to an increase in price and stimulate increased supply by expansion of firms already in the market, or through the entry of new firms. Similarly, firms which are producing unwanted goods, or producing goods in demand with an inefficient mix of resources, will find their unit costs rising above the market price, and will be driven out of the market by bankruptcy. But in some quasi-markets, the price signals which connect purchasers and providers operate in a rather different fashion. In education, as we shall see in Chapter 6, the pricing mechanism operates through a formula administered by the purchasing agency. In health and social services, the pricing of services is determined by a process of contract negotiation between purchaser and providers. Thus the prices established on the quasi-market are not formed directly by the interplay of demand and supply, and so are not what might be called free market prices, but rather are either administered prices, or negotiated prices. On the demand side, the ultimate consumers do not influence the price, which is regulated by the government agency. The budget constraint of the agency, which limits the level of prices it can offer, is set by the government, and so cannot be influenced by the resources which the individual users might like to make available. Thus price formation is unlikely fully to reflect user preferences, unless the agencies concerned are highly sensitive to consumer needs. This suggests that user participation in the decision making processes of the agencies may be a precondition of efficient price setting on the demand side.

On the supply side, in a conventional market, price-setting behaviour is determined in a context of profit and loss accounting, private ownership rights and firm or 'hard' budget constraints. In a quasi-market, however, there are a variety of forms of ownership including state ownership, municipal ownership, trusts, and collectively owned non-profit-making organisations in addition to privately owned organisations. If these organisations do not face hard budget constraints, the consequences of loss-making decisions are not necessarily bankruptcies. In this situation, price-setting behaviour on the supply side, to the extent that providers are able to influence prices, may not properly reflect cost constraints. This can be expected to lead to weaknesses in the ability of the quasi-market to attain satisfactory levels of efficiency. Hence an important requirement for quasi-market efficiency is that the relevant providers have hard budget constraints, and therefore face a real risk of losing their provider status if they exceed those constraints – that is, if they bust their budget.

Information

An important condition for markets to operate efficiently (in the sense defined above) is that both sides of the market concerned have access to cheap and accurate information, particularly concerning the costs and the quality of the service concerned. Providers must be able to cost their activities so as to be able to price them appropriately. Purchasers must be able to monitor the quality of the service they are purchasing, so as to limit the opportunity for providers to reduce costs by lowering quality.

Costing activities that have never been properly costed before can itself be a costly activity, as almost anyone working on this problem in the public sector can testify. However, it would not be appropriate to lay all such costs at the door of the quasi-market reforms, since in many welfare areas the process of improving costing procedures was already under way (under the Resource Management Initiative in the NHS, for example). This illustrates the fact that, even in a planned system, costing procedures can be an important management tool.

However, there are aspects of the use of costing procedures that are specific to quasi-markets. One example is the process of billing.

Billing operations, particularly if they involve debt collection, can be expensive, and, together with the expense of the costing and pricing procedures that necessarily accompany them, may be a offsetting factor to any cost-reducing tendency of quasi-markets.

The monitoring of quality also has to be an essential part of any quasi-market system. Otherwise providers may engage in what Williamson (1975, 1985) calls opportunistic behaviour, exploiting their informational advantage to reduce costs at the expense of quality. There are two kinds of opportunistic behaviour to which the theoretical literature draws attention: moral hazard and adverse selection. Moral hazard occurs where providers put in fewer resources into the provision of the service than is consistent with the terms of their contract; an example would be where a hospital skimps on its accident and emergency service that it provides under a block contract. Adverse selection occurs where providers possess certain characteristics that may adversely affect the provision of the service and that are known to them but that they do not reveal to the purchaser; for instance, a private residential home may try to conceal the dubious financial status of its proprietor from the social services department with which it contracts. In either case there would be a reduction in one or more dimensions of quality. The reduction could be prevented if there were continuous monitoring by the purchaser (of, for instance, the accident and emergency service provided by the hospital, or the financial state of the residential home). But monitoring consumes resources, the cost of which has to be taken into account in any overall assessment of a quasi-market's contribution to efficiency.

Opportunism would be less of a problem in the case of a competitive market, because service producers who behaved opportunistically would find it difficult to renew their contracts in the face of competition from more reliable producers. However, opportunism can give rise to persistent difficulties in formulating quasi-market contracts when the number of participants in a market is restricted. Moreover, in practice, a competitive situation with *ex ante* large numbers of providers can easily be transformed, *ex post*, into one of small numbers, as the initial contractors develop an established position in the market.

In theory, opportunistic behaviour should be controlled through the contracting process and its associated enforcement procedures. But there are considerable difficulties involved in practice, as illustrated by Bartlett (1991a) with respect to the NHS reforms. NHS contracts can be of three types: block contracts, cost-per-case contracts, and cost-and-volume contracts. Under the block contract, the purchaser pays the provider an annual fee in return for access to a defined range of services. Under the cost-per-case contract, each case has a price set under the contract either on an average cost basis, or where there is unplanned excess capacity, on a marginal cost basis. The cost-and-volume contracts are essentially a mixture of the other two types of contract. They fund a base-line level of activity to be undertaken by the provider, beyond which all funding is on a cost-per-case basis.

The cost-per-case contract is close to a complete contingent claims contract. As such it is obviously subject to the principal difficulty with such contracts: the costs of getting the information necessary to write and to administer them. Block contracts, on the other hand, are incomplete and hence subject to the possibility that opportunistic strategies will be pursued by the provider units, resulting in some areas in a reduction in the quality of service provision, and in others in an over-emphasis on prestige treatments and to an increase in the absorption of the 'organisational surplus' in the form of increased perks and side payments to staff. In addition, block contracts involve a shifting of risks on to providers; to protect themselves, providers will try to negotiate fees with a risk premium incorporated within and thereby inflate contract prices. Both of these factors will tend to increase the overall costs of service provision.

Overall, this analysis suggests that any improvement in efficiency due to the introduction of quasi-markets may be partly wholly or partly offset by a number of factors. These include the likelihood that providers will adopt opportunistic strategies in the face of incomplete information; the increased risk premia required by the risk-averse providers of services; and the increased administrative costs of fully specified cost-per-case contracts.

Transactions Costs and Uncertainty

The transactions which take place in quasi-markets are often quite complex and multi-dimensional, involving the provision of sophisticated service activities rather than the relatively basic provision of material commodities with which traditional markets deal. There is also often considerable uncertainty surrounding the future needs or demands for these services. As a result, the creation and management of these markets may involve a relatively high burden of what have been termed 'transaction costs'.

As developed by Williamson (1975, 1985), transactions costs can be usefully divided into two kinds: *ex ante* and *ex post* exchange. *Ex ante* transaction costs are the costs encountered in drafting, negotiating and safeguarding an exchange agreement. These tasks can be done with a great deal of care, specifying as many contingencies as possible and detailing all the appropriate reactions in each contingency for all the contracting parties, in which case the associated costs are likely to be high; or they can be done in an incomplete fashion, if indeed at all, in which case the costs will be low. *Ex post* transactions costs are the costs of monitoring the outcomes of the exchange to check compliance with the exchange's terms after the transaction has taken place, and the costs of any haggling or other forms of dispute resolution if the terms have not been complied with. *Ex post* costs are likely to be greater, the less care has been taken in drawing up the terms and conditions of the exchange in the first place. Hence high *ex post* transactions costs may be associated with low *ex ante* costs and vice versa.

In a seminal article, Coase (1952) pointed out that, where transactions costs are sufficiently important the market, as a system of resource allocation, may be set aside and transactions can be internalised within firms. Within firms, resources are typically allocated by non-market, administrative methods. In this light, large hierarchical organisations such as the NHS and other large producer organisations such as multinational corporations can be viewed as alternatives to markets as methods of allocating resources. Their existence can be explained by the high levels of transactions costs which would be generated should such organisations be broken up into smaller units, with markets being organised to allocate resources between them.

Of course, the balance of advantage over the extent to which production should be centralised within large organisations or decentralised into smaller units within an economy varies from one sector to another, and moreover, shifts over time. For example, there is substantial evidence of changes in the industrial structure of many advanced industrial countries towards smaller sized units of production. The trend towards decentralisation seems to be rather general

(Loveman and Sengenberger, 1991), and may indicate that technological change (particularly in the area of information technology) is
reducing the transactions costs associated with market exchange.
The quasi-market reforms, designed to replace administrative by
market methods of resource allocation in the public services, appear
to be following this trend (Hoggett, 1990).

Problems arise, however, where the transactions require investment in assets which are specific to the particular transaction, or set
of transactions, involved. The existence of such specific assets, which
could be specialised equipment or skills, ties the parties into the
contract and makes it costly for purchasers to turn to a new provider
and for providers to turn to a new purchaser. For example, where
the transaction involves investment in skills which are specific to a
particular task, an incumbent supplier will 'learn by doing' in the
process of contract execution, and so will be in a favourable position
to undercut potential rivals when the time comes to renegotiate the
contract. Other examples occur where investments must be made in
equipment and machinery which have no use in any other activity.
In this case, the provider who has invested in specific assets may
become tied into a particular purchaser and be vulnerable to future
reductions in contract prices. This in turn may act as a disincentive
to investment. Thus the existence of specific assets may make the
integrated organisation of service provision a preferable alternative
to the market in many situations.

The costs associated with market transactions may be particularly
acute in the presence of uncertainty, and this we must discuss in a
little more detail. The existence of uncertainty and risk is an
inevitable context of economic life, and has a particular salience in
welfare quasi-markets. This is perhaps more so in health and social
care than in education or housing, since present and future health
status and hence the level of future demand for health and social care
is so much less certain than levels of future demand for educational
and housing services. This is one reason why insurance schemes,
whether public or private, are so widely used to finance health care
provision.

The existence of uncertainty may threaten the efficient operation of
quasi-markets because it restricts the ability of both purchasers and
providers to plan ahead for the level of service which will be required.
The problem is compounded when uncertainty about the consequences of transactions or about the circumstances within which

transactions might take place is combined with 'bounded rationality' (Williamson, 1975). The concept of bounded rationality refers to the limited ability of individuals to process all the available information with which they may be presented in a complex situation. In such circumstances it is often costly, or even impossible, to specify all future contingencies, and all possible adaptations to unforeseen circumstances which may at some point be required, in a written contract which would serve to underwrite market exchange.

Williamson (1975) argues that this particular source of market failure explains the recourse to bureaucratic 'internal' structures within hierarchical organisations. Within such organisations, continual adaptations to uncertainty are accomplished through administrative processes, through the instructions given by superiors to those lower down the hierarchy, or by agreement within a work team or 'peer group'. Responses to unforeseen events can be devised, and appropriate actions can take place, in a sequential fashion as problems arise. In this way it becomes unnecessary to foresee all possible contingencies from the outset of the transaction period. Rather, the future is permitted to unfold, and appropriate actions can be taken to deal with events as they occur.

Thus the internal organisation of productive activities permits parties to a transaction to deal with uncertainty and complexity in an adaptive and sequential fashion. Where the degree of uncertainty about the future state of the world is high, and where bounded rationality is a limiting factor on the formulation of complete contracts, the costs of contract formulation may outweigh the benefits which might be expected to arise from greater flexibility of market exchange between independent agents. Decisions taken within an organisation may deal with the existence of bounded rationality more efficiently than the market is able to, because future contingent prices do not have to be specified in advance.

The existence of uncertainty also explains the widespread recourse to contracts as a context within which to structure quasi-market transactions. Contracts are ubiquitous in any process of exchange, although they may not be explicit (implicit contracts in the labour market, for example, have been studied in depth in recent years). Often the transactions involved in the process of market exchange are rather straightforward and the associated contract is easily specified by a verbal agreement. However, where transactions are multi-dimensional, and outcomes are contingent upon an uncertain

environment or 'state of nature', then the associated contracts
(which Williamson refers to as contingent claims contracts) may
be difficult to write, implement and enforce, and the associated
transactions costs may be high. This dimension of quasi-market
transactions, and in particular the issue of risk-sharing between
purchasers and providers, is analysed in more detail in Chapters 3
and 4 which consider the role of contracts in the quasi-markets for
health services in the USA and the UK.

What are the implications of this for the success or otherwise of
quasi-markets? Simply that, if they are to be more efficient than the
systems they replace, any extra transactions costs they create must
not be higher than any cost savings that may be generated by the
forces of competition or by other aspects of the quasi-market. That is,
for a given level of benefit (a given level of cost and quality) the costs
of contracting for a welfare service, including *ex ante* and *ex post* costs,
must be less than the costs of the administrative systems they are
replacing.

Overall, therefore, quasi-markets must have mechanisms for
dealing with transactions under conditions of uncertainty, and, if
they are to be more efficient than the systems they replace, these
mechanisms should not be too costly.

Motivation

The third condition concerns the motivation of both purchasers and
providers. Providers ought to be motivated at least in part by
financial considerations. If they are not, they will not respond
appropriately to market signals. It makes little sense introducing a
market to create profitable opportunities, if the participants in the
market are not interested in making profits.[*]

---

[*] Strictly a motivation of profit-maximisation is not always necessary
for market efficiency. Other motivations in other contexts, for
instance income maximisation by labour-managed firms, can lead
to efficient outcomes given free entry and exit (to compete away
surplus incomes); see Dreze (1985). However, another motivation
that it might be plausible to suppose motivates some non-profit
organisations, namely, output-maximisation, will not lead to effi-

In practice this condition might be difficult to fulfil, particularly during the transition stage from bureaucratic systems to quasi-markets. Many people working in welfare services are not commercially or financially motivated, and find it difficult to make the shift from considering, say, the welfare of their users to the financial state of their provider unit. (Indeed, this is not only difficult for people working in welfare, but probably also for many of those who are studying the quasi-market reforms and who might otherwise be sympathetic to them.)

Issues concerning motivation arise on the purchaser side as well. For the quasi-market properly to respond to the needs and wants of users, purchasers must be motivated to pursue the welfare of users. Now if the purchaser were the user, then, barring outright irrationality, there would be little difficulty in this respect, since a user who was also a purchaser could generally be relied upon to be motivated by concern for his or her own welfare. However, in most of the reforms with which we concerned, for a variety of reasons, users are not entrusted with the purchasing decision. Parents take schooling decisions on behalf of children; GP fund-holders, hospitalisation decisions on behalf of their patients; care-managers, care decisions on behalf of social service clients. In some cases, the purchaser is quite remote from the user; the district health authority, or the social services department. In all these situations, where an agent is acting as a purchaser on behalf of users, there clearly is a problem in ensuring that purchasers will act in the interests of users and not pursue their own agendas: a problem that increases, the further the distance between purchaser and user.

Cream-Skimming

In conventional markets who receives services is determined in large part by the ability to pay for those services. Since ability to pay is not necessarily correlated with need, market allocations are unlikely to be equitable, at least in the sense that we have defined it here.

---

ciency, since an output maximiser will earn zero profit by definition, and will therefore have dissipated the potential surplus of new entrants, without ever using resources in a way that equates marginal costs and marginal benefits.

In contrast, quasi-markets do not suffer from this problem – at least not directly. Eligible consumers receive services free of charge, but are only entitled to make use of the services to the extent that they fulfil the criteria of need established and verified by the relevant agency. The quasi-market thus establishes a correspondence between need and consumption. Where this correspondence is achieved, the quasi-market will meet the criterion of equity in the use of services.

However, there is a complication. If inequity is completely to be avoided in quasi-markets, there must be restricted opportunities for what is termed cream-skimming. Cream-skimming is discrimination by either purchasers or providers against the more expensive users: the chronically ill patient, the incontinent, confused, elderly person, the disruptive child from a deprived background. If purchasers can choose for whom they will purchaser, and providers can choose for whom they will provide, that is, if they can skim off the cream, then welfare services may not reach those who need them most and equity will not be achieved.

Cream-skimming is often termed adverse selection (see, for example. Glennerster, 1991) and indeed has much in common with that concept.[*] Both involve selection; and in both cases the consequences are adverse, at least for some groups of users. Also, both arise from an inability by the relevant actors to price-discriminate. If purchasers received a payment (a 'price') that related directly to the likely impact of the user's requirements on the purchaser's budget, and/or, if providers could charge the potentially more expensive user a price that was in line with the costs concerned, then there would be no disincentive to providing users with the service that they need.

However, if cream-skimming is a form of adverse selection then it is worth noting that it is not quite the same as the adverse selection that was described above under the information heading. Here. the problem does not appear to be the result of an imbalance of information, but one of the pricing or contract structures through which purchasers and providers are funded. So, for example, if, through formula funding, schools received larger weights for potentially expensive children, or, if fund-holding GPs were financed by a

---

[*] Our treatment of this point has benefited from discussions with our colleague Gervas Huxley.

formula that included a special weighting for potentially expensive patients, they would have no incentive to cream-skim; indeed, if the weighting were large enough, the incentive might be reversed.[*] (This is the idea behind the positively discriminating voucher discussed in Le Grand, 1989.)

On the provider side the problem arises because of the contract structure. If the contract takes the form of a block contract or a generalised service agreement, whereby the provider is contracted simply to provide a service without any specification concerning volume, then providers have the incentive to cream-skim. If the contract is of the cost-per-client type and if the agreed price is the same for each client, regardless of differences in the need for care, then again providers will have an incentive to cream-skim. Only if the contract price varies in an appropriate fashion with the needs of the client will cream-skimming not be a problem.

Conclusions

We may summarise the arguments of this chapter as follows. If quasi-markets in welfare services are to achieve the goals of improved efficiency, responsiveness, choice and equity, they need to meet certain conditions. These are:

Market structure. The quasi-market on both sides should be competitive: that is, there should be many purchasers and many providers. The only real exception to this condition concerns a situation where a monopoly exists in one part of the market that it is impossible to break up; in that case it may be necessary to have a monopoly on the other side in order to exercise countervailing power.

Information. Both providers and purchasers need to have access to accurate, independent information, providers primarily about costs, and purchasers about quality.

Transactions costs and uncertainty. Transactions costs, particularly those associated with uncertainty, should be kept to a minimum.

---

[*] Currently the size of a GP fund-holder's budget is determined by past referral patterns; however, it is envisaged that this will be eventually replaced by a formula based on capitation payments.

Motivation. Providers need to be motivated at least in part by financial considerations; purchasers, by user interests. Both raise particular difficulties in the quasi-market context. On the provider side, there are commonly non-profit providers, whose motivation is unclear; on the purchaser side, there are commonly third parties who act on behalf of users and whose interests may not always be identical with users.

Cream-skimming. There should be no incentive for providers or purchasers to discriminate between users in favour of those who are least expensive.

One final point should be noted concerning these conditions. If it is impossible to meet one of them, this does not necessarily imply that the 'second-best' position is for the other four to be met. It may be that it is better for another condition to be violated so as to 'compensate' for the failure to meet the first condition. So, for instance, if, for structural reasons, a particular quasi-market is not competitive or purchasers have inadequate information, it may be preferable to have providers that are *not* motivated by financial considerations, so that they will be less tempted to exploit their monopoly power. This is a point to which we return in the last chapter.

Quasi-Markets, Contracts and Quality in Health and Social Care: The US Experience

3

Carol Propper

As we have seen in earlier chapters, the recent reforms of the mechanisms for delivery of care in health and social care markets in the UK are intended to establish internal or quasi-markets; markets in which government agencies arrange care for their clients by placing contracts for the delivery of care with independent, 'arm's-length' suppliers. The supporters of these reforms argue that the separation of provision and finance will allow competition on the supply side, resulting in increased efficiency in service delivery, increased choice and increased responsiveness to the needs of clients. However, while government monopoly in both finance and delivery may be associated with inefficiency and a lack of responsiveness to consumer needs, so too can contracting relationships have associated inefficiencies (Bartlett, 1991a). The central problem is the asymmetry of information between provider and purchaser under a contracting relationship. The separation of purchaser and provider means that the purchaser has less information about the technology and conditions of production than the provider. The provider can exploit this to extract rent from the purchaser and/or engage in inefficient production, so increasing the amount the purchaser has to pay for a given level of the service.

Economic analysis suggests that this inefficiency may be partly overcome by the choice of services which are to be contracted for, the choice of method by which these services are put out to contract and the design of the contract between purchaser and provider. (This set of choices is often referred to as franchise design. In this chapter the term franchising design is used to refer to the choice of services to put out to contract and the term contract design to refer to specific features of the contract.) Economic analysis also indicates the importance of industry specific factors in determining the efficiency of the contracting process. Contracting arrangements which result in increases in efficiency in one industry may not have similar results in another. One feature common to all parts of the health and social care markets which, at least in its importance and intensity, distinguishes them from other markets is the difficulty of measuring quality of output. As a consequence, in all health and social care markets there is a high degree of concern over the effect of the introduction of contracting and quasi-markets on the quality of services delivered.

The aims of this chapter are to examine the effect of limited observability of quality on the process and outcome of the establishment of quasi-markets in health and social care and to consider possible features of contracting and franchising design which may be able to overcome some of the inefficiencies which are associated with the use of contracting in these markets. The quasi-market changes in health and social care have only just been implemented. In both sectors limits on the operation of contracting are currently in place, so it is not possible to draw any very robust conclusions from current changes in these markets. However, the US health and human services sectors share many features of the UK health and social care sectors. Internal markets have been in operation for over two decades in many US human services (hereafter social services) sectors. Contracts have been widely used to regulate price in the US hospital and nursing home industries. The possible effects of the introduction of contracting in the UK health and social care (HSC) sectors, can be judged in the light of the experience of these US markets. Specifically, this chapter examines the impact of the industry structure, and the partial observability of quality of output on the outcome of the contracting process in the USA. It then uses this evidence to draw out the implications for the design of contracts and the franchising process in the UK markets.

The chapter falls into two parts. In the first part I examine evidence from both the general economics literature on contracting and from the US health and social care markets. I present a very selective discussion of some economic analyses of government contracting for services in which quality is not at issue; provide an outline of the industrial structure of the various parts of the US health and social services markets and reviews the evidence from these markets; discuss evidence from the creation of internal markets in human services on the outcome of the contracting process; and examine evidence on contract design, drawn primarily from the experience of price (rate) regulation in the hospital and nursing home sectors. In the second part I ask whether there are lessons which can be taken from this experience and applied to the newly created health and social care markets in the UK. I examine the technology of production, the motivations of provider and purchaser and the information held by the purchaser and provider in the UK markets in order to assess those sources and types of inefficiencies which appear most likely, given the US experience, to occur in the UK. Given this, I examine those features of contract design which could potentially be used to overcome some of these sources of inefficiency. The final section summarises and concludes.

Government Contracting for Services where Quality is Observable

When the government buys services through contracts, the central problem it faces is that it has less information than the seller (hereafter referred to as the provider) of services about those services. In particular, it has less information about the technology of production. The government, as purchaser, could try to find out this information, for example, by auditing the provider. However, obtaining this information is costly. In addition, the information the purchaser obtains may not be verifiable in a court of law and so could not be used in the event of a dispute with the provider. This information asymmetry gives the provider the possibility of extracting rent. That is, it can use the fact that it has better knowledge of the technology of production to inflate the price it charges the purchaser, for example by engaging in inefficient production and/or by cost-padding. These actions mean that the government pays more for the services than it would have done had it had full information.

The purchaser can attempt to overcome this problem by encouraging competition at the bidding stage and through design of contracts. In cases where the output is single-dimensioned (so it is assumed any quality dimension of output is totally verifiable) and the government's aim is to minimise the cost of the services it buys, McAfee and McMillan (1987) have analysed the nature of the contract and the franchising process. (It is generally assumed that the aim of the government, as the representative of the electorate, is to maximise social welfare. In the context of contracting for one service, the assumption that the government minimises costs, rather than maximises social welfare, seems plausible.) Providers (potential bidders) are assumed to be risk-averse. In other words, in order to accept risk they need to be paid more than the expected costs of the services they are going to supply. The government is assumed to be risk-neutral (in other words, it does not require a risk premium in order to take on a risky project). Given its relative lack of information, the purchaser can attempt to minimise the cost of the services it buys through design of the contract for a service and by taking steps to increase the number of bidders for contracts. The two sets of tools are linked, as certain types of contract induce more bidding.

McAfee and McMillan argue that the precise form of the contract that will minimise the cost to the purchaser will vary from case to case, depending, for example, upon the amount of risk associated with the project, the amount of competition in bidding and the extent of risk aversion of the firm. However, they argue that the most common form of government contract, the fixed-price contract, is rarely optimal. Under a fixed-price contract the government, as purchaser, pays a pre-agreed sum for the goods, where the sum is determined in the bidding for the contract. While such a contract gives the winning bidder an incentive to hold down costs (because all cost overruns are borne by the supplier) the lack of cost-sharing means that a risk-averse firm will need to be paid a premium over and above the expected costs for taking on this contract. This increases the price the purchaser will have to pay. In addition, there will be few bidders for such a contract. Costs will be higher than if there was more competition for the contract and if the provider had not had to bear all the risk.

The authors also argue that the polar opposite to the fixed-price contract, the cost-plus contract (in which the provider receives all his costs plus a fee), is never optimal if there is more than one potential provider. Because the cost-plus contract does not require the firm to bear any risk, it will be attractive to firms. Competition in bidding, which holds down the price, will be stimulated. But there is no guarantee that the lowest cost firm will win the bid, because there is no relationship between the bidding price and the price the firm will receive. In fact, the firm with the lowest bid is likely to be the most risk-averse, not necessarily the lowest-cost. In addition, unless there is monitoring, cost-plus contracts will give the firm incentives to cost-pad. The contract which will minimise the cost the government will have to pay is one that allows some risk-sharing (so increasing incentives for a risk-averse agent to bid for the contract) but does not have complete risk sharing (so the bidding process will reveal a firm's expected costs). (The optimal amount of cost-sharing will be a positive function of the variance in bidders' expected costs and the risk aversion of the bidders and a negative function of the gains from cost-reducing effort and the number of expected bidders.)

The price the purchaser has to pay can be lowered by increasing the number of bidders. It is therefore argued that in the case where output is verifiable, the franchising process (which includes the choice of what services should be put out to contract) should be designed to increase the number of bidders. McAfee and McMillan (and others) suggest that if providers are risk-averse, actions a risk-neutral purchaser might take include reduction of the transactions costs of bidding and reduction of the risk of the project. High transactions costs of bidding (for example, the requirement to submit very detailed bids or a long bidding process) will reduce the attractiveness of the project for risk-averse bidders. It is also more likely to deter smaller bidders, since they are less able to spread the risk of not being awarded the contract across their activities. If the risks within one project are correlated, the purchaser can reduce the risk of the project by breaking it up into smaller components, though this gain must be offset against any transactions costs borne by the purchaser arising from an increase in the number of contractors. The use of operating contracts (where the provider does not own but leases the assets required for production of the service) will also reduce the risk inherent in the contract. The purchaser can also vary the length of contract to increase the number of bidders. Other authors have stressed the importance for contract design of the ability of the purchaser to monitor or audit the provider (Laffont and Tirole, 1991) and of considerations of dynamic as well as static efficiency (Sappington and Stiglitz, 1987).

In general, the literature on contract design stresses the importance of industry-specific factors. The technology of production, the relative risk aversion of purchaser and provider, the number of providers and the ease with which the product can be defined are all important in determining the optimal design of contracts and the efficiency of contracting (Tirole, 1988; Kreps, 1990). These factors need to be taken into account even where quality is not of concern. In health and human services markets, not only is the technology of production not observable by the purchaser, but the quality of output is also only partially observable. This lack of observability of quality is likely to have an impact on the bidding process, the type of contracts used and the outcome of contracting for services. I therefore turn to an examination of the experience of contracting in a specific set of markets; the US health and human services industries. I begin with an outline of the technology of production and the nature of demand in these markets.

The US Health and Social Care Sectors

The term 'health and human services' is applied in the US to those industries which deliver health and social care services. Common to all these industries is the importance of the professional in service delivery, a lack of complete observability of outcomes, social concern over the distribution of services and the importance of the government as a buyer of services. But the services produced, the technology of production, the nature of demand and the information of actors in these industries differ.

The Hospital Care Sector

Key features of the production of hospital care are the importance of professionals in the supply of care and the very high search costs for the consumer of care. The existence of professionals on the supply side means production tends to be dominated by professionals who have a set of standards and a common code of ethics, which may be more or less loosely binding on individual members. (The professions may be either self-regulating, and/or required by law to meet minimum quality standards.) Individual consumers have less information than the provider of care. The consequence is that the provider acts as the consumer's agent, providing both information as to the services required and the service itself. It is generally assumed that this agency relationship is less than perfect; in other words, the provider pursues its own goals, as well as, or constrained by, those of the consumer of care.

As a consequence, hospital markets tend not to be competitive, but are monopolistic in nature. A high degree of monopoly for each provider is ensured by the high information search costs for consumers. The tendency to local monopoly may be reinforced by economies of scale or scope in production. Care is supplied by professionals working in both not-for-profit and for-profit organisations. (It is not always clear precisely what the aims of non-profit-maximising organisations are in the health care market, but they are often modelled as the maximisation of the income or utility of the providers, subject to break-even (and sometimes ethical) constraints.) The product supplied is multidimensional. The aspects of care rated most highly by providing physicians are not always those rated most highly by consumers. In recent years, the threat of a malpractice suit has acted as a constraint upon the behaviour of the provider.

The social concern for the distribution of use of medical services in this market is reflected in the proportion of finance provided from public funds. Approximately 40 per cent of health care expenditure is met from the public purse. The public sector has not generally acted as both provider and purchaser; rather the state has acted as a third party insurer, buying care from both for-profit and not-for-profit providers through the Medicaid and Medicare programmes. Accompanying the high level of public finance is a high level of regulatory activity, designed primarily to control the growth of expenditure in the sector. The level of Medicaid and Medicare reimbursement is set through price regulation. Expansion of capacity (both through new entry and the expansion of existing facilities) is controlled through the Certificate of Need (CON) regulations. Such regulations continue to operate even as supply-side measures to promote competition have been actively introduced.

The Nursing Home Sector

In this sector the role of the physician is weaker, the influence of for-profit providers is greater and the importance of malpractice as a constraint on quality is smaller than in the hospital sector. While the agency role of providers may not be as great as in the hospital sector, consumers have been argued to have less information about the nature of the product and its effect than providers, partly on the grounds that entry into nursing homes occurs when consumers are unwell and/or elderly and frail.

The size of US nursing homes is large (Day and Klein, 1987), perhaps evidence of the existence of scale or scope economies (economies of scope arise when a firm manufactures more than one product and there are economies in production across the products). Nursing home costs have grown very rapidly, and at a faster rate than any other component of health care costs. At the same time, public expenditure, largely borne by the Medicaid programme, has risen. In 1985, total expenditure was in the order of 35 billion US dollars, accounting for around 55 per cent of all expenditure. Again, the government does not act as a direct provider of care, but instead acts as a third-party insurer. Despite a large increase in expenditure, there is continuing concern over the quality of and access to nursing home care for Medicaid-funded patients. As in the hospital sector, the high level of government funding has been accompanied by a high degree of regulatory activity. Through regulation, the federal government (in conjunction with state governments) has attempted to control entry, costs and increase quality and access for targeted groups.

The Social Services Sector

This sector provides services to a range of clients, including older persons, those with learning difficulties, those with mental health problems or physical disabilities. These services broadly correspond to social services in the UK. The technology of production and the information of consumer and provider varies across these services. For some, the consumer may be relatively well-informed relative to the provider. For others there may be asymmetry of information between user and provider (for example, psychiatric services) or an element of compulsion in consumption (for example, programmes for offenders). The level of specificity of capital in production, both human and physical, varies across services. Similarly, there are variations across the services in economies of scale or scope.

The form of government intervention in the US social service sector is close to that of the UK quasi-markets in health and social care. During the 1960s most social service programmes in the US were both funded and supplied by a bureaucratic public provider. Over the last two decades states have significantly increased their use of competitive bidding to purchase services from private agencies, thus splitting the purchaser and provider role. The arguments supporting these changes were very similar to those used recently in the UK. Contracting, it was asserted, would overcome the limitations of government provision, argued to be overly bureaucratic, hampered by restrictive regulations and political constraints and unresponsive to consumer needs. Private providers would be more innovative and responsive to the recipients of services and so contracting would lead to increased quality and increased efficiency in service delivery.

The Contracting Process: Evidence from US Social Services Markets

As the quasi-markets created in the UK are most similar to those set up in the US social services market, the evidence from these markets is particularly relevant. This section focuses on the market structure which emerges under contracting. Inferences about efficiency are drawn from the structure of the post-contracting markets and the type of providers in these markets, rather than from the direct measurement of efficiency, costs or quality.

Extent of Competition in Bidding and the Nature of Contracts

The experience from these markets appears to be that once the contracting process has been in place for a few rounds, the extent of competition in bidding becomes limited. In an analysis of contract-ing for mental health services in Massachusetts, Schlesinger, Dorwart and Pulice (1986) found that while there was an expansion in the number of providers at the introduction of contracting, the level of competition once the process was under-way was less than initially hoped for. In principle, for the programmes analysed by Schlesinger, Dorwart and Pulice, between one-third and one-half of direct service contracts in any one year were opened to competitive bidding. The authors found that in practice the proportion was about 20 per cent. Moreover, the extent of provider expansion was uneven. Entry of new providers was greatest for services that had previously not been available; for preexisting services, agencies already supplying the services received much of the contract funding. In a study of contracting in Michigan, DeHoog (1985) found similar patterns. Rather than compete directly, contractors attempted to differentiate themselves so that competition, if it existed at all, was not so much between agencies offering similar services, but between different agencies each requesting a share of a county's grant to provide a different service. In a review of the contracting process in several states and for several types of service Kramer and Grossman (1987) concluded that the bidding process has generally been characterised by relatively few bidders.

Lack of actual competition at the bidding stage does not necessarily mean that the firm which wins the contract is ineffi-cient. The more bidders, the greater the potential competition, but only one bidder in addition to the winning firm is needed to pose a threat of possible replacement at the contract renewal stage. This threat may be enough to ensure that the winner of the contract engages in efficient production. However, both Schlesinger *et al.*, and DeHoog found that bidding was dominated by large providers who tended to differentiate themselves from each other. This may indicate a lack of potential competition, as well as a lack of actual competition. In addition, all the research cited above found that unless the particular programme has been abandoned incumbents tended to get contracts automatically at the renewal stage. This is likely to limit the number of potential bidders, as the chances of winning the contract are small. Thus the threat of competition is limited. (These studies did not examine directly the costs or the efficiency of the contract winner. Implicitly, both studies assumed that lack of bidders was evidence of inefficiency. But it should be noted that if the transactions costs of the franchising process are very high, or the output is such that a long term relationship is the most efficient, then lack of bidders is not necessarily evidence of inefficiency.)

Evidence on the nature of output, in particular its quality and cost, is limited (in part, precisely because it is difficult to measure quality in these services). However, one dimension of quality on which there is some evidence is innovation in production. The study by Schlesinger, Dorwart and Pulice indicated that contracting led to a lack of innovation in care delivery. In order to meet the quality standards set by the purchaser, contracts tended to be placed with a provider who could meet certain input specifications, say a certain ratio of staff to patients. Contracts were less likely to be given to providers who might be more willing to try new methods of care delivery.

Both Schlesinger *et al.* and DeHoog found that contracting was also accompanied by a reduction in some of the legal protections that could be used to promote quality of care prior to the introduction of contracting. Schlesinger *et al.* argued that the role of the purchaser as the consumer's agent, and the arm's-length relationship between provider and purchaser, conducted through the medium of a legal contract, make it more difficult for those protecting consumer interests other than the purchaser to play a role. The process of contracting changes the legal relationship between purchaser and provider, and strong provider interests may be reflected in legal judgments. DeHoog cites evidence of protected ('sweetheart') contracts between contractors and the state of Michigan. She also notes that legal rulings that contractors in Michigan could not be held responsible for failure to meet performance goals on contracts were part of the reason why the watchdog role of contractors was rendered almost ineffective under contracting.

The evidence presented above suggests the following patterns emerge in contracting for social services. The creation of internal markets in US social services has not resulted in a great deal of competition for the market. Once the programme is initiated, the number of bidders for contracts tends to fall, the contracts tend to be awarded to incumbents, and a close relationship is established between provider and purchaser. Economies of scale in the provision of multiple services and in bidding for contracts encourages the consolidation of service provision into a small number of large providers. In what follows, I argue that these outcomes are the result of the lack of total observability of quality of output, coupled with the concern of the purchaser over the quality of output. These two factors influence the behaviour of the purchaser and so affect the type of contracts written, the bidding process and the outcome of the process.

Effects of Partial Observability of Quality on the Behaviour of the Purchaser

Risk aversion of purchaser

In the economics literature on contract design and government purchasing reviewed above it is assumed that the purchaser of services behaves as if risk-neutral. This is because the purchaser is identified as the government. Risk-neutral behaviour on the part of the government is usually supported by reference to its size. Its large size permits it to engage in both risk-pooling and risk-spreading and so allows it to self-insure. It can then act as if risk-neutral. This behaviour can be used in contract design to decrease the costs of services purchased. In dealing with risk-averse providers, the government can carry some of the risk in return for a lower contract price. However, there would appear to be features of the creation of an internal market in social services which may either make the purchaser risk-averse and/or may prevent a risk-averse purchaser from risk-spreading and so behaving as if risk-neutral

The organisational changes which accompany the introduction of contracting for health and social services often have the consequence that the purchaser becomes relatively independent from the rest of the government. The purchaser may have an earmarked budget. The process of contracting may be accompanied by a political process which emphasises the divorce of the provider from a monolithic state bureaucracy. This means the purchaser is unable to spread financial risk with the rest of the government. In addition, the nature of the goods the purchaser seeks to buy may be such that risk-spreading is not possible. In social services markets, the government acts as an agent for certain consumers precisely because they are thought to be weak and vulnerable (the poor, the sick and the handicapped). The political process may be highly sensitive to poor outcomes for these individuals (for example, nursing home scandals, deaths of children in care or protected by social work departments). It may therefore not be possible for the purchaser to spread risk, to pool poor and good quality outcomes in services bought in social service markets. Thus the purchaser, the government, may not be able to act as if risk-neutral.

Type of franchise, contracts and the bidding process

In the literature examined in the first section of the chapter, it is assumed the government cannot observe the production process, but can at least observe the output, including its quality. In HSC markets, it is difficult to observe the quality of the output produced. The fear of poor *ex post* quality, coupled with the high transactions costs involved in (or the impossibility of) writing complete contracts contingent on quality may encourage two types of purchaser behaviour. First, the purchaser may try to build up long term relationships with a provider. This will mean that the purchaser will not want to solicit bids from a large number of bidders, some of whom will be unknown to the purchaser. Evaluation of these bids has transactions costs and the eventual cost of a poor selection may be very high (in political terms). Switching providers may be perceived to conflict with the goal of provision of quality care. It is thus likely that few bids will be sought. In addition, those that are sought will be from providers whose performance is known to the principal. Similarly, at the contract renewal stage the incumbent, whose performance is better-known to the purchaser, will be more likely to get the contract.

Second, the purchaser may attempt to specify those measurable aspects of quality (or inputs believed to relate to quality) in some detail in contracts. Detailed specifications of the production process, in an attempt to ensure some aspects of quality, increases the transactions costs of bidding both for provider and purchaser. This is likely to reduce the number of bidders. It may also reduce the number of small bidders relative to large ones, as small providers are less able to carry the costs of a lengthy contract specification process.

Both these factors tend to reinforce the position of larger providers. If there are economies of scope or scale (for example, if users of the service are served by several programmes, which are cheaper if provided by a single supplier) this will further reinforce the position of large providers. The result is likely to be either oligopolistic competition for contracts, or no competition. The lack of competition for contracts is likely to lead to inefficiency in production and the transfer of rent to incumbents. Thus rather than creating a competitive market on the supply side, contracting leads to monopolistic providers.

Political power of the provider

The economic dominance of large providers may spill over into political power over the purchaser. In the USA, the large for-profit providers of some types of social services often operate in several states. This gives them considerable power relative to the purchaser of services, who by definition will only operate in one state. For example, the provider may be a large employer of labour in the state. If an imbalance of power in favour of the provider exists, it can be used to extract rent from the purchaser. Such power may also be supported by regulatory actions of the government. The 'non-public interest' theory of regulation (for example, Stigler, 1971; Peltzman, 1976) argues that the introduction of regulation, the particular form it takes and its operation over time reflect a complex interaction between interest groups that stand to lose or gain from different types of regulation. Regulation exists because it serves particular interest groups. Regulation is thus endogenous rather than exogenous to the market. A strong supply side, often a large employer in a state, has considerable political influence relative to the purchaser of services, a small part of the state bureaucracy. Thus regulation may be designed such that the incumbent is more likely to get the contract at the renewal stage.

Finally, the contracting process also appears to lead to the supply of certain types of product. Attempts to obtain output of a certain quality may also have dynamic efficiency consequences. In the absence of an ability to monitor output, quality specifications in contracts tend to be in terms of inputs or throughputs. In other words, the production process to be used by the contractor is specified in the contract. Detailed specification of input quality standards, particularly if coupled with penalties for violations of these input standards, discourages innovation (which essentially means using a production process other than that specified in the contract). Thus the nature of the product becomes more homogeneous. In addition, contractors who wish to innovate will be discouraged from bidding. If these are the smaller voluntary sector organisations, innovation is not only limited, but the position of the large for-profit provider, supplying a uniform product, is further reinforced.

The Form of the Contract: Evidence from the Hospital and Nursing Home Sectors

In these markets the evidence on contracts is drawn mainly from the use of contracts in price regulation, rather than from the use of contracts in an internal market. However, a limited amount of evidence exists from the selective contracting experiments in hospital care in California and Arizona. In these states, contracting for services was introduced to promote competition in the health care market. The evidence on the extent of bidding from these two experiments is similar to the experience in the human services sector. Although initially there were many bidders, the number of bidders fell at each stage of the bidding process (McCall *et al.*, 1987). In addition, after the initial bidding rounds, price became less important as a determinant of contract allocation. In Arizona, concern for the continuity of provider plans led to a greater emphasis on criteria related to financial viability and quality assurance (McCall *et al.*, 1987).

The remaining evidence on contract design to be discussed is drawn from the use of different forms of contract in price regulation.[*] In this case prices are imposed on hospitals, rather than established in negotiation between purchaser and provider in the contracting

---

[*]Culyer and Posnett (1990) provide a detailed survey of the impact of rate regulation in the US health care market.

process. I examine evidence both on costs and on other aspects of production, including outcomes, for both fixed and cost-plus contracts.

When price regulations are imposed to keep down expenditure, it is implicitly assumed that a decrease in costs indicates an increase in efficiency. However, when quality cannot be perfectly observed, falling costs may indicate not the desired increase in efficiency, but falling quality. If quality were completely unobservable and a provider derived no utility from the production of quality, then any contract (fixed-price, incentive or cost-plus) would result in production of output of the lowest quality. Even if the provider cared about quality, unless production of quality was cost reducing, the provider who produced the lowest-quality output would get the contract (because it could always set its price to just below that of the producer who produced higher quality). In the health care market, where quality can be partially observed and providers have some interest in providing quality, Holahan and Cohen (1987) have argued that fixed-price contracts will decrease the incentives to provide quality and cost-plus contracts will allow providers to provide quality. There is evidence to suggest that this is not necessarily the case in practice.

Fixed-Price Contracts

Theoretical models of the hospital sector generally conclude that the use of fixed-price contracts will decrease quality, whether hospitals maximise profits or have some other goal.[*] The empirical evidence is

---

[*] Ellis and McGuire (1986) model hospitals as profit maximisers. In their model, physicians act as agents for patients and hospitals, and so are interested in both hospital profits and patient benefits. Patients are assumed fully insured. If physicians give greater weight to hospital profits than to patient benefits, fixed-price contracts will lead to too few services being provided. Morrissey *et al.* (1984) develop a model in which the hospital is a not-for-profit organisation and where quality of output is not completely observable. They show that when faced with a fixed-price contract the hospital will

mixed. This may in part be because many studies did not, or were not able to, distinguish between different types of contract. In practice, a fixed-price system may not operate as such. For example, permitting organisation specific inflation turns a fixed-price contract into a cost-plus contract. Further, most studies look at costs, rather than quality *per se*, and therefore researchers have had to draw inferences from cost changes for quality changes.

Lanning, Morrissey and Ohsfeldt (1991) conclude, both from their own empirical research and from a survey of previous research, that fixed-price contracts decrease costs. Thorpe and Phelps (1990) reached similar conclusions. In both studies, cost was the dependent variable, and neither set of researchers was able to distinguish between increases in efficiency and decreases in quality. However, Lanning *et al.*, concluded that some of the decreases in cost must have been due to reductions in quality. There is some evidence on the effects of contracts on the quality of patient care or outcome from the introduction of Prospective Payment Systems (PPS) under Medicare in 1983. PPS is essentially a fixed-price contract for hospital care. Evidence suggests that PPS leads to a more rapid discharge from hospital (Culyer and Posnett, 1990). This may indicate that patients are getting poorer-quality treatment. It may alternatively indicate that services are being provided more efficiently. Early discharge to appropriate facilities is not quality reduction. However, Gaumer *et al.* (1989) suggest that contracting has been accompanied by a decrease in the clinical quality of care.

––––––––––

have an incentive to lower quality. Thorpe and Phelps (1990) develop a model of a not-for-profit hospital in which utility is derived from quantity and quality of output and which has some degree of monopoly power (so faces a downward-sloping demand curve). In this model, the imposition of a binding price control will unambiguously result in a fall in average costs. To decrease costs, quality will always fall (assuming there was no slack in production prior to the imposition of the fixed-price control). Coyte (1987) develops a model which explores the interaction of price regulation and other aspects of the markets. In this model, the impact of price regulation depends on the other aspects of the markets, but in several cases, fixed-price regulation decreases quality of output. In general, therefore, these models indicate that fixed-price contracts in hospital services will reduce quality.

Shortell and Hughes (1988) found that competitive environments were associated with an increase in inpatient mortality (though the authors were not studying contracting *per se*). Culyer and Posnett (1990) conclude that at present the true impact on patient outcomes of prospective pricing policies and contracting remains unclear. *

The effect of fixed-price contracts on quality would be less of a problem if the quality of care prior to the imposition of price controls was 'too high'. There is some belief that this was the case in the US hospital sector. The operation of third-party payment systems prior to the imposition of price controls was widely argued to lead to cost and quality spirals. This arose in a context in which fee-for-service providers had incentives to maximise the cost of treatment given. This led to high-quality treatment which in turn resulted in high cost premiums. As premiums were paid for by employers, consumers of care had no incentive to minimise expenditure and a spiral of ever increasing cost and quality developed. In this case a decrease in quality would not necessarily be associated with a reduction in efficiency.

However, there is also the question of which elements of quality are cut in response to fixed-price contracts. Health and human services have a number of dimensions. Inputs to increase the quality

---

* The nature of the market may account for some of the differences in the results of empirical studies. Holahan and Cohen (1987) found that following the imposition of price controls the costs (and so the quality) of patient care fell more than that of nonpatient care. From this they argued that incentives should be tailored to allow cost-pass through on patient care and strong cost control on non-patient care. However the differential response in costs observed by Holahan and Cohen may simply be the effect of a decrease in competition which accompanied the regulation of price. In the absence of competition organisational slack increases (because the home faces no competition). If organisational slack is present, there may be expenditure on inputs which benefit managers. Thus costs related to non-patient care will increase. Thus if price controls are accompanied by a decrease in competition, we would expect to see a positive difference between non-care-related and care-related costs. If this is the case, then differential rate-setting for different types of cost will have little impact on quality.

of one service may not be joint with inputs that increase the quality of other dimensions of the service. Empirical studies have not always been able to distinguish between various aspects of the service provided. Thorpe and Phelps suggest that savings were made in non-medical staffing. Lanning, Morrissey and Ohsfeldt (1991) concluded that not all the savings that result from price constraints were due to increases in efficiency; some must be due to reduction in the quality of care (either clinical or amenity). In a study of the effect of rate regulation in nursing home care, Holahan and Cohen (1987) concluded that the use of fixed-price contracts has decreased the quality of inpatient care.

While fixed-price contracts contain incentives to cut costs, they also give incentives for providers to manipulate output to increase reimbursement. From the PPS reimbursement system under Medicaid there is some evidence that providers are less likely to accept high-cost patients (to cream-skim), to discharge patients sooner and to transfer patients into treatment not covered by fixed-price contracts (Culyer and Posnett, 1990). Medicaid reimbursement of hospitals for inpatient care is made under a system of fixed-price contracts with different reimbursement rates for treatments of different severity (DRGs). It has been argued that this system is open to 'DRG creep', the practice of classifying patients such that hospitals maximise the reimbursement per patient. While such provider actions increase the treatment patients receive, since patients do not need such intensive treatment, the level of quality delivered is inefficient (too high). Similar evidence comes from other settings where price controls have been used to control physician behaviour and so expenditure on health care. In a study of physician response to fixed-price and quantity caps in Quebec, Rochaix (1991) found that quality was manipulated upwards to increase physician revenue (near full insurance cover permitted this cost-pass through). Physicians undertook higher quality treatments to increase their incomes.

Cost-Plus Contracts

In reimbursing providers for all costs incurred, cost-plus contracts give more incentives for the production of quality than fixed-price contracts. However, while cost-plus systems offer the possibility that quality will be increased, it is not necessarily the case that providers will respond to cost-plus contracts by increasing quality. In the absence of any monitoring, and if internal incentives to produce quality were low, providers could simply cost-pad. The actual effect of contracts depends on the internal incentives facing providers, and on other aspects of the market and regulatory regimes. Evidence on the impact of cost-plus contracts from the nursing home sector suggests that cost-plus contracts do not necessarily increase quality of provision.

Concern over the quality of care being delivered under fixed-price Medicaid contracts for nursing home care in the late 1970s resulted in the introduction of cost-plus contracts, the explicit aim being to increase quality of care and access of Medicaid patients. However, it is unclear whether this objective has been attained. Nyman (1986, 1988) has argued that the interaction of cost-plus contracts and regulation may have even decreased quality. Nyman (1988) and Gertler (1989) both develop models which show that the Medicaid programme cannot use cost-plus contracts to purchase both increased quality and increased access. They argue that the existence of capacity constraints on the size of a home, together with the presence of private fee-paying patients alongside Medicaid patients, creates a situation in which attempts to increase the return on Medicaid patients will increase access, but will reduce the quality of care supplied. Under cost-plus reimbursement the nursing home receives the marginal cost of a Medicaid patient plus some proportion of total fixed costs. The model assumes that private patients' demand depends on price and quality, and that the quality of care received by each group of patients (in any one home) is identical. All homes face a capacity constraint (the CON constraint). Both authors assume that at (or just above) the mandatory quality limit imposed by regulations there is excess Medicaid demand. Thus the capacity constraint is binding; a home will always be full.

Under these arrangements, an increase in the amount paid for a Medicaid patient will not increase both the quality and number of Medicaid patients. An increase in the amount paid by Medicaid will reduce the gap between the amount earned on a private patient and the amount earned on a Medicaid patient. Medicaid patients then become more desirable. In order to remain within their capacity constraint, the home must reduce quality and/or increase price, so decreasing private demand. Access for the Medicaid patients has increased but quality has not. Nyman goes further and argues that quality will necessarily fall. If the Medicaid rate is high relative to the private rate, homes will have little incentive to compete for private patients, thus will gain nothing from producing quality. Therefore quality will fall. Where the quality of care is a joint product, the interaction of cost-plus reimbursement and binding capacity constraints reduces, and in the end eliminates, the competitive incentive to improve quality. The determinant of quality is not the cost-plus contract, but the extent of competition in which quality is a dimension. With no competition on the quality dimension cost-plus contracts will not increase quality.

Thus, the evidence from the use of contracts to regulate price in the hospital and nursing care markets in the USA provides four key lessons for the operation of quasi-markets. First, providers do respond to the incentives given by contracts. Second, the impact of contract specification depends on the extent to which providers have greater information than the purchasers. Third, opportunities to circumvent price controls exist if there is an unregulated sector, or clients whose fees are not regulated alongside the regulated sector, and when providers have discretion over the patients they treat and the location of treatment. Finally, if quality is not fully observable, opportunities for cutting quality exist under both fixed-price and cost-plus contracts.

Implications for the UK Health and Social Care Quasi-Markets

It is clear that the contracting process as used in the US health and social care markets has been characterised by less competition than originally envisaged. Competition in bidding has been limited. Contractual relationships have been lengthened, provider and purchaser have developed close relationships and the incumbent has often come to dominate the market. The lack of competition appears to be a function of both the purchaser's concern with quality (which leads to high transactions costs in the evaluation of bids, a fear of contracting with a provider who appears to be low-quality and the development of long-term relationships between provider and purchaser) and the tendency to monopoly on the supply side (due to economies of scale or scope in either production or the bidding process). In addition, attempts to control prices give incentives for manipulation of inputs and output, because neither quality nor the technology of production can be easily observed. Will the same problems arise in the UK?

It is too early to answer this question fully, as the quasi-market changes are being phased in slowly in both health and social care. It is, however, possible to examine whether some of the features which have emerged as important in determining the efficiency of contracting in the US markets are also present in the UK. The features of most importance appear to be the quality concerns of the purchaser and the provider, the extent of political vulnerability of the provider, and the tendency toward monopoly on the supply side of the market.

Purchaser Concern with Quality

It is clear that the purchasers in both the health and social care markets have a concern with quality. The explicit brief of purchasers in both the health market and the social care sector is to meet the needs of their client populations. Chapter 4 of this volume and Harrison and Whistow (1991) give evidence of this concern in health service purchasers (district health authorities); Chapter 5 provides evidence of a similar concern on the part of the local authority as purchaser. In both the health and social services markets, in drawing up service agreements (contracts for services) much effort has been spent trying to ensure that providers meet quality goals. Thus, for example, throughput measures of quality (for example, waiting-times) have been features of many contracts in the health care sector. Hoyes and Means in Chapter 5 found local authorities in their study were taking steps to ensure that quality was met.

It is not yet clear whether the reforms have made purchasers more risk-averse or less able to spread risk. On the one hand, it is clear that the reforms have put greater emphasis on the role of the individual purchasing authority. In health care, responsibility has been moved from the centre to the local level. The district health authority has been explicitly made responsible for the health care needs of its local populations. In addition, a new set of smaller purchasers, the GP fundholders, has been established. This latter group is small in size. On the other hand, in response to the near monopoly in provision that providers have under the current 'steady state' operating in the health sector, DHAs are linking together to form larger purchasing authorities (Harrison and Whistow 1991; Chapter 4 of this volume).

In social care, the reforms emphasise the responsibility of the local authority for the needs of their populations. As the client groups served are the vulnerable, the reforms probably do not diminish the political sensitivity, and so the riskiness, of the local authorities' task. On the other hand, they may not increase it either. To the extent that it is implemented, the identification of care-managers with earmarked budgets may reduce the extent of risk-spreading

Provider Concern with Quality

Purchaser concern to achieve particular standards of quality may be unnecessary if providers have a similar concern. The incentives for quality on the supply side are difficult to determine without specific models of the various industries. The strength of the professional in service delivery varies across different parts of the quasi-markets. There is a spectrum which runs from hospitals to nursing homes to residential care to domiciliary care along which the importance of professional ethics becomes weaker. Perhaps as a corollary, the role of the for-profit producer is less important in health care and more important in residential and nursing care. While the ability of the end user to judge the nature of output, including its quality, may actually increase along this spectrum, purchasing agents may not always able or willing to use this information to constrain the activities of providers. Finally, even where professionals have quality goals, these may not be the same as those of the purchasers.

Tendency to Monopoly in Production

Monopoly on the supply side may result from the technology of production, demand conditions and the contracting process itself. It has generally been argued that economies of scale or scope exist in the US hospital sector, though recent research (Vita, 1990) has challenged this. In the UK, it has been argued that small hospitals are uneconomic and government policy has been to close them. The empirical evidence on the existence of economies of scale is inconclusive (a review of findings is provided in Bartlett and Le Grand, 1992). Findings indicating an absence of economies of scale amongst hospitals currently in operation may simply indicate an absence of smaller hospitals with higher average costs. The technology of production in the social care markets is an empirical matter on which there is little detailed evidence. Hoyes and Means in Chapter 5 cite evidence of scale economies in the provision of both residential care and of sheltered housing, though they also note that demand levels may be such that these economies are not necessarily obtained.

Monopoly may also arise as a result of consumer unwillingness to shop around between different providers (say because of asymmetries in information). This clearly arises in the US health care market. However, the UK quasi-market arrangements which make the purchaser the user's agent may reduce the strength of this source of monopoly. The DHA, as purchaser, is better-placed than the individual user to acquire and use information. Therefore this source of monopoly is considerably weaker than in the US hospital market. In the social care field, the care-manager is also more likely to be able to gain information than the individual consumer. Moreover, the problem of asymmetry of information between provider and eventual consumer may be smaller in this market than in the hospital market regardless of institutional arrangements for purchase and provision.

Lack of consumer willingness to travel may also put providers into a local monopoly position. Again, willingness to travel is likely to differ between services. In health care, there is some evidence to suggest patients would travel to avoid long waiting lists or for specialist services, but willingness to travel for accident and emergency services is likely to be considerably more limited. Given the requirements on provision of accident and emergency services under the current quasi-market arrangements, many hospitals could remain local monopolists for the bulk of their activities. In the social care market, monopoly arising from users' willingness to travel is likely to differ across services. For example, there is a large difference between willingness to travel for services provided in or near clients' homes and those that replace home care, such as nursing or residential care homes. Finally, the extent of possible competition also depends on the 'rules of the game' established by central government. The imposition by central government of a 'steady state' in the first year of operation of the health care market meant little competition was possible. The requirement that all hospitals provide accident and emergency related services (which account for over 50 per cent of all activity) also strengthens local monopoly power.

It appears likely that there will be differences between the markets, with the tendency to monopoly in production perhaps being stronger in the hospital that the social care sector, but the risk aversion of the purchaser and the role of for-profit providers perhaps being stronger in the social care market. These technical and institutional differences suggest that purchasers seeking efficient contracting arrangements are likely to use different franchising procedures and different forms of contracts in the different markets.

Contract Design to Reduce Possible Inefficiencies in UK Quasi-Markets

The literature discussed inthe first section suggests that the purchaser may be able to design contracts both to overcome lack of competition in, or for, the market and to achieve a desired quality of service. The tools available to the purchaser include the specification of services to be delivered under the contract (within the framework established by the current rules set at central government level), the length of contracts, the method of reimbursement and the design and use of sanctions.

Measures to Increase Competition for the Contract

The analysis of the first section of the chapter and the US experience suggest a number of ways of increasing the incentives to bid for contracts, and so increasing the extent of competition for the market. The first is to design the contract so that provider risk is reduced. This will attract risk-averse providers to bid for the contract. If risks are correlated across various parts of the service put out to contract, breaking the service into subprojects and placing contracts for each of the subprojects may increase the number of bidders. It may also increase the number of small organisations entering the bidding process. Against this potential gain must be set any losses in efficiency arising from loss of economies of scale or scope. If larger organisations can more cheaply provide a range of services than smaller ones, and bidders are prevented from bidding for a number of contracts, breaking a service up may entail a loss of productive efficiency. Contracting for a large number of small projects may also increase transactions costs, both for purchasers and, where potential providers bid for more than one contract, for the potential bidders. It therefore seems that encouragement of a large number of small bidders may be appropriate where there are no scale or scope economies, or where small bidders have a history of innovation and high quality as, for example, in some social care provision. This approach would appear less useful where scale economies may exist as, for example, in the hospital sector.

Uncertainty over the nature of the quality required by the purchaser increases the riskiness of the contract. This uncertainty will therefore reduce the number of bidders, and may increase the ratio of large to small bidders, as the former are more likely to be less risk-averse. Where quality of output is difficult to specify, one way to let bidders know what production will entail, and so to reduce the risk of the project, is to announce the total size of the desired expenditure on each programme being put out to tender. This method was used in the contracting process in Massachusetts (Schlesinger, Dorwart and Pulice, 1985) in an attempt to encourage small bidders. The gain from the potential increase in the number of bidders has to be set off against the loss from the incentives for cost-padding offered under such contracting arrangements.

This strategy, in common with that of breaking up a project into smaller parts, shifts the risk from provider to purchaser. In those cases where the purchaser is more risk-averse than the provider, such contract design is not likely to be efficient. Therefore this strategy may be less useful in the hospital sector where providers are large and perhaps less risk-averse than the purchaser. However, it may be useful where small scale providers are thought to be able to provide a high-quality service, as perhaps in some areas of the social care sector.

Asset specificity gives opportunities for opportunistic behaviour by either the purchaser or the contract winner (Dnes, 1991; Ferguson and Posnett, 1990). It also gives the incumbent provider an advantage over competitors at the contract renewal stage. Thus a high degree of asset specificity is likely to reduce the extent of bidding. One method of limiting the power of an incumbent, and so of increasing the number of bidders, is to reduce the length of the contract. This will mean the incumbent has less time to invest in task-specific assets. It will thus be less dominant at the contract renewal stage. On the other hand, decreasing the length of a contract will reduce the extent to which the contracting process can mimic a long-term trust relationship, which may be desired if quality cannot be observed. The length of contract is also likely to depend on the degree of specificity of assets in production; if the assets are very specific, bidders for a contract will want longer contracts to compensate for the need to build up project-specific assets. Longer term contracts will therefore be more appropriate where capital is asset-specific (for example, as in the hospital sector), or where quality is hard to evaluate and the purchaser needs to rely on the 'track record' of the provider, or where there is considerable uncertainty over the nature of production.

Another measure to increase the number of bidders is to alter the nature of the franchise from one that requires the winner to supply all assets to an 'operating-only' contract. Under such a contract, providers bid to provide services, leasing the assets required for their provision from the purchaser. This would essentially mean that bidders compete for a management franchise, with the non-human capital assets remaining in the public sector. The scope for asset-leasing will depend on the importance of non-human product-specific capital relative to human capital. There is more non-human capital in the hospital and residential/nursing home sector than in other social services, so asset-leasing would be more suited to the former markets. In essence, this is what has happened in the case of NHS Trusts, except that there has been no competition for the right to manage these assets. As with all methods to improve the incentive properties of contracts, asset-leasing has associated drawbacks. As the capital is not owned by the winning bidder, it has little incentive to maintain investment in the leased capital, and so the capital stock may deteriorate over time. If asset-leasing were adopted, contracts would have to be written so that winners had incentives to keep up investment in the assets.

Measures to Provide Incentives for Production of Quality Through Contract Design

The theoretical analysis of contract design discussed in the first section of the chapter suggests that fixed-price and cost-plus contracts have very different incentive properties. Fixed-price contracts encourage providers to reduce their costs, perhaps at the expense of quality of service. Cost-plus contracts give greater incentives to provide a higher quality of service, but encourage cost-padding. The empirical evidence of the first section of the chapter suggests that in quasi-markets in which quality is not fully observable, the distinction between fixed-price and cost-plus contracts may be less important than other features of the contract. Nevertheless, in general in HSC markets, the incentive properties of full risk-sharing (cost-plus) contracts do not seem very useful. Limited observability of output gives incentives for cost-padding. Some degree of risk-sharing in contracts will be appropriate where the purchaser is less risk-averse than the provider, say in the hospital sector, where the purchaser may be larger in relationship to the provider than in the social care market. Risk-sharing will not increase efficiency when the provider is less risk-averse than the purchaser, say in the case where a large for-profit nursing home provider is the provider to a small local authority purchaser. Where quality can be relatively easily observed, and the purchaser is more risk-averse than the provider, fixed-price contracts, which place all the risk upon the provider, may be most efficient (Note that the purchaser's gain from the reduction of risk to zero will have to be weighed up against the decrease in number of bidders induced by this type of contract).

Payments may be linked to the severity of illness, thus discouraging the providers from 'cream-skimming'. This is essentially what the Diagnostic Related Group (DRG) pricing system widely used in US hospital care is designed to do. However, such a system will not eliminate the incentive to put patients in as remunerative a category as possible (for example, the so-called 'DRG creep'). In addition, categorisation of patients has transactions costs for the purchaser. Different qualities of care must be specified in the contract and a patient's need for care must be assessed by a purchaser or regulatory body. Where the purchaser of care already makes some assessment of patient illness severity (for example, as part of the referral process) the additional monitoring costs may not be large. This may therefore be useful in the social care market where the care-manager will assess the needs of individual clients as part of the contracting process.

Where privately funded patients share facilities with publicly funded patients information provided by private consumers could be used in contract design to increase incentives for provision of higher-quality care to publicly funded users. In the US nursing home context, Nyman (1986) has suggested a reimbursement system that makes the Medicaid payment a positive function of the proportion of private patients in the home. As private patients are assumed to be able to identify levels of quality of service, higher proportions of private patients are signals of higher-quality facilities. Higher-quality facilities will receive higher Medicaid reimbursement rates, so an incentive for provision of higher-quality services is given.

For such a contract to have desirable incentive properties, private consumers must be able to identify levels of quality of service, and the transactions costs to the purchaser of determining quality directly must be higher than those incurred by inferring quality from the behaviour of private patients. Nyman argues that in the nursing home context, given that private patients are going to live in the home (perhaps until they die) they have a strong incentive (or their relatives do) to collect information on quality. Thus observing their actions may be more cost-effective than either detailed specification in the contract bidding process or direct monitoring, the latter also being open to regulator capture. In the UK in both the hospital and nursing home sectors, private patients do not currently share facilities with publicly funded patients, but there may be increasing opportunities for this to occur (say if the purchaser were to increase the use of private sector hospital providers). However, in the case of hospital care, neither private nor public users may be able to assess quality. In nursing home care, users may be better able to assess quality, and so this approach may be more appropriate in this sector. For the effective operation of such a contract mechanism, the state reimbursement rate must be far enough below the private price that the provider has an incentive to take some private patients. In addition, if all quality improvements are not patient-specific, there is a danger that providers will cross-subsidise from state-funded patients to private patients, creating a two-tier structure within a single facility.

Concern over quality may lead to detailed specification of input or throughput standards in contracts. But such action increases the transactions costs of bidding and so reduces the number of bidders. It may also decrease the proportion of small bidders as they are less likely to be able to bear the costs of a lengthy contract-specification process. One possible solution is to specify verifiable output standards and punish non-achievement of these standards. Providers can thus use whatever production process they wish, subject to the constraint of meeting the required output standards. This approach obviously requires that some dimensions of the quality of output can be measured and verified. However, it does not require that all dimensions can be observed. Typically, the dimensions which may be observed are negative ones, indicators of absence of quality. New York State operates such procedures in its regulation of nursing homes. A set of negative outcome indicators is defined. If the incidence of these events in a home is above a level defined with respect to all facilities, the home is investigated and appropriate sanctions are brought to bear (Day and Klein, 1987). This procedure has the advantage that the purchasers need not be involved in giving advice on inputs or on appropriate production functions. Thus monitoring costs are lowered and the charge of regulator capture avoided. This strategy also avoids the loss of dynamic efficiency which may be associated with detailed input specification.

Such a strategy requires that appropriate output standards can be defined (and to avoid large bargaining costs, these probably must be such that there is a high degree of consensus over their relevance). It also requires that sanctions for non-performance can be implemented. In order that sanctions are effective they must be credible. Experience in New York (Day and Klein, 1987) indicates that the hands-off stance implied by this approach is not always followed. There is an acknowledged difficulty in preventing regulatory staff from playing a consultancy role. There is flexible implementation of sanctions, fines are used rather than closure, and not necessarily collected. Enforcement becomes a matter of political judgement in which a trade-off is made between the encouragement of a surplus of facilities which allows closure and the financial costs of such a policy.

This approach could be useful in designing contracts for certain services provided in the social care market. An example is the residential care market in which there has been considerable invest-igation into quality standards (for example, Department of Health, 1989a). However, it is possible that the required hands-off behaviour of purchasers would be difficult to achieve in the UK social care market. Flynn (1990b), for example, has argued that care-managers need to learn to operate more as brokers and advisers and less as agents making all the decisions, indicating that a hands-off stance may not currently be adopted in the transition to a quasi-market. In order for this approach to operate successfully, the sanctions for non-performance must be implementable. Nyman (1986) has argued that in the case of nursing home care, closure is limited as a sanction because it is politically unappealing and therefore difficult for a legislator to do. An alternative to sanctions is the takeover of the management. This avoids the need to close the facility, thus allowing continuity of care. This is probably politically more appealing (and is similar to asset-leasing discussed above). The use of management takeover as a punishment for not meeting contract specifications may be more successful where this does not threaten continuity of care than in parts of the market where continuity of care is an important dimension of quality. So it is likely to be a more useful sanction against providers of acute hospital services than against providers of long-term residential care, though it may be more useful in other parts of the social care market. Finally, the use of indicators for only a subset of the quality dimensions of output will encourage inefficient production. Providers have an incentive to concentrate upon those aspects of production which mean output meets the (negative) indicators of quality and to ignore other dimensions of quality.

Finally, one strategy a purchaser may adopt to ensure quality is to build up long-term relationships with providers. Within a contract-ing framework this means increasing contract length and awarding contracts at the renewal stage to incumbents. The evidence reviewed in the third and fourth sections of this chapter suggests this is common following the adoption of contracting in US HSC mar-kets. If quality is very difficult to observe and professionals with high-quality standards have strong representation within the provider organisations, this may be the most efficient strategy. However, it leaves the purchaser open to provider opportunism, may limit the extent of variety in the market and may reduce dynamic efficiency.

Each aspect of contract and franchise design has associated advantages and disadvantages. The relative balance of incentives will depend on the technology of production, the verifiability of output, the extent of information asymmetry between provider and purchaser and the degree of relative risk aversion of provider and purchaser. As these factors differ across different segments of the HSC markets, efficiency will require different contract specification in different parts of the markets.

Conclusions

The efficiency gains from the replacement of a monopoly public provider with an arm's-length relationship between purchaser and provider depend upon the nature of the market that will evolve after separation of purchaser and provider. Economic analyses stress the importance of industry specific factors in determining these gains. The quasi-markets established by the recent reforms of the health and social care markets in the UK are currently insufficiently developed to make an assessment of the impact of the reforms. This chapter has therefore examined the experience of contracting in the US health and human services markets.

This experience indicates that competition for contracts in these markets has been limited. After initial interest, few providers bid for the franchise, the incumbent often receives the franchise, and both the bidding for and the delivery of service are dominated by large, often for-profit, providers. Price becomes relatively unimportant in the assessment of bids. Providers and purchasers together seek to replace competition with long-term relationships. These patterns appear to be the result of purchaser concern over quality, the partial verifiability of quality of output or inputs, and purchaser inability to spread risk.

The evidence on contract design, taken from the use of contracts in price regulation in the hospital and nursing home industries, indicates that fixed-price contracts appear to limit cost increases, but perhaps at the expense of quality of service. Cost-plus contracts potentially provide more incentive for improvements in quality of service but do not in practice necessarily result in a higher quality of service. Asymmetry of information between the purchaser and the provider subject to regulation may give the provider incentives to cream-skim and to under supply care to high-cost users.

The chapter has assessed the implications of these findings for the newly emergent markets in health and social care in the UK. The discussion indicates that the technology of production, the relative size of provider and purchaser, their relative extent of risk aversion and the extent of information asymmetry between provider and purchaser will vary across these markets. Thus the efficiency gains from the introduction of competition in provision will also vary. Given this, the chapter has discussed the possible features of the contract and franchise design which may encourage efficient production and give incentives for the provision of quality in service delivery. There is no single blueprint for all quasi-markets; the different structures of the markets require different forms of contract and franchise design.

Quasi-Markets and the National Health Service Reforms

4

Will Bartlett
and Lyn Harrison

By far the greatest part of health care in the UK is provided through the National Health Service (NHS). The NHS is one of the largest organisations in the world, employing over a million people throughout the UK. Throughout the 1980s, the NHS increased its share of public spending, and the Department of Health is now the second largest spending department, with an expenditure of £21.57bn on the NHS in England alone in 1990/91. Moreover, by some measures the efficiency of service delivery has been improving throughout the 1980s: the number of patients per bed has increased from 16 in 1980 to over 23 in 1988/89; average bed occupancy stands at 80 per cent, compared to 55–65 per cent in the residual private health care sector.

Yet some problems remain. There is a large and growing waiting list, which passed the one million mark in 1990. Inefficiencies and inequities can arise in the way in which priorities are set to manage this large queue. More significantly perhaps, it is claimed by some critics of the system that there are high levels of micro-economic inefficiency in the allocation of resources, both spatially on account of the historically-determined geographical allocation of resources, and across different types of health care, due to the implicit nature of decision criteria.

The NHS and Community Care Act was introduced by the Thatcher Government in 1990, partly in response to these criticisms, and partly in reflection of the general policy trend towards the extension of the domain of operation of market forces into the provision of welfare services. More recently, the post-Thatcher Conservatives have been at pains to stress the merits of the National Health Service, and have cast the reforms as an attempt to improve its efficiency, rather than as an attempt to replace it with something entirely new and different.

The Act, as with other elements of the quasi-market reforms, introduced both a decentralisation of control to independent provider units, and elements of a transfer of state ownership to organisations with a non-profit status. The decentralisation of control is effected through a splitting of the NHS into two sets of 'purchaser' and 'provider' units. Firstly, in the new system the District Health Authorities (DHAs) and budget-holding General Practitioners (GPs) (still a minority of GPs) become the *purchasers*, along with private individuals, insurance companies and employers. Second, services are supplied by *providers* which include the hospitals which remain under DHA control (Directly Managed Units), GPs, and other newly independent 'provider units': the 'self-managing' NHS Trusts.

It is intended that the new system will address some of the critics' concerns, principally about the microefficiency of the system. Concern with the choice and equity issues was less prominent, although some features of the reform of the funding system do address them. For example, both DHAs and GP budget-holders receive their revenue on a capitation basis: DHAs on the basis of their resident population (by 1995), in line with previous trends towards a more consistent spatial allocation of resources; GPs on the basis of their patient list size, with the intention of promoting responsiveness to patient choices. New GP contracts, and the devolution of budgetary control to GP fundholders were intended to introduce more effective systems of incentives to stimulate GP effort.

One of the most significant new departures from previous arrangements is to be found in the creation of a system of independent non-profit NHS Trusts. The first wave of NHS Trusts accounted for 41 000 (15 per cent) of the total number of 298 000 available beds in the NHS, and for £1.8bn out of its total £13.3bn expenditure budget (Newchurch, 1990). They employed 110 000 employees (representing 13 per cent of the total NHS workforce), had assets valued at over

£3.8bn and had planned capital programmes of over £930m for the period 1991–4. Most first-wave NHS hospital trusts were formed by general acute hospitals (25 cases). Others were formed by provider units of entire district health authorities (DHAs) opting out of DHA control (9 cases) or from providers operating district community services (6), mental health and mental handicap services (6), specialist hospitals (7), and ambulance services (3). The Trusts are widely spread geographically, with each of the 14 health authority regions having at least one first-wave NHS Trust. They were followed by a second wave of conversions in April 1992, when a further 99 NHS Trusts were established.

An NHS Trust is run by a board of directors, which consists of a chairperson, five non-executive directors, and five executive directors. The non-executive members of the board consist of two 'community directors' appointed by the regional health authority, and up to three others appointed by the Department of Health, and are likely to include people with top-level management experience in finance, information technology, legal services and personnel management. The executive directors, drawn from the upper echelons of the medical and administrative staff, represent the employee and professional interest, and give substance to the Act's description of the Trusts as 'self-managing' units.

The board is able to run the Trust as an independent business, so that Trusts can establish their own input mix (type and mix of staff, materials and so on), and to agree output levels with the various purchaser units with which they draw up contracts. They are able to set levels of remuneration, bonus payments, and working conditions for their own workforce. For example, the Homewood Trust in Surrey signed the first NHS no-strike deal with labour unions in the NHS in March 1992. They are able to retain financial services, and reinvest such surpluses in the Trust. Income is generated on the basis of contracts drawn up with a variety of purchasers, including DHAs (not necessarily entirely with the parent DHA), GP budget-holders, insurance companies, employers, individuals and other NHS Trusts and Directly Managed Units.

The assets of the hospitals and other service units which comprise a new NHS Trust are transferred to its ownership when it is established (NHSME 1990). The Trust becomes the new owner, free to dispose of any of the assets as the directors see fit, within broad limits, and to purchase and develop new sets of assets. Sales of assets are subject to the veto of the Secretary of State for asset disposals valued at over £1m, whilst development schemes with a value of over £10m require approval from the NHS Management Executive.

At the same time a Trust receives a debt equivalent to the current market value of the transferred assets. This debt is held in two forms. The first part will be a fixed interest rate loan in the form of interest-bearing debt (IBD). The second part, however, is a public equity stake in the form of 'public dividend capital' (PDC). The exact proportions in which these two types of debt are held by each individual Trust is declared by the Secretary of State at the time the Trust is established, and generally lies between a two-thirds/one-third split and 50/50 split between PDC and IBD. The important point however, is that the dividend on the PDC is a contingent cost, payable only when the Trust is in financial surplus. In this way, part of the debt service payment is made contingent upon the state of the world prevailing at any particular time, and this has the effect of shifting a proportion of the risk involved in managing an NHS Trust on to the State.

Central to the operation and performance of the new arrangements for health care provision is the system of contracts which links the purchasers and providers on the new quasi-market, and on which the new system of resource allocation will rest (Bartlett, 1991a,b). It is envisaged that contracts will be of two types. The first type will be a cost-per-case contract. This, as one can imagine, sets a cost, or price, for each type of treatment. Contract prices can be set on an average cost basis, or on a marginal cost basis where there is excess capacity. Prices are regulated so that Trusts make a 6 per cent return on their assets when entering into contracts with NHS purchasers, although they are allowed to exceed this target when entering into a contract with the private sector. The cost-per-case contract cannot be a complete contract, in the sense of specifying a separate price contingent on every set of circumstances. Nevertheless, any such contract is likely to require a far greater degree of price information than is currently available, since in most cases, individual treatment costs are not precisely known. In addition, such contracts are likely to be costly to write, implement and enforce, the more so the more complete the nature of the contract. It is not surprising therefore that an early survey of the intentions of those units which applied for Trust status in the first round found that only 14 per cent of such applicants intended to operate mainly on the basis of cost-per-case contracts (Newchurch, 1990).

The second type of contract which is in common use is the block contract. This is an incomplete contract in which the purchaser agrees to pay the Trust an annual fee in return for access to a broadly defined range of services. Broad performance targets, such as an increase in the proportion of day cases, maximum target waiting lists, reduced lengths of stay, and so on, are also laid down in the contract. The contract will also specify the mechanisms by which quality is to be monitored, and the remedies available if a Trust fails to meet the terms of the contract. However, such contracts are inevitably incomplete, in the technical sense that they are not able to specify a fee structure which is contingent upon every possible state of nature (that is, every contingency). Moreover, an asymmetry of information exists between purchaser and provider concerning the level to which the contract is fulfilled, despite the implementation of medical audit procedures designed to monitor service quality. Since block contracts are incomplete, and since information is asymmetric, they are open to the problem of what Williamson (1975) calls 'opportunism'. This problem occurs once an incomplete contract is agreed, and purchaser and supplier are locked in to the contract. The provider unit is then in a position to vary its performance strategy and choose an imperfectly observed set of actions in pursuit of its own private interests, resulting in a level and mix of service quality which may not optimise the purchaser's interest. In the present context, this could just as easily be a level of service quality that is too high in some prestigious areas (relative to the efficient level), as a level that is too low due to an excessively lax set of working practices. This 'opportunism' effect (a form of moral hazard) may work to increase the costs of service delivery over and above that which would obtain under an integrated purchaser/provider system (such as existed before the reforms were introduced).

In addition, the existence of uncertainty about the exact costs involved in meeting an incompletely specified set of obligations can impose a high degree of risk upon the provider, given that under a block contract the contract fee is fixed, even though the delivery costs are variable, and only partially controllable by the provider unit itself. In the case where Trusts are risk-averse, such uncertainty over cost outcomes may increase the desired fee for any specified quantity and quality of service delivery, since the contract fee will have to include an element to cover their risk premium. This may be an additional factor tending to increase the cost of operating a contract-based system of health service delivery, the more so the greater the extent to which risk is shifted on to the provider, although in practice an element of risk-sharing is built into the system through the use of Public Dividend Capital to fund a Trust's debt.

Thus, the new system of health service provision is likely to have two offsetting effects on efficiency and performance. On the one hand, the increased incentives provided to suppliers of services by the operation of market-type price signals, and by the possibility which the new arrangements will give to the independent provider units to appropriate financial surpluses, will tend to increase efficiency and reduce costs. On the other hand, there are a variety of factors which may work in the opposite direction. These include the increased risk premia required by risk-averse providers; the increased administrative costs of fully specified cost-per-case contracts; the increased labour costs which may follow the break-up of the NHS monopsony on the labour market; and the possibility that providers will adopt opportunistic strategies in the face of incomplete 'block' contracts. These factors will all tend to reduce efficiency and to raise the costs of supplying health services. The outcome of these opposing factors is as yet indeterminate, and careful empirical research will be required to estimate and determine their relative impact.

In the rest of this chapter we consider one example of the way in which the new system has been established and operated in its early stages, based on case study research carried out in the second half of 1989 and early 1990. The example is the Bristol and Weston DHA in whose area two newly independent Hospital Trusts, each comprising a group of several hospitals and community care services, were established on 1 April 1991. (Since this study was carried out Bristol and Weston Health Authority has been merging with the two other health authorities in the conurbation of Bristol, forming the Bristol District Health Authority.)

Introducing the Purchaser Provider Split in one Health Authority

Bristol and Weston Health Authority includes central and southern areas of the city of Bristol along with a cluster of rural and urban communities around the seaside town of Weston-super-Mare (WSM) and the towns of Nailsea and Keynsham. There two CHCs within the district, one for Bristol and one for Weston.

Bristol and Weston Health Authority is within the county of Avon, and this includes three other health authorities (HAs), Frenchay, Southmead and Bath (see Map 4.1).

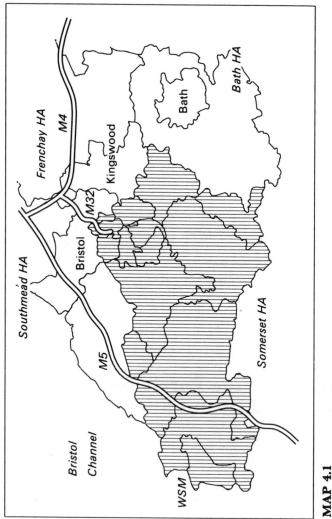

MAP 4.1
Bristol and Weston Health Authority Showing Neighbouring Health Authorities
Source: Bristol and Weston Health Authority (1990).

Bath Health Authority is under the Wessex Regional Health Authority, while the other three Avon health authorities fall within the South Western Regional Health Authority. The revenue cash allocations in 1990/91 were £118 million for Bristol and Weston HA, £60 million for Frenchay HA and £64 million for Southmead HA. The move to per capita funding will most adversely affect Southmead and Bristol and Weston HAs. There is considerable patient flow between the districts with, for example, Bristol and Weston HA accounting for approximately 10 per cent of Frenchay's inpatients and approximately 15 per cent of Southmead's.

Bristol and Weston HA's main hospitals are located on a site around St Michael's Hill, close to the university. The Royal Infimary, Children's Hospital, Maternity Hospital, Radiotherapy and Oncology Centre are all within this precinct. This site is close to the city centre and is positioned on extremely steep hills.

Implementing the Reforms

Bristol and Weston Authority responded positively to the proposals in the White Paper and this was reflected in two key areas. First, it implemented the split into purchaser and provider units from the beginning of 1989 and second, both Bristol and Weston were in the first wave of applications for Trust status. In each case the application was for all hospital and community services to be considered as a single unit. The timing of the restructuring of the management units within Bristol and Weston, along with the South Western Region Health Authority (SWRHA), and the introduction of contractual arrangements for cross-boundary flow during 1990, means that there was general agreement that this authority was further advanced than the average in terms of 'preparedness' for April 1991.

The purchaser/provider split was made both at the level of the health authority membership, and within management structures. A purchaser committee and two provider committees (one for Bristol and one for Weston) were established as committees of the health authority. These three committees were chaired by members of the health authority, and each consisted of officers and members.

The district general manager was the only manager to retain joint membership, attending both purchaser and provider committees. All other managers were designated either purchasers or providers. These committees reported back to the full health authority and replaced five member/officer committees which had previously supported the district health authority. The departments of Planning, Information and Finance continued to support both the purchasing and providing function.

On the provider side, in addition to maintaining the services within both Bristol and Weston, members and officers were involved in drafting business plans for Trust status.

Distinctive Factors

It is perhaps worth considering at this stage, before moving into a more detailed consideration of developments within Bristol and Weston, in what ways this authority may be seen as distinctive in the context of implementing the White Paper.

Bristol and Weston is a teaching authority and historically this has been a very strong part of its tradition, shaping the development of the hospital complex. Bristol does not, however, share the problems of many of the London teaching hospitals which may be characterised as an overprovision of specialist beds in the context of a declining but highly disadvantaged inner-city resident population. The teaching dimension does, however, mean another powerful set of interests are involved in the complex processes of implementing a quasi-market.

Bristol, like some of the London health authorities, has close neighbouring health authorities (Bath, Frenchay and Southmead) which were already providing some services to its community. A pan-Avon perspective has persisted, despite the removal of the area-level health authority, and provided the opportunity to ensure a more coordinated provision of services within this geographical area. Bristol and Weston carried this broader view, and the related complex negotiations with adjoining health authorities, through the implementation process.

While reorganisation within any service will always coincide with other ongoing developments and therefore never be at the 'right' time, Bristol and Weston was already in the process of implementing a number of key developments which impinged significantly on the implementation of the White Paper. First, the process of rationalising the size and location of services which was already under way required a commitment by purchasers to a significant level of future funding for particular services. In this case, since the development was on to a more costly site, the need to secure appropriate funding was particularly sensitive. Second, Bristol and Weston was in the final stages of a shift of resources into priority services, and this provided little room for manoeuvre in terms of allocation of revenue expenditure. This situation was exacerbated by the fact that the annual resource allocation to Bristol and Weston was to be reduced from its previous level by the order of 6 per cent. This meant that all new expenditure would have to be made through efficiency savings if existing services were not to be cut.

Bristol and Weston health authority may also be viewed as unusual in that it wished to transfer all its services into two Trusts. This was perceived as more complex and possibly involving more risks than for a non-teaching authority, because of the size of the teaching hospital unit and the 'pioneering' style of its 'first wave' application.

The Interviews

In order to illuminate what was happening in the Bristol and Weston Health Authority and to make some assessment of its significance, information was gathered through attendance at meetings and interviews with a small number of key individuals during the period from April 1989 to March 1990.

Three main groups could be distinguished in terms of their perspectives on the developments following the White Paper. These were the purchaser committee, the team developing the proposal for Trust status, and a much larger and heterogeneous group including the employees of the health authority and some health authority and CHC members. While the objectives and views of the first two groups were reasonably clear and consistent, the latter group was characterised by higher levels of uncertainty and lack of clarity about what could be achieved within the rapidly changing environment.

Setting Up the Purchaser Role

The purchaser committee had the challenge of a new explicit function. This engaged the members of the team, both officers and members, and visible progress was made towards achieving a number of goals. These achievements were associated primarily with the process of assessing the needs of the community and converting these needs into contracts which could specify cost, quantity and quality. While it was acknowledged that it was an enormously difficult task to achieve these objectives, the team appreciated the space which had been created by the purchaser/provider split. This provided an opportunity for the assessment of service requirements to take place independently of the pressure from existing service providers. How effective the group would be in shifting the pattern of services in the long term was something about which no-one was very certain.

The key officers involved in the purchasing committee included the director of public health, a manager concerned with contracts and quality, and a finance officer who acted as general manager for the purchaser committee. While these officers were only concerned with the purchaser function, some staff supporting them through financial and information systems were also providing a similar function for the Bristol provider unit.

For community physicians assessing local needs was not entirely a new role, but it certainly had taken on a greater prominence and priority in the functioning of the health authority; it meant that their skills and training could be applied directly to the function of purchasing health services, rather than being subservient to the preoccupation with the clinical functions of hospital consultants. The short-term objectives then for this team was to obtain a better understanding of GPs' views on the adequacy of existing services in meeting the needs of their patients, and to foster methods of working with or through community groups to obtain more direct views on the health needs of the population. The process of translating these into contracts was taken forward in two ways: first, through feeding back the views of GPs to clinicians and the other officers and second by four more formal pilot projects on contracts. Much of this work was informed by the objectives set by the regional health authority, and involved particularly finance officers at region and district working closely together. It was recognised that establishing the structures for contracting could easily become an end in itself. It was therefore felt important by some members of the group to keep in mind the broader strategic issues and to try to identify what was the real potential for purchasing.

The purchaser group's actions were constrained by the messages from the Regional Health Authority which were emphasising the need to proceed slowly, and for the bulk of services from 1991 to be purchased in similar volume, and from the same providers, as in the previous year and with costs broadly in keeping with previous years' budgets. In addition to this 'steady state' restriction, the purchasers indicated that factors such as the lack of appropriate staff, and the failure to distance themselves sufficiently from the providers, were also impeding the development of the purchasing function. In particular, the lack of resources to set up the appropriate information systems meant that the contracting process was slowed down. While clearly there had been costs in establishing the purchaser role, mainly in withdrawing staff from their previous management functions, this was seen as relatively low compared with the costs of developing the Trust proposal.

Setting Up the Provider Role

The team involved in developing the Trust proposal included the ex-chair of the health authority and the district general manager. Within this group the objective was to establish a successful Trust within Bristol. This objective was seen to reflect the wishes of the Secretary of State and there was little critical debate about the strengths and weaknesses of Trust status as compared with directly managed units (DMUs). However, greater freedoms to act outside Regional control were anticipated as a potential benefit.

The draft proposal for the Trust, therefore, did not attempt to show why a Trust was more desirable than a DMU, but argued that Bristol would be able to deliver a Trust combining hospitals and community services successfully. The distinctions between the work done within the authority on developing both the Trust and the purchaser and provider functions were to some extent blurred. Until June 1990 no separate work was done in exploring the management structures and implications of a DMU. The group working on the Trust proposal felt that energy put into developing new personnel functions or financial management would be equally required, whether a Trust or a DMU finally came into operation.

This focus towards the Trust did, however, mean that the provider committee's role was not as stimulating and innovative as that of the purchaser. It was more concerned with receiving reports and routine operational matters. Indeed, some of the members began to doubt whether the meetings were an effective use of their time.

The work on the provider side which absorbed most resources during this period was that undertaken by the financial officers. This would, however, have been required regardless of whether a Trust or a DMU was to be developed. Time had also been specifically spent both by managers and clinicians in developing the Trust proposal and this could be seen to be distracting from the normal management functions. In the area of resource management, the authority was lagging behind those hospitals where specific initiatives were being undertaken.

Reactions and Conflicts

Outside these two groups, the purchaser committee and the group involved in developing the Trust proposal, which had clearly defined short-term goals, there seemed to be high levels of uncertainty about how to assess the merits of the White Paper proposals and their implications for the functioning of the NHS. These uncertainties in part indicated an absence of much opportunity for detailed discussion, but also reflected a lack of information about how the proposals would work out in practice. There were few formal statements about the way in which the 'rules of the game' of the new system would be formulated and enforced at the local level, and so it came down to having to wait and see what would emerge over time.

It was not surprising then, given these different dimensions of uncertainty, that the views of many individuals or groups were influenced by professional bodies, trade unions or political parties at a national level. These views tended to be based on bold differences of principle which distinguish political parties or which inform bargaining by occupational groups. They were, however, not sufficiently 'finely tuned' to deal with the complexities and uncertainties surrounding the implementation of the White Paper proposals. Many individuals recognised the problem of 'throwing the baby out with the bath water' in adopting a blanket acceptance of or resistance to the White Paper. Since many individuals had only these rather crude frameworks for making sense of the White Paper, it was perhaps to be anticipated that the overall reaction of the Bristol and Weston Health

Authority workforce was negative. The 'party' lines from the Labour Party, health service unions and the BMA were against the reforms. They were influential because in situations of uncertainty the most appropriate reaction is often to hang on to the familiar and known and opt for the status quo, or at least its nearest equivalent.

Within this turbulent and uncertain environment individuals' reactions reflected the extent to which they had some control or influence in their work situation, and the extent to which they perceived key individuals being able to determine outcomes locally. These considerations were important for individuals or groups to assess what the changes meant for them in the day-to-day sense. Broad-principled and often emotional debates about the provision of health care through a market or public sector mechanism were accompanied by speculation and anxieties about how status, pay, and job satisfaction would be affected in the new environment.

It is therefore possible, given these limited frames of reference which could be applied to the developments, to appreciate how specific local factors had considerable potential to influence perceptions and progress. The transition to Trust status could be represented not as a new and radical approach to health care but as a reversion to the old hospital management boards which existed pre-1974. Thus Trusts were represented as close to a structure, which if not the status quo was still familiar ground for those who had been in the NHS for some time and embodying the same values.

The overall reactions to the proposals of Trust status also differed between Bristol and Weston health services. There was a higher level of support for the latter than for the former. While this could in part be explained by the compactness and relative simplicity of the Weston unit compared to Bristol, for some people it was their perceptions concerning the differences in the objectives underpinning the two bids which provoked contrasting responses.

Towards Efficiency, Responsiveness, Choice and Equity in Health Care?

The conditions for the successful operation of a quasi-market across a wide range of social welfare services in terms of their impact upon efficiency, responsiveness, choice and equity have been established in

Chapter 2 above. Each of these will now be considered in turn in the light of the developments in the Bristol and Weston Health Authority.

Market Structure

The outcome of the first wave Trust applications was that two Trusts, one in Bristol and one in Weston, were created in April 1991. Two further Trusts were established in Avon by April 1992 in the second wave of bids. Within Avon (and for the moment excluding Bath Health Authority) there were initially three purchasing health authorities which were subsequently combined into one large pan-Avon purchasing authority in autumn 1991. In addition there were initially two GP budget-holders also purchasing services. The Trusts are themselves able to purchase services from each other and from DMUs. In practice, however, given the rules imposed on the quasi-market by the Department of Health through the regional health authorities, each purchaser has reflected the existing pattern of service provision which involves around 60 per cent of services being purchased from a dominant local provider.

The situation therefore within the health authority more nearly resembles the situation of a bilateral monopoly in terms both of purchasers and suppliers. There is no process of bidding between many suppliers and many agents, and little evidence that the district health authority sees the stimulation of an competitive market structure as a high priority. However, the regional health authority actively encouraged the merger of the purchasing authorities in Avon: given the complexity of the contracting process across three districts and the staff and time involved, it is not surprising it supported a rapid move to a pan-Avon purchaser. This was promoted predominantly on the grounds of the possible savings in staffing, but little if any consideration was given to the possibility that a single purchaser might distort the market and create inefficiencies, or to the structure which would best support the necessary dialogue between the health authority and the community.

Quasi-markets share with other markets the need for constant or decreasing returns to scale to support the activity of several suppliers. However, large fixed costs give rise to increasing returns to scale and reduce the possibility that many producers can fill the market. In this respect, the fixed costs of a large general hospital complex would make it difficult for Bristol or Weston to support more than one unit, and may enforce a non-competitive situation, although Southmead and Frenchay hospitals are sufficiently close to be accessible for some services.

This situation does not apply to the same extent to community services, where there is not the need for expensive complex equipment, so that it is perfectly feasible for several suppliers to coexist in the 'market'. Similarly, it may be that certain interventions which at present take place within the general hospital may in fact, particularly with new techniques, be possible within the primary care setting. This would imply that there could be more suppliers both of community health services and minor operations. This clearly would depend on the extent to which GPs opt to become budget-holders and extend the range of services they provide, and the extent to which the private and voluntary sectors, and the local authority, offer community services in competition with those of the health service. Thus in non-teaching districts in particular there may be a trend towards less-centralised hospital services and in general a move towards a more mixed market for the provision of community services. However, the 'start up' costs for new and/or small organisations may restrict the structure of the market to larger, well-established and resourced providers.

The teaching dimension does complicate the issue of the extent to which resources, including those which relate both to research, and to service delivery, need to be concentrated on one site and so contribute to the very high fixed costs of a teaching hospital complex. At this stage it is not clear whether the funding for teaching and research will completely cover these extra costs.

Information

In a quasi-market both purchasers and providers should, ideally, have equal access to information. Suppliers are responsible for generating both quality and quantity, but purchasing agents need to know both the effort put into production and the characteristics of the suppliers if they are to avoid:

(a) purchasing less effort than they have paid for; or
(b) choosing a producer of low quality because it is impossible to distinguish between good and bad producers.

In a quasi-market the effort put in by suppliers and the characteristics of the suppliers may only be controlled through the contracting process. This means that the contract has to be sufficiently tight so that agents can tell whether the suppliers are providing the agreed level of service and can assess the quality of service delivery.

The separation of the purchaser and provider function, particularly if this involves the creation of a Trust, raises considerable problems associated with access to information and these have not as yet been addressed in the process of contract specification. They are, however, recognised by a number of key 'actors' within the authority. Individuals expressed their hopes in the very early days, for example, that the purchaser authority would continue to have physical access to Trust facilities and the option to witness the delivery of services and talk with staff. It was also assumed that the data generated within the provider unit would be available to the purchaser authority. On a different level, the whole area of defining what constitutes 'good quality' care, both collectively for a population and at the individual level, and how to monitor the quality of care being delivered, is enormously difficult. The purchaser authority is to a large extent dependent on its own providers to indicate what models of care, forms of intervention, expected outcomes and so on constitute 'good quality'. It is unclear to what extent regional or other professional bodies will develop as alternative sources of information.

The development of medical audit and consultant contracts are some of the mechanisms through which it is intended that information will be gathered about hospital practice, about outcomes, and about the way in which the medical profession assesses the quality of the services provided. However, the extent to which this information circulates freely between purchasers and providers is something which will be worked out locally and may or may not be formally built into the contract specification.

Transactions Costs and Uncertainty

The problem of providing reliable information on the quasi-market is compounded by the existence of a high degree of uncertainty about key aspects of the information environment. For example, it is desirable that reliable predictions about future prices and the number of referrals should be available to both purchasers and providers. The key instrument defining this information environment is the contract between the purchaser and the provider. Some idea of the probable mix of contract types which has emerged in the new system can be gained from looking at the contracts which were actually proposed in the first wave of NHS Trust applications. In these applications, the block contract was the most common form of contract which the NHS Trusts expected to be operating. Some 25 per cent of Trusts expected to operate entirely on block contracts, while a further 61 per cent of Trusts expected to operate mainly on block contracts. Only 14 per cent of the applicants for Trust status expected to operate mainly on cost-per-case contracts (Newchurch, 1990). Thus far, reflecting these general trends, the prime form of contracting in the case study area has been the use of block contracts. In the 1991/92 accounting period, for example, as much as 95 per cent of the DHA cash limit was placed in block contracts with the six local NHS Trusts in the Avon area.

However, the difficulties involved in writing complex contingent claims contracts of this type are formidable, especially considering the uncertainty surrounding the resource requirements of medical interventions in particular cases. This difficulty was explicitly recognised in the Government's Working Paper on Self-Governing Hospitals:

it is unlikely that a District will have placed contracts for all foreseeable referral possibilities (BMA, 1989, p. 30).

In addition a 'contingency reserve' is held by the DHA, to cope with the problem of extra-contractual referrals to hospitals outside the district, so that GPs can send their patients to hospitals with which neither they nor the DHA have a contract. But if all extra-contractual referrals were permitted, overspending could not be contained, and so a policy of selective rationing of such referrals, in consultation with GPs, has had to be adopted, even though this limits consumer choice to some extent.

Thus it seems likely that the use of block contracts will be subject to all the difficulties of writing, implementing and enforcing complex contingent claims contracts which have been identified in Chapter 2 above. In consequence such contracts will inevitably be incomplete, in the technical sense that they will not be designed to specify a fee structure which is contingent upon every possible state of nature (that is, every contingency). Such incomplete block contracts are likely to be subject to a variety of defects which hinder the efficient provision of services. According to the DHA in this case study, many problems have been encountered in drawing up block contracts. Among the main problem areas were issues to do with the degree of uncertainty surrounding the contracting framework. In particular these involved huge variations in the adequacy of activity, price and service data on which to contract; differences in the contracting capabilities of providers; and a lack of consistency in the terms of contract specification.

Motivation

A further difficulty concerns the motivations of the agents in a quasi-market situation, and the behaviour of providers who are not simply profit-maximisers. Economic theory provides little guidance as to the way in which the variety of agents' motivations (monetary reward, career development, 'empire building', 'pursuit of excellence') can be expected to impinge upon the efficiency of service delivery. Conflicts of interest may arise when a purchaser focuses on efficiency to the exclusion of choice and equity.

The motivations of both purchasers and providers are critical in ensuring that a quasi-market can operate in a responsive manner. The Government has stressed the role of the quasi-market in delivering value for money and choice for consumers. The prevailing values and culture of the NHS also embody the principle (if not the reality) of ensuring that all citizens have access to the services they need, regardless of their ability to pay or geographical location.

Within Bristol and Weston Health Authority the motivations of the purchasers and providers have so far been couched in general and, one may suggest, rather ambiguous terms. Statements about 'utilising available resources to optimise the health status of the local population' or 'committed to the continuing excellence of teaching and research in Bristol' have been offered to indicate the objectives of purchaser and provider respectively. This does not, however, make explicit the relative priorities to be given to efficiency, responsiveness, choice and equity, nor how the complex issue of the definition of quality is to be addressed. The majority of providers of services within the quasi-market for health care are unlikely to be 'profit-maximisers', and purchasers may be seeking a mix of services which in the first instance is informed by some understanding of equity. Only in the second instance can they be expected to be concerned to do that in the most cost-effective way. While it is widely accepted that a conventional market, with all agencies operating in order to maximise profits, is not desirable for the delivery of health care, because of the almost insuperable problems of the imperfect nature of the information available to consumers, a quasi-market is more likely to achieve greater efficiency if both purchasers and providers are explicit about their motivations.

This ties in closely with the present preoccupation with business plans inasmuch as it requires each agent to have a clear 'vision' of what they are aiming for in the future and a strategy for achieving these aims. However, being explicit about motivations does also imply that each agency has a shared set of values which informs its strategy. In the case of the Bristol United Hospitals, the desire to maintain the resources and environment which supports its role as a teaching and research centre may not necessarily be shared by the purchasers of its services, nor totally compatible with the objective of providing comprehensive services to meet the needs of the community. While the particular motivations of the agencies may not directly contribute to the efficiency of the quasi-market, being explicit about them may well reduce some of the uncertainties within the system, which would in itself be a beneficial outcome of the contract system.

Implementing Markets In Health Care: A Discussion

The Government has introduced competition into the provision of publicly funded services in a belief that this element of a market will improve efficiency: services will be more cost-effective and offer better value for money. In addition, as indicated earlier, the Government was eager to address the problem, identified by many other commentators, of the failure of the NHS to be responsive to the preferences of its users. It was argued that market provision in health care would offer users choice and high quality of services. Historically, the NHS has also been concerned with equity in the provision of services, and this has also been the focus of recent debate. Each of these issues and some of their interrelations will briefly be considered in the light of the earlier description and analysis.

This case study of the delivery of health care in Bristol and Weston suggests that it is likely that the quasi-market will fail to operate in a competitive fashion in many local areas. The absence of a range of suppliers, and the likelihood of services being purchased almost exclusively by a single purchaser, suggests that competition does not exist in any real sense of the word. The potential for altering these conditions rests in part with the DoH and regional health authorities, but at a local level it may be argued that it is equally important for the purchasers of services to be willing to stimulate a range of suppliers, as to draw up well-structured contracts for the purchase of services. This would require a range of interventions which might include, on the supply side, grants and other forms of support for alternative providers to establish themselves, training, and help with business development. These are activities not normally associated with the health authority and resources would have to be allocated for them, not least in order to develop the relevant skills and knowledge within the 'enabling' authority.

The effects of competitive pressures may be felt more on a broader national level. This applies particularly in the London regions. There, the more costly London hospitals have begun to lose contracts for patient care to the cheaper provider units in the home counties. The impact has been observable during the April 1992 contracting period as health authorities have been permitted to switch contracts to different hospitals if they believe this is in the patients' interests.

Markets are more efficient where there is a range of purchasers and new suppliers may be more attracted to enter the market where they are not dependent on a single purchaser (see Chapter 2). While the model for a pan-Avon purchaser has attractions in that it may enhance the extent to which the purchaser can impose terms on the providers, a more efficient market, in terms of value for money and choice, may be more likely to emerge where suppliers are able to negotiate with a number of purchasers.

In broader terms the relationship between the purchaser and its provider, especially where this is a teaching hospital, needs to be reviewed. Norms have often been internalised as standard practice which in fact specifically relate to the needs of teaching and research and comparisons with non-teaching hospitals outside the county may be useful sources of reference.

The purchasing health authority has to balance the objectives of equity, choice and efficiency. These are not necessarily contradictory but there are, for example, more and less efficient ways of achieving equity. Again, it would seem important that the purchasing health authority is explicit about the nature of the trade-offs being made.

The purchasing authority needs to be aware of the strengths and weaknesses involved in increasing the scale of its activities and to develop structures and strategies which will ensure it is able to purchase services which are sensitive to local needs. It would be easy for the neighbourhood or patch perspective to be lost for the sake of administrative convenience in placing and monitoring contracts.

In addition, under the prevailing system of block contracts, independent providers bear a high share of the risks resulting from cost uncertainty in the absence of some mechanism to share the burden of any unforeseen excess costs with the purchaser. Whilst providers may keep any surpluses arising from improved productivity performance, they must also bear a large part of the burden of any losses which result from an uncertain and variable pattern of referrals. This arrangement is designed to give an incentive to the provider units to improve their performance. However, if such units are risk-averse, uncertainty over costs may increase the desired fee for any specified quantity and quality of service delivery, since the contract fee will have to include an element to cover their risk premium. It is desirable under such circumstances to build into the contract some element of risk-sharing between the purchaser on the one hand, and the provider on the other. The properties of 'incentive contracts' of this type have been analysed by McAfee and McMillan (1987) and are discussed in more detail in Chapter 3 above.

Given the lack of a competitive market structure, it is in the interests of both purchasers and providers to maintain some distance between them. This is likely to enhance the efficient functioning of the quasi-market. It should also enable more of the 'stake-holders' involved with health care (particularly users, carers, community and voluntary groups) to have their values expressed in the planning, delivery and monitoring of services. Purchasers and providers should therefore preserve separate agendas and negotiate with a wide range of purchasers or providers.

This is not, however, to suggest that a competitive, 'cut and thrust' and secretive environment is being advocated, but rather that both competition *and* cooperation are desirable. It is essential, in order to overcome the problems of contracting in an uncertain environment, that information is shared, and that a dialogue is maintained between purchasers and providers and key issues are discussed and resolved in a spirit which reflects bargaining between equal partners. The partners do not share the same values or seek the same objectives; rather, they are explicit about their respective perspectives and negotiate from these differences, seeking an acceptable outcome for each side. This is different from a cosy alliance where it is assumed (either rightly or wrongly) that both sides operate with a shared agenda informed by a single culture or set of values.

The split between purchaser and provider is important, not just because it makes explicit how resources are being allocated within the health care system, which is desirable on economic efficiency grounds, but also because it enables both sides to clarify their respective positions without explicit or implicit pressures to comply with a dominant view.

The purchasing authority has a number of new roles which will take time to develop. These include:

(a) stimulating a market of suitable suppliers which will be able to meet the needs identified within the community;
(b) encouraging a dialogue with a wide range of users and potential users of services in a systematic and ongoing way;
(c) leading an informed debate within the population on the issues and problems of allocating resources to health care;
(d) ensuring opportunities occur within the health authority for discussions about the way in which priorities are to be set. This should include both the values and technical devices involved.

Since it is evident that the conditions under which quasi-markets are being developed (both nationally and locally) fall short of those required for competitive behaviour, it follows that the mechanism through which quality could be assured by users exercising the option of taking their custom elsewhere (the exit option) will not operate effectively. Alternative means of ensuring high-quality services are therefore required within the system. This process is made additionally problematic in a system where the client or user is not the immediate consumer, and where professionals have traditionally defined needs, allocated resources and assessed quality. Quality may be defined differently by different users, purchasers and providers of services and may well conflict with other values which are used to inform the allocation of resources.

Hoyes and Le Grand (1990) have argued that 'ensuring quality is essentially about the ability to measure performance in all activities'. However, as indicated in the previous paragraph, performance measures are themselves derived from arbitrary and diverse values and objectives. The link between whatever performance measures are adopted to assess quality, and the values which underpin them, should be made explicit, and this requirement should apply equally to purchasers and providers. In addition, the measurement of performance should, ideally, draw on information which relates both to aspects of the services being provided and to the characteristics of existing and potential clients. This suggests that in addition to the systems for data collection and review which are being developed to record various aspects of services and professional views of quality, *ongoing* and *systematic* inputs from users and carers are also required.

Purchasers will need to devise systems to ensure that, on the one hand, defining quality is no longer seen just as an objective professional exercise and, on the other, that the most articulate users do not prevent services from being easily accessible and acceptable to all groups within the population.

Providers, including NHS Trusts, need to develop a small number of indicators against which they can assess performance and internal systems for monitoring progress against these indicators. In particular the definition and recognition of quality within the services delivered is something on which Trusts should develop a corporate view.

The extent to which individual patients or users are able to make choices about the health care they receive seems more likely to be restricted by the introduction of a quasi-market than to be enhanced. This is because the main customers of the service providers are local district health authority purchasers and budget-holding general practitioners. Certainly the constraints they are likely to introduce in order to make the system run 'smoothly' and to limit the adverse effects of uncertainty of patient flow on service delivery, are likely to limit rather than enhance the patient's choice of hospital.

In reality, individual users may place a higher value on certain aspects of quality, such as accessibility and the coordination of services, than on being able to make choices between services. It may therefore be more sensible for both purchasers and providers to work on issues of flexibility and the availability of appropriate information than to work up 'genuine' market conditions for the provision of all services. However, where real choice cannot be expressed by users (and carers) it is essential for the models of care not to be informed exclusively by the priorities of either health professionals or purchasers. Users, carers and community groups need to be given the 'voice' option in that they are involved in strategic planning, setting performance measures and establishing priorities. This again implies the development of a participatory framework in which this involvement may routinely take place in a sufficiently finely-tuned way.

Conclusions

While it is not possible to draw any generally valid conclusions on the basis of one case study alone, the research has provided a number of valuable insights into some of the difficulties which are likely to arise in the operation of quasi-markets in secondary health care. The principal problems are associated with an absence of a competitive market structure. The simple separation of purchaser and provider roles has done little to disturb the monolithic approach to health service delivery on a local level, and it remains to be seen whether competition between large purchasers and between large providers across localities will have much impact on the allocative efficiency of service delivery, a conclusion supported by other studies (for example, McGuire, Fenn and Mayhew, 1991). However, it should be noticed that the new flexibility given to purchasers has enabled them to achieve specific goals in some dimensions of quality such as a reduction in the overall waiting-lists. At the same time, the separation of purchaser and provider roles has introduced new problems associated with an asymmetric distribution of information between the two sides of the quasi-market, resulting in increased costs of monitoring the quality of provider performance and of operating block contracts in an uncertain environment. In addition, there is a particular problem of coping with extra-contractual referrals. It remains to be seen whether the new system will yield net benefits to the users it is designed to serve.

Quasi-Markets and the Reform of Community Care

5

Lesley Hoyes
and Robin Means

The White Paper, *Caring for People: Community Care in the Next Decade and Beyond* (Department of Health, 1989a) was published in November 1989. Its main recommendations were subsequently included in the National Health Service and Community Care Act 1990. This chapter looks at the early attempts of social services departments in two shire counties to think through their response to the emphasis of the White Paper on the need for social services to develop an enabling role which makes maximum use of the independent sector. This emphasis upon developing a range of service providers flows from a belief that the introduction of market elements into the provision of social care services will improve their efficiency and consumer responsiveness. The first section places the case studies into this national context not only by looking at recent debates about community care and the proposals of the White Paper but also by reflecting upon the broad trend to introduce market elements into a wide range of public services. This is followed by a description of community care arrangements, both present and proposed, in the two shire counties and a consideration of the extent to which the future pattern of provision is likely to possess the characteristics of an efficient market. The paper concludes with a general discussion of implementing markets in social care.

Caring for People: The National Context

Community care services for older people and those with learning difficulties, physical disabilities and mental health problems were largely neglected in the welfare legislation of the 1940s (Means and Smith, 1985). Care for these groups tended to be institution-based, whether provided through the National Health Service or local government and, partly in consequence, they were often starved of funds relative to resources available for the acute sick or for children's services. Despite incremental progress over the next forty years, including some important legislative changes, the fundamental difficulties remained. These included administrative complexity and often hostility between local authorities and the NHS; the failure to shift resources from institutional to domiciliary care; the failure to target and plan resources effectively at a client or authority level; and the failure to empower the consumer.

In the mid-1980s, community care services began to shake off their 'Cinderella' image and to achieve a much higher political profile. Among the factors precipitating this were concerns about the growth in the numbers of 'old old', the explosion in social security payments to support residents in independent residential and nursing home care and the difficulties associated with the Government's 'Care in the Community' initiative to close down large mental handicap and psychiatric hospitals (Means and Harrison, 1988). A succession of official and semi-official reports, most significantly those of the Social Services Select Committee in 1985 and the Audit Commission in 1986, criticised existing provision and called for change, culminating in Sir Roy Griffiths' report in March 1988 (Griffiths, 1988) and the White Paper, based on Griffiths' recommendations, published 18 months later (Department of Health, 1989a).

The White Paper agreed with Griffiths that local authority social services departments should be given the lead role in community care planning. It also confirmed that their role at the client level would increasingly be confined to the assessment of need, the designing of care arrangements to meet that need by appointed 'care-managers', and the provision of funds to finance those arrangements. They were to be discouraged from directly providing all care services themselves; instead, services were to be provided increasingly by a 'mixed economy' based largely on the private and voluntary sectors. Local authorities were to become 'enablers' through the allocation of funds; they would have a declining role in direct service provision. Social services were to set out their strategy for achieving all this through a new system of community care plans. Finally, a new funding structure for those seeking public support for residential and nursing home care was proposed with local authorities taking over responsibility for financial support of people in private and voluntary homes, over and above their entitlement to general social security benefits. This was to be funded through a transfer of money from the social security budget to local authorities. However, local authorities would have discretion to use some of this money to fund domiciliary services which might reduce the need for so many people to enter residential care.

These proposals were enacted through the National Health Service and Community Care Act of 1990 with a view to implementation in April 1991. However, the Government announced an implementation delay soon after on the grounds that local authorities would not be ready in time (although more cynical observers believed that the principal motivation was concern about local authority expenditure implications at a time of high sensitivity about poll tax levels and poll tax capping). Implementation is now being spread over three years; the first community care plans were introduced in April 1992 and the change in residential care funding is now scheduled to take place in April 1993.

In the 1990s, whilst government at central and local levels will still finance most community care services, its role as provider will be reduced to a residual one. The assignation by Griffiths of lead role to local authorities, at a time when central government was clearly seeking to limit their influence, was seen by many as paradoxical and the main reason for the long delay in any official response. However, if, as seems increasingly clear, central government is permitting the continued decentralisation of operations and administration whilst further centralising strategic control and resources, then local authorities are merely being asked to 'manage' care and oversee the residualisation of social services (Walker, 1989).

A major justification for the introduction of quasi-markets is that, because they are competitive, they will be more efficient. The White Paper argues that its proposals will result 'in better value for money and a more cost-effective service'. However, the indeterminacy of organisations' objectives (profits, turnover, social welfare) makes it difficult to predict how they will respond to market incentives. Consumers of community care, even if aided by a care-manager, might find it difficult to shop around to find the best 'value for money'. It has also been shown that variable 'transactions costs' can sometimes make services provided through competition less cost-effective than through direct state provision (Williamson, 1975, 1985).

The second set of issues concerns choice. An important justification for markets in social care is that they will increase the range and quality of consumer choice. Again, the White Paper expresses the confidence that:

> *stimulating the development of non-statutory service providers will result in a range of benefits for the consumer, in particular: a wider range of choice of services [and] services which meet individual needs in a more flexible and innovative way.*

But to what extent can the consumer really choose what he or she actually wants and how far is access to services dependent upon the assessment and negotiating skills of a professional care-manager? For many potential consumers, choice may be illusory, since it depends upon the individual's power to exercise it and the existence of genuine alternatives (Walker, 1989). There is ample research evidence to show that elderly people and people with learning difficulties often have little say in their admission to residential care (Bradshaw and Gibbs, 1988; Hoyes and Harrison, 1987). Moreover, as the need for regulation of the quality of the 'market' provision is not disputed, the scope for innovation may well be decreased, thus reducing variety and hence choice (Knapp, 1989), the reason for this being that innovation may be seen as 'too risky' by the regulators.

A third set of issues linked to that of choice relates to equity. A common criticism of conventional markets is that they create inequalities and therefore inequities. Private residential homes often exclude more dependent (and therefore more costly) consumers (Association of Directors of Social Services, 1986; Hoyes, 1990). This kind of discrimination is likely to affect disproportionately the poorest and minority ethnic groups. Users of the increasingly residualised public services may then suffer stigma and reduced choice as these contract. As one commentator has predicted, "residualisation" of the poor may be the price of freedom of choice for the rich' (Knapp, 1989). Against this needs to be balanced the growing evidence that high-income households have received more from welfare state services since the 1940s than low-income families (Woolley and Le Grand, 1990).

Community Care in Two Shire Counties

Research Focus and Methodology

The initial focus of the two community care case studies was to be narrowly upon the production of the first community care plans for April 1991. The delay of these plans meant that a wider focus needed to be taken, and so interviews covered a broader range of issues relating to present services, attitudes to markets and prospects for the future. The two social services departments were chosen because they were seen as likely to be positive about the proposed changes while previous contact meant that access could be negotiated quickly. In each case study, the Director of Social Services defined key staff and/ or councillors who needed to be interviewed together with important managers from other key agencies, such as housing departments, health authorities and voluntary organisations. Overall 15 interviews were carried out. Seven of them were from social services and eight were from other agencies. Fieldwork was carried out between summer 1990 and early 1991 so that social services were still at an early stage of thinking about their implementation strategies. However, these case studies raised a series of crucial issues and questions about implementing quasi-markets in community care services.

Case Study A

Case Study A covered a mainly rural area with a population of just under 600 000 people. The county council was a hung council, although it has traditionally been controlled by the local Conservative party. Arrangements between the parties seemed quite fluid with

Labour/Liberal Democrats tending to set the annual budgets, but with the Conservatives/Liberal Democrats tending to control committee affairs on a day-to-day basis.

Eight interviews were carried out. One of these was with the Director of Social Services and two others were with senior social services staff (a Divisional Director and a Principal Officer for Community Care Planning). In addition, the unit General Manager (Community Services) of the district health authority, the Chief Housing Officer for one of the five district housing authorities, and a Development Officer with a large housing association were all contacted. Finally, the professional adviser of a voluntary sector care attendant scheme, and the professional adviser of a local branch of a national mental health charity were also interviewed.

All respondents expressed positive views about some aspects of the White Paper on community care. Many were enthusiastic about its stress on consumer choice and support for carers, while the emphasis on domiciliary services was viewed with particular favour. Some stressed the opportunities the White Paper created for the development of a more pluralist system, based on extensive service provider roles for a wide range of private and voluntary agencies. However, various concerns were expressed, the most common of which was whether sufficient resources would be made available by central government to allow good-quality flexible services to develop throughout the county.

The level of enthusiasm for a quasi-market system varied. All saw a role for the contracting-out of some services, and all expected the process to speed up in the next five years. Some supported the large-scale contracting-out of services over time as the only way to enable flexibility to develop and as the best way to avoid the inefficiencies of cumbersome bureaucracies. Others were less sure and, whilst accepting the case for limited contracting, made the point that the monitoring and supervision of a fully contracted-out social care system would be very expensive. The Director felt that residential care was only being contracted out in most social services departments at the time because financial incentives encouraged this to happen. The contracting-out of residential care facilitated access to social security benefits for residents, and enabled other agencies to help with the required capital reinvestment to bring former local authority homes up to the standard demanded by the 1984 Registered Homes Act.

The social services respondents stressed that they worked in a traditional shire county which had been proud of its social care services. As a result, the vast bulk of services remained 'in house' and not particularly flexible or innovative. Clients were expected to adapt to services rather than vice versa. However, important changes had been taking place, especially over the previous three years. These changes concerned both the provision of services by the independent sector and internal changes within the social services department.

The independent sector

Social services respondents identified four important changes with regard to the independent sector, over and above the generalised growth of private residential care. First, the department was negotiating with housing associations to develop very sheltered housing schemes. The most advanced scheme was on a site which was originally going to be used for a cottage hospital and included a respite care element. Social services were to contribute £900 000, the Housing Corporation was to provide £550 000, the health authority was to provide £400 000 (for the respite care unit) and the district council sold the land at a discount (perhaps worth £150 000). Negotiations were at an earlier stage with four other schemes which all involved local authority residential homes in poor repair. Second, well-established voluntary organisations already ran day centres in some parts of the county either for frail elderly people or for adults with mental health problems. Social services had decided to support these new developments through contracting out rather than running them themselves. Third, social services had for some years made arrangements with some trusted voluntary sector agencies to contract out the care of highly dependent clients on an individual basis. The best example of this arrangement was with the care attendant scheme. Out of a total annual income of £110 000 from social services, the care attendant scheme received nearly £70 000 through individual client contracts. Finally, social services had given a principal officer the remit to replace yearly grant arrangements with voluntary organisations by three-year service agreements. In exchange for more secure finance, the voluntary organisations were being expected to guarantee the delivery of certain services. Social services saw this as an important mechanism for moving towards a contract economy. Both the voluntary sector respondents emphasised that the longer-term funding of care services was much appreciated although one indicated that some people from his organisation had expressed fears about a social services takeover.

Change within the social services department

Important internal changes were also taking place. The department had pilot schemes for care management and resource management; a forthcoming departmental reorganisation would facilitate the process of devolving budgets and developing cost centres; and a series of strategy papers were being developed for each client group setting out long-term objectives. Responses to the White Paper on community care would be led by the need to achieve these objectives, rather than to pursue possibly short-term organisational fashions. As a result the forthcoming reorganisation was not based on an attempt to separate out purchaser and provider functions within the department. Above all, extensive research had been carried out by the Personal Social Services Research Unit at Kent University on the match between services, resources and need throughout the county. This had identified a need to redistribute resources geographically, and to shift the balance of resources from residential care to community services. This was to be achieved through the differential allocation of extra resources, and through the selective protection of some areas but not others from financial cutbacks.

However, several significant obstacles to change were identified by the social services respondents. First, the development of computer-based information and cost systems was still at a very early stage, and yet was essential to the smooth development of new service delivery systems. It was hoped to obtain a major capital injection for computer equipment in the next budget (1991/92), although this would be hard to achieve given concerns about poll tax levels amongst members. Second, there was a need for a cultural change amongst all staff to encourage them to think in terms of flexible individual care packages, rather than sending the client perhaps 20 miles to standard local authority provision. Interestingly, the health authority respondent backed up both these points, and stressed how a resource management culture now existed in the health authority with, for example, nurses having control over their own budgets.

Immediately after the publication of the Griffiths Report in March 1988, the social services department had set up an implementation group from which many of the external and internal changes described above had flowed. The group was composed of some senior managers and others central to community care planning. Overall, the three social services respondents felt that good progress had been made, and the social services department, the Family Health Services Authority (FHSA), and the district health authority (DHA) had agreed to a joint planning agreement. Relations with the DHA were positive and senior staff from social services and the DHA meet two or three times a year.

With regard to housing, social services was developing, jointly with health and housing agencies, an action research project to look at the housing dimension of community care. There were regular meetings between the Director of Social Services and the five Chief Housing Officers at district level. The Director attended regular meetings of private and voluntary residential home managers. Liaison with the voluntary sector was improving all the time. There was extensive contact at the divisional level while joint planning meetings in the health authority provided another mechanism for voluntary sector representation. A Joint Planning Forum had recently been established of voluntary sector representatives from all joint planning committees and this was chaired by one of our voluntary sector respondents (the ex-chair of the mental health charity). The forum was supported by a joint finance grant which employed a part-time coordinator. Overall, social services were keen to include the voluntary sector in strategic thinking at the county and divisional level. This was easier where a single organisation had the lead voice for a client group (as with disabled adults and those with mental health problems) but was more difficult to achieve where a plethora of different organisations were involved (the situation with elderly people).

The five respondents from other organisations were all very positive in general terms about the social services department and the ability/commitment of its senior management team. The expression 'the situation is improving' was frequently used, although the financial constraints upon social services were frequently acknowledged. The Development Officer from the housing association was working in several different counties and he described the working relationships between social services, the health authority and the district councils as excellent, compared to the situation in many areas. However, this did not imply complete satisfaction with, or clarity about, the community care planning process. The Chief Housing Officer said the district council had taken the initiative in asking for regular meetings with the Director of Social Services. The Joint Planning Forum was seen by the ex-chair of the mental health charity as coming from a voluntary sector recognition of the need to coordinate their inputs into the joint planning system.

Senior managers from all the key organisations recognised the need to place a high priority on developing clearer understandings about roles and responsibilities. The health authority respondent was particularly aware of the need to carry out further work on the boundaries between home care (a social services responsibility) and district nursing (a health responsibility). Another complex issue was the role of general practitioners as service gatekeepers. It was observed that this would only work if they were aware of the full range of services and the criteria for access to them. The two voluntary sector respondents argued that voluntary organisations needed an input into strategic proposals which went beyond the chance to comment on the planning proposals of others. One of the respondents saw this as a pivotal future role while the other felt such planning must not be allowed to expend energy to the detriment of service delivery. Both the health authority and housing department emphasised that all the statutory agencies were experiencing enormous changes and were under severe financial pressure, which made joint working difficult. One danger in such a situation was that each agency would fail to fully understand the constraints facing the other. For example, the housing association respondent observed that social services were not fully aware of the difficulties of obtaining funds from the Housing Corporation.

Directions of change

All respondents expected a further move towards a mixed economy of social care over the next five years. The Director of Social Services said that 90 per cent of services were provided directly by social services and only 10 per cent of services were contracted out. By the mid-1990s, he expected that this would be close to a 50/50 balance. However, future changes depended on the presence or absence of financial incentives to contract out, and also on the general attitude of future central governments to local authorities: a government hostile to local government might introduce a far greater use of the private and voluntary sectors to provide all care services.

Views about the difficulties of contract selection and contract regulation varied. Social services respondents felt the necessary expertise could be developed; although with complex housing schemes they expected to invite only those with previous experience to tender. The ex-chair of the mental health charity expressed some concern that small non-traditional voluntary organisations might be disadvantaged within the tendering process because they were not seen as reliable, and because they did not know the rules of the game. Both the health authority and housing department respondents expressed some general doubts about the cost of organising and regulating the tendering process. And the housing association respondent indicated that social services needed more development officers who would understand the practicality of building sheltered housing schemes, since the technical quality of briefs was often poor, and it was not clear if the tender award would be made primarily on cost or quality criteria.

A variety of views was expressed about whether the majority of contracts would go to large providers or small providers; to the voluntary sector or the private sector. With social services, the emphasis was upon finding reliable providers in a context of a dialogue with a wide range of potential providers. Scope for small-scale providers in home care was felt to exist through the use of specialist private sector suppliers, small voluntary agencies or through diversifying the activities of some private residential homes. However, ideas about this were still at an early stage and so it was difficult to predict the future pattern of services. The two voluntary sector respondents doubted if there was sufficient 'profit' in their clients to attract large-scale private providers, and they expected service contracting in non-residential services to occur mainly through established voluntary organisations. The housing association respondent emphasised that his association was keen to develop and diversify its service delivery role into running residential homes and supplying domiciliary services. However, this was a general policy direction, rather than a specific statement about what was likely to happen.

The overall impression from all respondents was of a desire to develop a more consumer-orientated community care system. Two main obstacles to this tended to emerge from the interviews. The first was a concern that services may be badly underfunded. The second concern revolved around the need to achieve greater clarity about the roles and responsibilities of the main statutory agencies.

Case Study B

Case Study B was also a large, mainly rural county of around 650 000 people, most of whom live in one medium-sized city and half a dozen smaller urban settlements. The county council has always been controlled by Conservative members. Prior to the 1989 local election, power rested with a small group of members; since then an evenly balanced and more moderate council has been controlled by the Conservative chairman's casting vote.

Seven interviews were carried out, including the chairman and the Director of Social Services. Two senior social services managers were interviewed, one of whom has overall responsibility for research and development, and the other has the task of coordinating the Community Care Unit. The county council area includes seven district council housing authorities and four district health authorities. The Director of Housing and the Unit General Manager of Community Services from the housing and health authorities covering the main urban area were interviewed. The final interviewee was the County Director of a national voluntary organisation for older people.

As in Case Study A, all those interviewed had some positive reactions to the White Paper. This may have been because, as one respondent commented, 'It is a bit like the Bible – something for everyone.' The Conservative chairman felt that even opposition members were not against its concept and principles, and that it was being viewed on an apolitical basis, with the means of implementation being the main area of challenge; this view was echoed within the Labour-controlled housing authority. All respondents strongly supported the aim to shift care from institutions to domiciliary care but several regarded the prospects for real choice for the consumer as 'disingenuous rhetoric'. Success was seen to depend upon the level of resources which would be made available. This was a significant concern of the county council social services chairman, who felt that money transferred from the social security budget should be 'preserved expenditure' to avoid it being diverted to more politically pressing uses, such as roads.

The independent sector

Most respondents saw advantages in encouraging a mixed economy to complement, but not to replace, local authority provision. Whilst at a political level the county council did not want to be providing services which were really the families' responsibility, there was a strong feeling that carers needed to be supported by good respite care, which the independent sector would be unable to provide at a price that social services could afford. Professionally, there was concern that over-reliance on the independent sector would, in fact, limit responsiveness, choice or flexibility (for example, by an emphasis on permanent instead of respite residential care). The result was a shared commitment within the county council to retain a core of high-quality targeted services alongside an encouragement for alternative sources of provision. Doubts about the existence of potential providers of domiciliary care were expressed by many respondents. In large rural areas it would be expensive to provide this type of care on a commercial basis, and the voluntary sector already had difficulty recruiting workers; also, both private and voluntary providers could be 'selective' in their choice of clients.

The county council therefore saw the residential care field as offering the best potential for expanding the mixed economy of service provision. The main aims were to promote 'alternative forms of management' and to access social security income so that the authority's own funds could be reinvested in domiciliary services. An original proposal had been made by the previous administration's policy committee to privatise a number of residential homes for older people, but this had created a public outcry. Instead, after the 1989 election, more moderate politicians decided to contract out the management of one newly built, unoccupied home. A competitive tendering process resulted in the management contract being awarded to a voluntary organisation. Private providers did participate, but failed because the selection was based not just on cost but also on guarantees of quality provision. The social services department retained rights to the first ten beds, and options on the rest.

At the political level, this development was regarded as a great success, and the authority was exploring other alternative management arrangements, including a request from the staff of another home to effect a 'management buy-out'. Officers regarded the increase in choice created by these mechanisms as indirect, in that they did not increase the options to existing residents. However, they did enable funds to be used for community care, so extending the range of choice between residential and domiciliary care for others.

Other previous 'arrangements' with independent service providers were gradually being put on to a more formal contractual basis. Some loose service agreements were arranged by individual social workers with voluntary sector residential establishments. A number of beds were 'sponsored' in this way, using a budget of over £1 million to 'top up' benefit payments. Approvals for such arrangements have had to be sought centrally and monitored by service advisers from the performance review section.

One private sector provider, offering up to 30 places in six houses to people with learning difficulties, had been used informally by the department. Inspection procedures raised doubts about the operation; it had, perhaps, expanded to the point where 'quantity exceeded quality'. A new contractual relationship was sought to develop an 'enabling relationship' between the authority and the provider, based on a pilot care-management project to ensure that all residents have Individual Programme Plans (IPPs), with a Principal Officer monitoring performance. In effect, the IPPs themselves became a form of 'contract'.

Previous grant aid to voluntary organisations was also being replaced by 'service agreements', which specified the services to be provided. In the case of the voluntary agency visited, a grant of around £8 000 had been put into a contractual format, with the specification including general development activities as well as the provision of direct services. The organisation felt it had little choice but to agree to the changed arrangement, but did negotiate the specification after challenging the county's original draft.

The organisation's director felt that such moves would increasingly fail to recognise the voluntary sector's need for core funding to support its administration and developmental work. The county council's 'contract' amounted to less than half of the agency's total costs. Nevertheless, she also feared a situation where the authority became its sole source of income. She pointed out that in another county, her counterpart had lost her post, and the organisation had been greatly reduced, when the county council was charge-capped and cut the grant upon which the agency was almost entirely dependent.

The formalisation of arrangements was beginning to be seen as offering scope for manoeuvre on both sides. For example, the voluntary organisation, which had been providing free day care within one of the social services department's residential homes, had recognised the potential for re-negotiation of the agreement.

Change within the social services department

From the social services' view, these developments reflected the evolutionary way in which the reforms would be implemented in the county. The policy was to avoid being 'panicked' into rapid changes and to do only what had to be done by April 1991 and to observe what other areas were doing and how the policy was being implemented nationally. The clear recognition that implementation has had profound implications for the organisation of the department, as well as for its contractual arrangements, led to an emphasis on the necessary restructuring as one of the more immediate tasks.

The department was organised in generic teams based on seven areas, coterminous with district councils. Whilst service delivery was decentralised, control of personnel and budgets was highly centralised and inflexible. Members kept a tight grip, making manoeuvre at area or frontline level difficult and were loath to loosen this control. The budget was allocated between client groups and services, with tight rules of virement which meant that 95 per cent of expenditure was fixed. This situation was seen as a major obstacle to the implementation of care management. The social services chairman appreciated the need for more discretion at local levels, and the implications of this for devolved budgets. He was keen to ensure that the budget was not held by the same person responsible for assessment of needs.

Optional proposals for restructuring during the 1991/92 financial year were being considered at the time of interview, and were likely to result in a reduction from seven to four areas, based on district health authorities, with strong local management and wide-ranging responsibilities and devolved control.

In parallel with planning the departmental reorganisation, a specially established Community Care Unit was charged with progressing implementation. Three project groups were set up in April 1990 to examine nine areas of implementation. These groups were:

   Community Care Plan (Planning Structures; Mental Health Grant)
   Business Requirement (Charging for Services; Financial Delegation; Financial Resource Generation)
   Professional Issues (Care Management/Assessment; Quality Assurance; Consumer Involvement; Complaints Procedures).

The groups included officers from other departments and, where appropriate, from other authorities. The health authority Unit General Manager interviewed was on the Care Management/ Assessment group, representing all four health authorities in the county and the city council's Director of Housing was a member of the Planning Structures group. The initial task of the project groups was to start off the thinking process. Some were task-orientated, whilst others were trying to conceptualise or to identify needs and future developments. For example, the planning group was examining information needs, starting with a consideration of what systems were needed; in the longer term it would go on to consider how information could best be collected; the health authorities were keen to promote the idea of joint assessments by health and social services staff, but this had not been accepted by the Care Management/ Assessment group.

As well as other agencies feeding into the county council's internal implementation machinery, structures for involving external organisations in service planning were also being reorganised. This appeared to be causing considerable confusion and concern in other organisations as new groups were established alongside existing ones, without adequate clarity of function or with less influence. The overall structure for external planning was far from clear. Former local consultative committees, based on district council areas and including housing, health and voluntary sector representation, had had the power to pass resolutions which the Director of Social Services had been obliged to take to his committee. This was replaced by much larger groups based on health districts which had no such powers. One respondent felt this had taken away its teeth and 'doesn't inspire confidence' in the social services' resolve to implement consultation procedures.

In addition to these concerns, there was felt to be scope for better understanding between different authorities' officers of the constraints each were facing, and an appreciation of the need to work together. Most felt that this was also needed at member level; in the case of the Labour-controlled housing authority, political hostility was seen as the main problem, whereas the Joint Consultative Committee for health and social services members was only concerned with allocating joint finance.

The health authority respondent felt that social services could learn a great deal from the previous four years' experience of health authorities since 'Griffiths I', particularly in relation to training staff for devolved responsibility on budget-holding; however, he did not feel that it had yet been recognised that it was possible to draw upon this learning.

The Director of Housing was concerned that social services should recognise the housing authorities' enabling and strategic role in housing provision, including coordinating the contribution of housing associations. He felt that there was still an expectation that housing departments should be able to make public sector lettings available on request for community care clients, but that this was now unrealistic. He also felt that housing authorities were often left to pick up the pieces of previous 'failed' community care policies, with lack of support from social services. It was clear that the social services department saw health authorities as their primary external link, and that housing authorities were not centre stage in their planning process. The cursory treatment of housing given by Griffiths and the White Paper was reflected in the lack of recognition by social services of the pivotal role housing plays in successful community care.

Consumer involvement

The involvement of consumers as partners in service planning and delivery was mentioned as a genuine desire by social services. Three parallel strands of action were being pursued to this end:

(i) a small unrepresentative group of four or five users and carers was asked to draw up an agenda of issues and to comment on proposals;

  (ii) a series of seven or eight 'search conferences', led by an external facilitator, represented an ongoing process to get feedback and priorities from existing and potential consumers;

 (iii) a pilot project was introduced in one of the social services areas to test micro-strategies for involving consumers in planning, staff recruitment, training and research.

In addition, the previous 'fairly safe' representatives on the social services committee were being replaced more by 'campaigners' and service users.

Interestingly, none of these initiatives was mentioned by the voluntary sector representative, who clearly felt that the organisation had a role to play in consumer involvement. It was accepted that at present it represented a very narrow range of older people, but a new post, funded by the national parent organisation, was to build up a liaison and information network based on clubs for older people throughout the county. It was intended that this should be developed as a means of widening the base of consumer feedback and strengthening the organisation's campaigning credibility with the county council.

Formal consultation between the county council and the voluntary sector appeared to be concentrating not on the sector's role as advocate/representative, but on its potential as service provider. A Consultative Day was organised by social services in July 1990 to discuss the White Paper and its implication for the voluntary sector (a similar event was organised for private sector service providers). Many voluntary sector representatives were reportedly alarmed at suggestions by an elected member that as voluntary organisations, they should be prepared to provide services free of charge.

The county-wide Rural Community Council was also taking an initiative to set up an umbrella organisation, linked to the National Council for Voluntary Organisations, to work with local groups on community care issues. The social services committee was to be asked to provide grant aid for a link worker to develop this.

Directions of change

Most respondents felt that the change to a 'contract culture' would be gradual and did not expect any dramatic change in the pattern of service provision over the following few years. These views were mainly based on doubts of the existence of potential providers which could supply the variety of services required to a high standard, and at a price the social services could afford. The Director of Social Services felt that they had been trying for years to encourage alternative suppliers of community care services to improve the very unequal provision of care across the county. The voluntary sector was already overstretched and could not recruit volunteers; the private sector was only interested in cleaning tasks, not providing care (even if they were prepared to get involved, it would be prohibitively expensive).

Another senior social services manager felt that it would be mid-1991 before contracting-out started in earnest, probably with a series of controlled pilots. A certain amount of block purchasing of residential beds for elderly people was anticipated, with spot purchase of out-of-county placements to cater for special identified needs. It was expected that eventually 50 per cent of the department's own residential provision would be transferred to alternative management.

The health authority respondent expressed some concern that the shift from residential to domiciliary care would increase the demands for health input, with resources having to come out of their mainstream allocation. He was not sure whether social services would purchase additional services or would expect them to be provided free of charge.

The voluntary sector respondent recognised scope for expanding into more varied service provision, but policy decisions needed to be taken in the light of possible implications for the nature of its role. This organisation's parent body had set up a Contracts Unit to advise groups; the emphasis was on quality, and it was hoped that the social services would appreciate and share this priority, using contracts to set high standards.

The social services respondents stressed the increased importance of the inspection team in ensuring value for money and compliance with explicit quality standards. The current team was felt to have considerable powers under the 1984 Registered Homes Act, and had a reputation for firmness. The activities of this section, working alongside social workers, would ensure that services would be delivered as specified. Adverse selection (choosing a poor contractor) would be avoided by the selection of new providers in whom the department had confidence. A portfolio of various contractual relationships would be needed, depending upon the level of trust between purchaser and provider.

The Director of Social Services found the concept of the purchaser/provider split strange and artificial. Some services would continue to be provided by the department alongside complementary services arranged with other providers. In the context of such a planned range of services, the draconian measure of splitting the organisation seemed artificial. Identification of costs could be achieved by other means. It would be necessary to define what would be purchased and what provided directly. This would involve a redefinition of the council's own residential establishments, reducing numbers and redeploying resources for respite care, day care and outreach support.

All respondents echoed each other's concerns that choice and quality were too dependent upon availability of resources to be taken for granted. The general view was that the the community care reforms offered great potential but enthusiasm was tempered on all sides by a fear that insufficient finance would be transferred to implement the reforms in a satisfactory manner.

Towards a Quasi-Market in Community Care?

In Chapter 2, it was explained that quasi-markets could be assessed in relation to their impact upon efficiency, responsiveness, choice and equity. Five critical factors were identified which influence the efficiency of markets and these relate to market structure, information, uncertainty, motivation and cream-skimming. This research addressed the first four of these factors specifically, and each of these will now be considered in turn in the light of likely future patterns of service delivery in our two case studies.

Market Structure

A conventional competitive market requires the absence of both monopoly producers and monopoly consumers. If there are several producers, then no single producer will be able to influence market prices upwards by temporarily reducing their output and creating scarcity. The existence of numerous consumers would mean that no single consumer could distort prices downwards by temporarily contracting their consumption.

The purchasing of services may be carried out directly by the client, by field level staff or by senior managers. In both case studies, the latter had tended to be the main purchasers and are likely to remain so in the short to medium term. However, both departments are involved in care-management pilots and so a strategy of pushing purchasing down the hierarchy might emerge. The Independent Living Fund meant both case studies had some experience of the client as purchaser. The care attendant scheme was extensively involved in providing a service for clients who were funded in this way. In Case Study B, a private domiciliary care agency, aimed at people in receipt of severe disablement pensions and Independent Living Fund payments, had approached social services about referrals. However, the impact of government decisions to curtail the Independent Living Fund scheme reinforced doubts about the possibilities of a market expanding in this field.

Both departments were in the process of thinking through their provider strategy. In Case Study A, social services expressed confidence that several providers could be found. This was a wealthy county that already had specialist private domiciliary providers and numerous private residential homes. The voluntary sector was well-established. However, there was no evidence of a strategy to ensure provider competition for each element of care provision contracted out. Expensive building schemes were put out to tender, but day centres and the care of the heavily disabled were negotiated with reliable individual voluntary agencies.

Similarly, in Case Study B, there was little doubt amongst social services respondents that the main area for contracting-out would be in residential care, where there were already many independent providers. Most of these operated on a small scale, with one or two homes. In rural areas there would be little choice between competing providers, and as it was an objective to place clients as near to their homes as possible, a 'good value' contract might not be possible.

In both areas, it was not clear whether a wide range of potential new providers existed who could provide the full range of domiciliary services. Whilst it was recognised that the voluntary sector could expand into more service provision, and the private sector could diversify from residential care, this was unlikely to happen on its own and would need to be nurtured.

Social services are generally in a strong purchaser position, but in wealthy counties they face competition from individuals who have the financial means to buy services at full cost without any social services assessment, although this was likely to be the exception rather than the rule. For example, in Case Study B over half of the residents in private homes were supported by state finance and 87 per cent of home-help clients were subsidised. However, if residential care continues to be over provided, homes may 'recruit' residents from outside the county, leaving social services to pick up the tab once private funds are exhausted.

There is obviously a danger that as strong purchasers, in a near monopoly position, but under financial pressure, social services departments might squeeze their providers financially. Core funding for administration, training, information technology and so on, particularly important for small voluntary providers, may be curtailed. However, the emphasis of social services upon dialogue with reliable providers suggests this will not happen.

The case studies also illustrate that there is a continuing ambiguity over the roles and responsibilities of local authorities and health authorities. It is also not clear which services should be provided by home care workers and which services should be provided by district nurses. And it is uncertain whether there are circumstances in which health authorities should buy home care from social services and whether social services should contribute to the cost of district nursing services from the health authority. In Case Study A, hip operations placed pressure on home care (mentioned by the Director of Social Services) and residential home closure placed pressure upon district nursing (mentioned by the Unit General Manager). In Case Study B, a regional joint working group which was set up to determine which elements of care were medical and which social, concluded that it was extremely difficult to distinguish one from the other, reinforcing confusion over the role of the health authority as provider. Joint assessment by staff of both authorities was seen as important because of this. The boundary between health care and social care remains blurred, and the activities of one agency have external consequences which spill over into the cost calculations of another.

Despite a recognition in both areas that the creation of a competitive market structure would need social services stimulation and intervention, there is little evidence that such strategies are yet a priority. Nor does it seem likely that they will be in the future, given the uncertainty about levels of resources available.

A further issue in relation to market structure concerns the issue of minimum efficient scale of production. In a conventional market, the average cost per unit of production decreases as production increases. In particular, large fixed costs give rise to economies of scale, reducing the possibility that many producers can fill the market.

The sheltered housing scheme described in Case Study A provides a good example of the tendency towards economies of scale. Such schemes are costly, complex and time-consuming to develop and build; it is very difficult for small local housing associations to compete successfully with large national housing associations with an established 'track record' in producing such schemes. The viability of such schemes depends upon successful financial performance and this, in turn, creates pressure to increase the number of units in each scheme, despite concerns that this may generate an institutionalised environment. Economies of scale may also influence residential care, with large providers beginning to dominate the market.

Several respondents recognised that established organisations had an advantage over new entrants. All three voluntary organisations visited in the case studies were part of national organisations, while the housing association also had a national structure. This provided them with ongoing national support so that they were enjoying some economies of scale, as well as strength from having already learnt how to organise and provide services. One organisation had access to its national Contracts Unit which had helped it to negotiate the terms of a service agreement. It was also about to begin to pilot and test a computer-based networked information service, and to build up detailed data on all services provided for elderly people. The costs of all equipment and software were being met by the national organisation.

In contrast, new or small organisations have to learn the rules of the game themselves, and may face high 'start up' costs. The emphasis within the case studies on negotiating services with known and trusted organisations indicates that existing larger agencies are likely to inspire greater confidence in social services as purchasers. It is difficult to speculate about the likelihood that the authorities would underpin development costs for newer organisations, but the current emphasis on negotiating service provision agreements rather than the direct provision of grants must raise doubts about the capacity or the will of social services to finance the provision of anything other than highly specific services.

There is also doubt about the likelihood that private suppliers of domiciliary services would be responsive to demands for small individually tailored packages of care. They may well be able to offer commercial large-scale services which would be cost-effective but standardised, representing no improvement over direct provision by the authorities.

The housing association was possibly the best example of a large, powerful provider who, in the future, could squeeze out small providers in both residential and domiciliary provision. One of the voluntary organisations recognised that it was the large housing associations which seemed to be preparing for getting into providing 'extra care' on a large scale. This voluntary organisation's local branches were moving to fill gaps in day care services, rather than in domiciliary care.

Information

Conventional markets are most efficient where information about prices and other attributes of goods and services is available at low cost to all market participants, who need to be able to assess quality with accuracy, to know how much they are paying (or being paid), and for what.

It is possible to identify at least three major difficulties that might emerge with regard to information and quasi-markets. First, these information flows depend upon a clear separation between the purchasers and the providers, and upon clarity about which provider should provide which service. This is not always the case (as we have seen with regard to community health services). Mobile wardens are another example; practice varies, even within one of the counties, concerning who should provide this service, who should pay for it and what are its objectives. Second, the purchaser would fail to buy an efficient level of service if adverse selection were to occur. Adverse selection arises when the purchaser picks a provider of low quality because of the inability to distinguish between good and bad providers. Third, the purchaser will experience the costs of moral hazard when the provider puts less effort into production than the purchaser has contracted for.

In both case study areas, we were struck by the absence of detailed service and cost data, and of sophisticated information systems. In Case Study A, most data remained heavily centralised, although they were trying hard to improve this situation. This suggests most purchasing will have to remain centralised, at least for the immediate future. There was also a reluctance to introduce a clear purchaser/ provider split within social services, and this might undermine attempts to develop a local dialogue about service availability within this very large county.

In area 'B', a variety of different information systems had been developed separately with little strategic planning. Some of these were simple indices, such as a register of people with learning difficulties. Other systems had generated only general statistics. Since the systems were neither area-based nor integrated, much of the quarterly statistics collected (on referrals, case loads and so on) were produced manually from area case records.

A working group looking at 'information for planning' was examining these systems with a view to creating an integrated networked system; a client record system – CRISP – had been piloted in one area and was to be introduced throughout the county by April 1991. Budgetary control was via a countywide LAFIS (Local Authority Finance Information System), and was consequently centralised, with local budgets being monitored locally rather than being under local control. These systems will need careful examination if they are to meet the needs of a locally determined pattern of market-led services.

The integration of other agencies into service planning and provision may also be limited by information inadequacies. Health authorities use a wide variety of information and resource management systems; one of the housing authorities visited appreciated the potential of being able to integrate various data relevant to community care needs, but felt that this could not be given priority without some financial incentive. The voluntary sector's access to information and its capacity to develop sophisticated costing and budgeting systems varies enormously; resources and skills are often very limited, although one agency saw the future potential for marketing its own service data base to social services.

Clearly, the information available to all parties – purchasers and providers – is currently in a highly imperfect state. Remedying this situation is likely to take a great deal of time and require considerable financial investment in IT, not an option open to all potential providers, one which will put severe strains on the budgets of purchasers. In the meantime, the implication of these information deficits may be serious. How are purchasers to guard against adverse selection and moral hazard if they do not have adequate information about the quality and costs of various sources of provision? In the case study areas, adverse selection is likely to be avoided, partly by purchasing only from well-established and known providers. However, this strategy in itself distorts other conditions for efficient market operations described in the earlier section on quasi-market structures.

The precise terms of service agreements, and the role of Inspection Units, may partially ensure against moral hazard. But without well-defined standards based upon collectable and retrievable information, inspection is likely to focus on easily observed features of quantity and costs, rather than on more relevant measures of quality and cost-effectiveness.

Uncertainty

In order to ensure efficient operation of conventional markets, either all future prices and conditions should be known, or it should be possible to devise contracts that cover all possible contingencies.

One of the common themes that emerged in nearly all interviews was the level of uncertainty that existed in all quarters regarding future numbers and types of providers, future levels and mechanisms for purchasing, and future costs and resources. Attempts to combat this uncertainty centred mainly upon the selection of reliable providers (see above) and upon the nature of agreements and contracts entered into. The prerequisite of good community care, that it should be flexible and responsive to individual needs, meant that it was difficult to draw up highly specific contracts which would allow for variation, whilst at the same time safeguarding both the viability of the producer and the resources of the purchaser.

In both case study areas, generalised service agreements were being introduced with voluntary organisations, acknowledging the importance of formalising relationships whilst at the same time endeavouring to maintain a degree of flexibility based on trust. This reflects an appreciation of the difficulty of producing detailed contracts for social services, and indicates that the quality of the staff running the contracting process may be significantly more important than the actual terms of the agreement.

One such service agreement between social services and a voluntary care attendant scheme required the organisation to:

carry out its objectives which are:

a. *to relieve stress in families or persons responsible for the care of disabled persons;*
b. *to avoid admission to hospital or residential care of such disabled persons should a breakdown or other failure occur in the household;*
c. *to supplement or complement, not to replace, existing statutory services, and to work closely with them;*
d. *to maintain a high standard of care.*

Another voluntary organisation had entered into a service agreement with social services on the basis of a list of its own current activities which were then incorporated into a similarly loose agreement. Whilst it can be argued that these types of agreement may well be an appropriate response to present circumstances, they fail to meet the competitiveness conditions for the efficient operation of a quasi-market as laid down in Chapter 2. And since the agreements are incomplete, they make monitoring and enforcement difficult.

From the provider perspective, there is some voluntary sector concern that formalised contractual relationships may take away their independence; this would make contract compliance easier for the purchaser but may well constrain the very nature of the sector – its capacity for innovation, responsiveness, and flexibility – and thus limit other objectives of both purchaser and provider.

Moreover, some types of contract are not amenable to presentation in a loose format, and require highly knowledgeable and detailed input. For example, the housing association in Case Study A expressed concern that social services staff might lack the technical skills to develop briefs for complex building schemes. The Director of Housing in area B felt that social services did not recognise the pivotal enabling role of his department in this regard, and that negotiations should not be carried out directly between social services and housing associations, but should rather include the housing authority.

Finally, providers were uncertain as to the relative emphasis which social services would place upon quality and price in determining which services to purchase. Social services, not surprisingly, insisted that quality was a primary consideration, but there was an acceptance that this would be quality within available resources – the biggest uncertainty of all.

Motivation

In conventional markets, providers would be primarily concerned to maximise profits. It is not yet clear what motivations will exist and what motivations should exist if quasi-markets in community care are to be efficient, equitable and to offer choice.

Both social services departments were concerned to achieve high-quality welfare outcomes, namely the maximum amount of well-being for any given amount of resources. Running efficient services was seen as critical to this, but the quality of services supplied was emphasised more than a narrower focus upon cost alone. In Case Study A, a heavy emphasis was also placed upon equity, in terms of a balanced expenditure on services relative to need throughout the county. The case studies demonstrated that resources and services were overly concentrated upon certain urban communities within the county. Choice was also seen as important, but difficult to achieve, and in reality, most consumers did not have a choice of providers for any given service. Achieving this was not seen as a priority when so many high-need clients lacked access to any service.

In area B, problems of achieving equity across a large rural county had always proved difficult. The Director of Social Services did not see quasi-markets solving this as there simply were no other potential providers in some areas, let alone any existing competition. Where profit maximisation is the provider's main motivation, there will always be some services which the private sector will not provide at an affordable price. Where motivations are more varied, as in the voluntary sector, other grounds for selection of clients come into play. In such situations, total freedom of choice is unrealistic and the best that can be hoped for is an informed choice between a small number of options. For both political and professional reasons, quality is often held to be a higher priority than financial efficiency.

Pressures to improve financial performance are, moreover, a potential source of tension between social services, the health authorities and the housing departments. All of these agencies are under considerable pressure to contain expenditure and this clearly creates potential conflict. For example, should social services be expected to pay for increasing demands for district nursing services if community care is to be promoted over residential care? In one area, considerable ill-feeling existed over the failure of proposed community care developments which involved land and financial deals between all three statutory authorities. Whilst real efforts at collaboration were taking place, a better understanding of each other's resource constraints may be needed.

The three voluntary sector respondents emphasised that their agencies were concerned to provide a high-quality service to consumers. They were not involved in making 'profits', although care was needed that they did not drift into a cash-flow crisis. If such organisations move more into direct service delivery on a larger scale, they will need to develop more sophisticated skills for management and costing of services. This clearly has implications for training potential providers.

Implementing Quasi-Markets in Social Care: Conclusions

The two case studies have revealed that an assessment of the impact of the introduction of quasi-markets into social care services will need to take into account a number of factors specific to the field of community care services. It will also need to take account of conditions which are important for the efficient operation of such quasi-markets, and consider to what extent these conditions are likely to be met in the world of welfare markets (Hoyes and Le Grand, 1991).

In the long term, any apparent 'policy failure' of quasi-markets will be open to several alternative interpretations. These include the following possibilities:

- quasi-markets are no better, and possibly worse than conventional markets or bureaucratic systems;
- quasi-markets were a good idea, but one that received little understanding or commitment from the supposed lead authority;
- the missionary zeal of the local authority was undermined by vested interests, low-quality staff or the service legacy of the last forty years;
- a major opportunity was lost through chronic underfunding by central government.

The response to the reforms will be subject to possible variations at all levels of the implementation process. First, the already substantial time-lag between the formal introduction of change and the filtering-down process through organisations and on to clients will be exacerbated by the phasing of implementation over a three-year period. The reforms will be open to negotiation and blockage as well as encouragement and this process will occur between central and local government, between officers and members, between managers and field-level staff and between field-level staff and consumers. Similarly, negotiations will occur between social services departments and other key agencies involved in service provision, including health and housing authorities and private and voluntary suppliers. Second, different localities will be responding from different baselines of provisions and traditions of service delivery; individual localities may vary in these respects between different groups of consumers. Third, a commitment to multiple suppliers can only be operationalised if these suppliers can be found, and their potential availability may well vary across the country. Finally, a multitude of factors outside of the community care reforms will impinge upon service provision in any given locality.

The role of the local authority in the successful introduction of a market-led pattern of services must not be underestimated. It is at least as important that the authority be prepared to generate supply as to purchase services, and the way in which authorities choose to award contracts may in itself have a profound effect upon the local market structure (Flynn, 1990a). The existing market structure varies enormously between areas; the uneven distribution of private and voluntary residential homes, with a concentration in seaside resorts, has been graphically demonstrated (Audit Commission, 1986). The independent market in domiciliary services is far less developed, with few large suppliers and many small ones; local authorities have little experience of contracting out in this field although, if future services are to be based on individual packages of care for people in their own homes, these are likely to assume greater importance (Flynn and Common, 1990; Booth and Phillips, 1990).

The White Paper recognised these potential supply problems, stating that one of its key objectives was:

> *to promote the development of a flourishing independent sector alongside good quality public services.*

Moreover, social services are expected to make clear:

> *where such providers are not currently available, how they propose to stimulate such activity. In particular, they should consider how they will encourage diversification into the non-residential sector.*

However, stimulating new and diversified markets may not be easy. The voluntary sector has expressed fears about losing autonomy and flexibility, and compromising its advocacy and campaigning roles; smaller groups in particular may not feel up to the demands of bidding for and fulfilling contracts (Gutch, 1990; Flynn, 1990b). The Government recognises the need for authorities to continue to provide core grant funding to voluntary organisations to underpin administrative infrastructure and developmental work, but it is questionable whether authorities will choose to spend their limited resources on other than the purchase of particular services. Diversification from residential provision may appear to be a logical step for suppliers in areas where demand is shrinking and interest rates are rising. However, it may not necessarily be a straightforward move for small, or even larger, organisations whose experience is limited to providing care in an institutional setting (Wright, 1990). Moreover, it would be a move which itself incurred financial penalties in the form of liability for the Unified Business Rate.

If a local authority is to stimulate a quasi-market, it will need to do more than contract out its residential care. Flynn has listed a range of other interventions on both the supply and demand sides which social services could engage in to encourage alternative supplies of services (Flynn, 1990b). These include, on the supply side, help with business development; grants, subsidies and credit for start-up and working capital; training; and licencing and regulation. On the demand side, care-managers need to operate more as brokers and advisers rather than as agents making all the decisions. There is clearly much scope here for authorities to promote or block quasi-market developments and the Social Services Inspectorate will have a crucial role to play in assessing individual authorities' efforts as set out in their Community Care Plans.

In addition to authorities' ability to stimulate alternative provision, they will also have scope for manipulating the quasi-market by the way in which they use suppliers. It is likely that in some areas, for some services, the social services department will be the only purchaser. Whilst this may make it easier for the authority to dictate terms, it may also deter potential suppliers from entering a market where they will be dependent on a single buyer. On the other hand, if an authority, for the sake of administrative convenience or economy, chooses to enter into block contracts with one or two suppliers, they risk squeezing out smaller suppliers and will find themselves faced with a monopoly and in a very weak position. Authorities will need to consider to what extent they are able, and wish, to guard against these situations by operating care-management systems which devolve responsibility and resources to many 'purchasers', and by encouraging the entry of new providers by adopting actively interventionist strategies such as those described above.

Quasi-Markets and Educational Reforms

6

Will Bartlett

The Education Reform Act of 1988 has brought about fundamental changes in the way that educational services are supplied in England and Wales (for a general overview of the administrative changes introduced by the Act, see Hill, 1988; Davies and Braund, 1989; and Hill, Smith and Spinks, 1990). The general aim of the reforms has been to introduce a more competitive, quasi-market approach to the allocation of resources in the education system, and to increase the range of parental choice over children's schooling (Glennerster, 1991; Dixon, 1991). This chapter analyses the impact of these reforms on the provision of education services in the light of the experience of a county local education authority (LEA). In particular, it addresses the issue of the way in which the introduction of a quasi-market has led to changes in the allocation of both resources and pupils, between schools.

The basic rationale behind the Government's reforms in the educational sector has been to attempt to bring about an improvement in the quality of educational provision by creating a system in which high-quality provision is financially rewarded. The idea has been that such a system of rewards works best when decision-making is decentralised, and successful decision-making is rewarded by an automatic, hands-off mechanism. This is the essence of the new quasi-market system, in that the size of a school's budget is linked to the numbers of pupils it can attract. And the school alone, largely independent of the direct influence of the LEA hierarchy, is now responsible for the way in which it manages and organises the

125

resources placed at its disposal. However, despite the fact that this system resembles a market system, the educational services are still provided free of direct charges to the consumers. The market is only a'quasi-market', in which producers are encouraged to compete against one another and consumers are encouraged to express their preferences, but in which no money actually changes hands.

The introduction of quasi-markets is usually supported on the grounds that they assist in the promotion of efficiency and the expansion of the range of opportunities and choices open to individuals engaged in them. Critics argue that they may have such effects under certain favourable circumstances, but that circumstances are not always favourable, and that they also tend to generate undesirable inequalities. This study of quasi-markets in education highlights some of these issues, and reveals that the education reforms have brought about surprisingly rapid changes in the structures of education provision in the case study area. Some aspects of these changes are widely seen to be beneficial; in particular the role of financial and managerial delegation and decentralisation of functions to individual school level has been positively received as a factor leading to increased levels of productive efficiency by most of the actors in the quasi-market. Other aspects of the reforms, such as formula funding and open enrolment, however, are found to have a partially negative impact in so far as they tend to increase levels of inequality in service provision. Choice, although widened to some degree, remains rationed at key points in the system. This study is designed to explore the way in which this quasi-market has begun to influence the provision of educational services in one local education authority.

The New Institutional Framework

Formula Funding

Formula funding was introduced in all maintained and grant-maintained schools in the county in April 1990 (see Thomas and Levacic, 1991, for an analysis of the variation in formula funding schemes across LEAs nationwide). Under the previous system, the education budget was allocated administratively, on a set of criteria which included a strong element of inertia. Any changes in its distribution from one year to another were incremental adjustments to the pattern established in the previous years. The budgetary process involved the initial construction of a 'commitment budget' based on the forecast of pupil numbers for the coming year. Using the existing pupil–teacher ratio, the required staffing level would be calculated. Then the budget would emerge as the product of the required staffing level and average teaching salaries corresponding to that staffing level. The commitment budget would then be discussed by the policy-makers in the education committee, and after possible modification, sent back to the LEA, who would then allocate the budget amongst the schools.

Although this process was administrative, and incremental, it was not inflexible. In fact it led to a situation in which the average pupil–teacher ratio in the county remained more or less constant in the face of a secular decline in pupil numbers (at secondary level). The system as a whole could be expanded or contracted by the opening or closing of schools in a planned manner: in the early 1980s, for example, this meant school closures at a rate reflecting the decline in pupil numbers.

From April 1990 the introduction of formula funding brought about a radical change in the process by which the county education budget was drawn up and allocated among schools. The basic principle of the new system is that the budget should reflect the number, and ages, of the children actually admitted to each school. Since 1990 the commitment budget has been drawn up as the product of the forecast number of pupils and the age-weighted funding per pupil (FPP), which plays the role of a parametric 'price' for pupils, identical for each school. The main differences to the previous system are that the concept of a semi-fixed pupil–teacher ratio does not enter the calculation; a parametric pricing system is introduced so that all schools operate on a 'level playing field'; and the allocation of funds between schools is essentially dependent on the number of pupils which they attract, rather than on a centralised administrative allocation of funds.

As yet, however, not all the budget is actually managed in this way. Part of the General Schools Budget remains outside the formula funding mechanism altogether. These 'exceptions' are referred to as mandatory exceptions, unlimited discretionary exceptions and limited discretionary exceptions. *Mandatory exceptions* include capital projects, capital financing costs and specific grant related expenditures. By law they are not allowed to be included within the formula. In the 1991/92 budget these mandatory exceptions accounted for 9.2 per cent of the General Schools Budget. *Discretionary exceptions* are areas of the service which the LEA may exclude from the formula at its own discretion. Some items, the limited discretionary exceptions, were subject to an overall limit of 10 per cent of the General Schools Budget. They included one set of items which consist of centrally supplied services such as educational psychology, peripatetic teachers, and resource centres, and another set of items of expenditure incurred at school level such as the structural maintenance of buildings, supplementary personnel costs such as maternity cover, nursery classes, and the cost of statemented pupils in special units. Non-limited discretionary exceptions included the central administration of the education service, the schools' advisers service, home-to-school transport, school meals, premature retirement and dismissal costs, and contracted-out services including grounds maintenance and cleaning. Taken together the discretionary exceptions accounted for 23.2 per cent of the General Schools Budget. Consequently, after the various exceptions had been taken into account the amount left to be allocated by the formula (known as the aggregated schools budget, or ASB) amounted to 67.6 per cent of the overall budget.

Further inroads into the proportion of the budget which was actually allocated on the basis of student numbers was made within the formula itself. In the 1991/92 budget, only 82.9 per cent of the Aggregated Schools Budget (the part of the General Schools Budget allocated by formula) was allocated on the basis of pupil numbers. The remainder was allocated on the basis of size of school (3.5 per cent); special needs (4.04 per cent); small schools protection (4.02 per cent); various lump sums for primary schools (1.31 per cent); various school specific items (3.93 per cent); and for transitional arrangements and a 'safety net' to limit the loss to any individual school resulting from the application of the formula to 5 per cent of its budget (0.3 per cent). Expenditure on the safety net was around £450 000 in 1990/91.

The combined effect of exceptions from the formula and fixed elements within the formula was to limit the amount which was actually allocated on the basis of pupil numbers to only 56 per cent of the overall General Schools Budget in 1990/91.

The funding per pupil (that is, the quasi-market price per pupil) is determined by by a formula which gives differing weights to different age groups. In the 1991/92 budget, the funding per pupil calculated by this method varied widely between age groups, from a low of £900.55 for 10-year-olds to £2 153.68 for the 16 + age group. The details of the age-weighted formula funding price schedule for our case study county is shown in Table 6.1.

The trend of development of government policy on funding has been to progressively diminish the extent of the various types of exceptions. For example, Circular 7/91 (Department of Education and Science, 1991) eliminated the category of unlimited discretionary exceptions, and ring-fenced the discretionary exceptions to a global limit of 15 per cent of the Potential Schools Budget, (itself a restricted element of the General Schools Budget). Whilst this may

TABLE 6.1
Age-Weighted Pupil Units, 1991/92

Age group	FPP (£)	Pupils	Funds allocated (£000)
4	1046.80	11 046	11 563
5	1006.65	11 078	11 151
6	1006.62	10 871	10 943
7	926.24	10 350	9 587
8	903.44	10 284	9 291
9	905.78	10 259	9 292
10	900.55	10 260	9 240
11	1427.72	9 753	13 925
12	1427.72	9 443	13 482
13	1427.72	8 929	12 748
14	1451.94	8 981	13 040
15	1589.03	9 278	14 743
16 +	2153.68	6 402	13 788

Total funds allocated = £152 816

Source: County Council budget statement 1991/92.

reduce the variation in funding per pupil between schools, by introducing further limitations on the discretionary elements in the formula it will tend to increase the unequal distribution of gains and losses which formula funding has brought about.

Delegated Budgets and Delegated Management

Although the funding for all schools in the county was put on a formula basis in April 1990, the process of delegating budgets to schools (a process often referred to as local management of schools, or LMS), is being gradually phased in over a number of years. With the introduction of delegated budgets, a school's governing body will be increasingly responsible for managing a school's finances. Although the budget is delegated, the LEA still provides central accounting services. Schools are connected to the LEA information and accounting system through a computer network, costing about £5000 per school to set up and install. In addition, a delegated school still has to operate within the LEA's regulation and constraints. In particular, it is not free to set its own pay levels, and is required to fund teachers' salaries through the county pay-roll. According to LEA officers, many secondary schools would like to go further and have the additional freedom of grant-maintained schools to enter into employment contracts with the teaching staff on their own behalf.

Initially it was intended that all secondary schools and primary schools with over 300 pupils on the roll would receive a delegated budget. Government policy, enunciated in Circular 7/91 (Department of Education and Science, 1991), has led to an extension of the intended coverage, so that all primary schools should be managing a delegated budget by 1995. In addition, the scope of budget delegation has been extended, so that all secondary schools should be operating a system of 'cheque book management' by 1994.

Open Enrolment

Under the old system, before the implementation of the 1988 Act, the number of pupils admitted to a secondary school could not exceed the planned admissions level (PAL). Often the LEA would set this artificially low, in comparison to the physical capacity of a school, as measured by the indicated admission level (IAL). This was done so as to even out the pupil numbers in different schools in a given locality in conformity with the LEA's overall plan for the district. The thinking behind this was that a school could become very costly to run if the pupil numbers fell very low, and in educational terms it would be difficult to offer a full range of curricular activities in a small school. Under the Education Act of 1980, parents were able to express a preference as to which school they would like to send their child, but the LEA could ignore this preference if 'compliance would prejudice the provision of efficient education or the efficient use of resources' (Admission and Transfer Arrangements, 1989/90, p. 5). The LEA used this power to restrict and even out the planned admissions levels of different schools.

The 1988 Act still gives parents the right to express a preference for a school of their choice, but it does not give parents an automatic right to send their child to a school of their choice if the school is already oversubscribed. This distinction is not always appreciated by parents. The provisions of the 1988 Act are identical to the 1980 Act regarding an LEA's right to refuse admission on the grounds of 'provision of efficient education or the efficient use of resources' (Admission and Transfer Arrangements, 1991/92, p. 6). But the new policy removes the ability of the LEA to set admissions ceilings which do not reflect fully the capacity of the school as defined by central government. Thus, whether or not the child is admitted depends partly upon the school's 'Standard Number' set by the Secretary of State. This is based on the highest admissions level achieved by the school since the 1979/80 academic year. Clearly, in some cases this could be considerably higher then the previous admissions level achieved immediately before the introduction of open enrolment, giving room for large shifts in the final allocation of pupils between schools. If the school roll is below the standard number, the school cannot refuse to accept the child. On the other hand, if the standard number has been reached then the school does not have to admit more pupils, although it may admit up to 10 per cent above the standard number with the approval of the LEA or through appeal. 'Open enrolment' in such cases is not equivalent to an 'open door', and rationing of places is still a reality in the more popular schools.

The effect of the change has been to bring about a general increase in the capacity limits for admission to schools in the county. The typical increase in the admissions limit was between 10 per cent and 20 per cent, with some schools having their admissions limits raised by nearly 60 per cent. Nine schools saw no change and one school had its admissions limit reduced. The system ensured that schools which were popular, and therefore had not suffered a decline over the previous decade, did not have their admissions levels raised, whilst schools whose intake had been falling experienced an increase, in some cases a dramatic increase, in the official definition of their capacity limit.

Opting Out

Two schools in the county have opted out of LEA control, and become grant-maintained schools. These opted-out schools receive their budgets directly from the Department of Education, but the initial basis of their funding was the same as it would have been under the LEA formula. They may also receive generous additional capital grants, and this provided a strong incentive for other schools in the case study area to actively consider the possibility of opting out. The grant-maintained schools also received their share of the LEA central service budget (which was deducted from the LEA budget by central government and paid directly to the grant-maintained school) and they were free to buy in those services, either from their home LEA or from elsewhere. In response, the local education committee decided that it would not offer to tender for these services from the two grant-maintained schools, and so the authority was faced with the inevitable loss of the corresponding amount from its budget (about £250 000). The two grant-maintained schools purchased the services in question from another LEA; and the public service labour unions protested about this action to the education committee on the grounds that it threatened jobs within the local central services. The reason why the education committee took this unusual step was to discourage other schools from opting out. However it seems to be a strategy which is essentially not credible in the long run due to the loss of income to the LEA budget which it incurs. Moreover, the direction of central government policy, revealed in the White Paper of July 1992, is to encourage more schools to opt out and to weaken the ability of local education authorities to obstruct this process.

The advantages to a school considering opting out are considerable, particularly in the case of the additional capital funding which the government has been prepared to offer the early opt-outs. However, this source of munificence will most probably be less available to late-comers. A further advantage is that employment contracts come directly under the grant-maintained schools' control, whereas in locally managed schools, teaching contracts are held by the LEA. Freedom to enter into employment contracts with teaching staff directly provides the grant-maintained school with substantial financial flexibility. On the other hand, the view of LEA officers who were interviewed was that the grant-maintained school may suffer from the loss of LEA support over budget costing and accounting, and over educational advisory support, which may affect the quality of the educational services which they can provide.

Case Studies

Several schools were selected for the case study section of the research according to whether they were oversubscribed or undersubscribed. These cases highlight some special problems of implementation of the system of open enrolment under the 1988 Act in the county.

Oversubscribed Schools

School A is an example of an oversubscribed secondary school having a local monopoly position in its area of prime responsibility (APR). The particular problem has been that the number of children of secondary school age living in the area exceeded the school's standard number of 240. The current policy for pupils living within the APR but who are not admitted to School A, is to provide transport to School B in a neighbouring area. Priority for admission to School A is given to pupils who have spent the longest time in local primary schools. However, many of the pupils bused to School B on this basis actually live closer to School A than some of the children who are admitted to School A. Consequently the Education Committee agreed to the recommendation of the LEA that applicants for a place at School B who live within School A's APR should be given priority. However, School B is itself oversubscribed and the headteacher and governing body have objected to this arrangement, as it would limit the school's ability to choose to admit local children. A partial solution to the dilemma was reached when the party spokespersons agreed to School A's request for a temporary increase of its standard number by 10 pupils for the 1991 admissions. The case indicates that the new system has not eliminated rationing of school places.

In another case, the LEA provides free transport to School C for children of parents who express a preference for the school but who live over three miles away from it. However, the bus on which these children travel passes by another secondary school, School D, which is the nearest coeducational secondary school to the parishes in question. This small rural secondary school is undersubscribed and is facing a continuous loss in pupil numbers. School C is over-subscribed despite having had its admissions limit raised following the introduction of the new standard numbers. The governing body of School D has objected to this effect of open enrolment, as they feel that the policy is disadvantageous to their school. Should it be forced to close, there will be no local alternative for the pupils in its APR.

Undersubscribed Schools

School E is an inner-city school which is undersubscribed. The school has a mixed ethnic intake with 24 separate langauges being spoken by its pupils. The numbers of pupils in the school have been declining for several years, from a peak of 2 250 in 1980 to around 816 in 1990, reflecting both the general decline in secondary school intake, as well as factors specific to an inner-city school with a high intake from minority ethnic groups. Over the past ten years the school has suffered from a rationalisation of the school capacity through the closure of three lower-school sites. Under open enrol-ment the school can expect little change in this pattern as extra capacity is opened up elsewhere in the school system. In addition the school's governing body has taken a decision not to engage in overt marketing of the school, due to a feeling that this could alienate many of the potential entrants to the school and so have a net negative impact on admissions.

Although delegated management is welcomed by the school's officers for the increased flexibility it provides in controlling and spending the budget on site, school E has lost heavily from the formula funding system. For the time being, however, it is shielded from the full extent of the losses by the transitional arrangements and the safety net system. Its budget has fallen significantly due to the loss of funding for special educational needs under the new system, especially in the field of provision for children with English as a second language. It has also had a disproportionate number of experienced older teachers whose salaries are not fully reflected in the formula which is based on average teacher salaries in the county as a whole. Despite the safety net, the school is projected to be in deficit over the next three years. This deficit was met initially by voluntary retirements of up to ten senior staff between the 1990/91 and 1991/92 school years. The school has few resources for publicity and the school brochure is funded by local businesses.

Some consideration has been given by the governing body to the possibility of opting out and become grant-maintained. Were it to do so, it would receive its share of the LEA's capital budget, which would provide a substantial financial boost to the school's budget. If the school were to opt out, it would enjoy some additional flexibility in buying in a pay-roll function, an educational welfare function, an educational psychology service, and a careers service. Senior staff interviewed thought there might be some advantage in this, for example in employing a child psychologist on site. In addition to the flexibility which local management provides over revenue expenditure, opting out would provide flexibility over capital expenditure, and some much-needed renovation and upgrading of premises could be carried out. For the time being it is held back from this step for ethical and moral reasons, and because of political uncertainty over future government policy.

The experience of School E illustrates some of the negative impact of formula funding for inner-city schools, in so far as its budget has actually fallen despite its relatively high level of special educational needs. Nor has it gained from the open enrolment system as it is in a weak competitive position in the expanding quasi-market for educational services in the county.

Responses and Conflicts

Headteachers have responded to the new system of delegated budgets with enthusiasm, and there appear to be no head teachers who have indicated that they would wish to return to the previous financial regime. Although their accountability, which is now directly to the governing body, has increased, they also enjoy increased freedom of decision-making and of control over expenditure decisions at a local level which is generally felt to be beneficial to the efficient day-to-day management of schools.

Teachers have responded less enthusiastically, being to an extent overburdened by the simultaneous and rapid introduction of new forms of organisation, and the new national curriculum.

Governing bodies now have much increased responsibilities. Many governors have resigned, and significant amounts of scarce resources have to be devoted to the process of governor training. Governors must devote far larger amounts of time than was previously the case to fulfilling their role, yet they receive neither expenses nor disturbance allowances. While an initial surge of goodwill may support their active involvement in the early years of operation of the new system, it is likely that the supply of effective and committed governors, especially in areas with above average economic and social stress, will require some more formal financial support in the long term.

Parents have responded to the new system by taking increasing advantage of the possibilities offered through open enrolment to exercise a greater degree of choice of school. In the context of the general raising of capacity limits in the school system, this has brought about substantial changes in the pattern of admissions to schools in the county. However, limits on admissions numbers are still imposed centrally, albeit by the Department of Education rather than the LEA. This means that admission to schools which are oversubscribed is still rationed, and it may be expected that such schools will adopt selection procedures designed to screen out pupils of lower initial ability, or with special educational needs.

LEA officers have been involved in a major input of additional time and effort in implementing the new system. Their general reaction is ambiguous: on the one hand there is a feeling of being 'under siege', and a perception that their position is being undermined as more and more of their powers are being stripped away; on the other hand there is a generally positive reaction to the change in roles from generalist administrators to that of specialist advisers and facilitators, responsible for training, monitoring, and reviewing, which will replace a less rewarding controlling function.

Conditions for Success

The Market Structure

One of the key criteria by which the operation and effectiveness of markets (whether 'quasi' or not) can be judged concerns the degree of competition to which providers of services are subject (see Chapter 2). As is well-known, where a provider unit in a market holds a monopoly position, it may choose to reduce the quantity or quality of the services it offers with no adverse consequences due to loss of trade to competitors. A parallel consideration concerns the existence of potential competition. If it is relatively easy for providers to enter and exit from the market, then the problems associated with any tendency towards even a local monopoly may be much reduced. A key element in the appraisal of the operation of the quasi-market in education in the county, therefore, must be an initial analysis of the existing market structure.

In 1991 there were 61 maintained secondary schools in the county, two of which were grammar schools, and two of which were grant-maintained. In addition there were 26 independent schools (primary and secondary) providing the county with the largest number of private schools in any county outside London. There had been four secondary school closures since 1981, whilst the number of primary schools had fallen from 402 in 1981 to 373 by 1987 reflecting falling school rolls in the first half of the decade.

The number of secondary school pupils on roll fell continuously throughout the decade, from 72 114 in 1981 to 51 745 in 1991. The decline in pupil numbers was matched by a corresponding, but proportionately slower, decline in teaching staff from 4245 full-time and full-time equivalent teachers in 1981 to 3267 in 1990. The simultaneous nature of these changes meant that there was relatively little change in the pupil–teacher ratio which fell from 16.99 in 1981 to 16.07 in 1990. Contrary to common perception this demonstrates the high degree of flexibility in the pre-reform administrative system which was apparently capable of bringing about a rapid adjustment and reallocation of resources in response to the shifting pattern of demand for education services.

In contrast to the situation in the county, at a national level the pupil–teacher ratio dropped much more sharply from 16.6 to 15.25

between 1981 and 1990. This figure can be further compared to the national average pupil–teacher ratio in independent schools which had fallen from 12.5 in 1981 to 10.9 in 1990. Public sector education trends in the county have been out of line with national trends. Not only have parents of pupils in independent schools been prepared to pay for far lower pupil–teacher ratios (possibly indicating higher quality of provision), but the public sector nationally was willing to support a more rapid decline in the pupil–teacher ratio than was supported in the county.

Table 6.2 shows the age profile of pupils in the maintained sector in the county. The figures show a sudden drop in numbers of pupils between the ages of 11 and 12, from 10111 to 8975. This reflects an exodus of pupils from the state sector into the private sector at this age. Thus, the state sector faces strong competition from the private sector, and this inevitably conditions the experience of the introduction of the education reforms in the county.

The size distribution of the primary and secondary maintained schools in the county is shown in Table 6.3. Primary schools are on average smaller than secondary schools, with most primary schools

TABLE 6.2
Age Profile of Pupils in Maintained and Grant-Maintained Schools in the County

Age	Full-time pupils	Age	Full-time pupils
2	4	12	8 975
3	441	13	8 853
4	10 838	14	9 153
5	11 283	15	9 502
6	10 572	16	10 067
7	10 386	17	3 413
8	10 411	18	2 326
9	10 171	19	206
10	10 488	20	14
11	10 111		
			Total 125 931

Source: DES data.

TABLE 6.3
Size Distribution of Schools and Pupils in the County

Full-time pupils	Primary schools	Secondary schools	Primary pupils	Secondary pupils
< 25	2		49	
26–50	12		512	
–100	42		3 196	
–200	144		22 297	
–300	128	1	31 240	227
–400	35	1	12 014	310
–500	7	3	3 009	1 380
–600	2	5	1 116	2 787
–800		16		11 175
–1000		16		14 532
–1200		12		12 797
–1500		6		7 617
–2000		1		1 673
Total	372	61	73 433	52 498

Source: DES data.

falling into the 100–300-size groups. In contrast, most secondary schools fall in the 600–1 200-size groups. The distribution of schools indicates that there are no particularly large schools which would be expected to hold a monopoly position in the market in the county as a whole (although some schools may be in a local monopoly, or near monopoly position in some areas within the county). This indicates that the market structure is broadly, if imperfectly, competitive, and that any failure of the quasi-market system in education is unlikely to be associated with a absence of alternative providers.

Admissions patterns

Open enrolment was introduced in the county in the 1989/90 school year, one year ahead of schedule. The general impression from interviews with LEA officers is that open enrolment has already had pronounced effects on the pattern of admissions. An example often quoted is the increase in the number of children who are taking school transport from urban to rural secondary schools on the city fringe.

More comprehensive evidence on the initial impact of open enrolment on the allocation of pupils to schools in the county can be seen from the following tables. If the new system had no effect, the variance in admission changes both between, and within, school groups would remain roughly constant over time. An increase in the variance of admissions changes would indicate a change in the underlying pattern of admissions. Table 6.4 reports the changes in admissions across school groups for various years.

TABLE 6.4
Annual Change in Admissions by School Group (%)

| Group | School year | | | |
	1987/88	1988/89	1989/90	1990/91
1	−0.85	−0.14	2.00	10.77
2	−5.10	−1.54	−6.08	16.11
3	−2.16	1.76	−3.47	17.07
4	0.82	−13.51	−2.81	14.47
5	−2.80	−10.75	1.76	−7.36
6	−4.17	−5.69	8.87	12.70
7	−6.47	−4.46	6.54	6.80
8	−1.99	−3.38	2.10	15.07
9	−3.20	2.83	−2.64	8.36
10	−1.51	−1.53	−5.11	17.89
11	−6.01	−5.69	−0.75	0.13
12	1.32	−14.38	20.04	−8.59
13	−4.88	−6.01	4.38	3.17
14	−0.85	0.43	2.36	10.69
Variance	0.05	0.27	0.43	0.69

Note: Percentage change in pupil age group 11 over same age group in previous school year.
Source: County Council summary of DES form 7.

As can be seen from the table, the average between-group variance in admission changes has been steadily increasing. The increase was already beginning to register in the entry to the 1988/89 school year, even before the formal introduction of the reforms, possibly reflecting increased parental awareness of the possibilities for the exercise of choice which existed even under the old system as a result of extensive public debate of the issues involved following the passing of the 1988 Act.

Table 6.5 reports the variance of rates of change of admissions within school groups. In 1987/88, for example, the variance of admissions changes in school group 5 was 2.55 per cent indicating

TABLE 6.5
Variances within Groups (%)

Group	School year			
	1987/88	1988/89	1989/90	1990/91
1	0.95	0.69	0.53	0.83
2	1.82	0.50	1.16	2.97
3	1.94	0.78	0.55	1.39
4	0.00	0.00	10.48	10.27
5	2.55	3.00	5.09	0.46
6	0.05	0.30	0.33	0.59
7	0.11	0.30	0.58	0.15
8	0.00	0.00	0.00	0.00
9	0.95	0.16	3.58	0.73
10	0.72	0.80	0.75	1.04
11	1.49	1.43	2.22	2.79
12	0.70	0.05	2.52	0.87
13	0.36	3.03	1.21	0.51
14	1.88	2.16	1.88	0.04
Average variance	0.97	0.94	2.21	1.62

Source: County Council summary of DES form 7 (full-time pupils between 10 and 19+ in secondary schools in the county, as at 31 August in the previous year, compiled 17 January).

that schools within this group were expanding or contracting at different rates, whilst schools in group 8 were apparently experiencing no variance at all in their admissions patterns.

The table shows the changing pattern of within-group variance, as parents switched children between schools within a group. The average within-group variance rose by over 100 per cent when open enrolment was introduced in the entry to the 1989/90 school year, from 0.94 per cent to 2.21 per cent. This suggests that large shifts began to take place in the pattern of secondary school entry. The extent of the shift was highest in the first year of the introduction of the new policy and fell back to 1.62 per cent in the entry for the following school year. This reflects the constraining influence of the upper limits to admissions reflected in the new standard numbers, which, whilst higher than the old planned admissions levels, still enforce some rationing of the educational services on offer.

This evidence indicates that there was a marked change in the pattern of admissions to secondary schools in the county following the introduction of open enrolment in 1990/91 (similar effects were observed in Scotland by Adler and Raab, 1988, following the introduction of the Education (Scotland) Act in 1981 which introduced open enrolment provisions similar to those subsequently introduced in England and Wales in the 1988 Act).

Entry and exit

A further key issue in the establishment of a quasi-market in education is the question of entry and exit of school units. A school which has a delegated budget is free to spend according to its own assessment of the best mix of services to be offered and of inputs to be purchased to produce those services. At the same time, the responsibility attached to delegated management should mean that a school which is failing to fulfil local needs should suffer financial loss, and either change its mix of inputs (teaching staff) or services offered (courses), or contract, or close down. Equally, where new needs are developing, say through population movements or new housing developments, the quasi-market should provide some mechanism for signalling the emergence of those needs and for establishing new school units.

In practice, neither of these requirements for an efficient operation of a quasi-market seem to have been established. First, in a technical sense there is no provision for a school to go bankrupt since it is not a trading organisation. Overspending in one year is carried forward to the next. Continuous overspending would most likely result in the LEA stepping in, in the role of administrator, taking the school back into direct management and restructuring the school. Provision for closing down and opening new locally managed schools, which occurs by the administrative decision of the LEA, subject to political ratification by the Education Committee, does not appear to have been altered by the introduction of the new system. Second, the opening up of new schools remains an essentially administrative decision to be taken by the LEA on the grounds of projections of future population changes. No direct or indirect market signals influence these decisions. Indeed, the small schools protection element in the funding formula means that capital costs of schools which are contracting will be automatically covered, and so closure is most unlikely to come about as a result of any quasi-market price signals.

Nevertheless, given the existing market structure, competitive forces appear to be increasingly active and under the quasi-market system, the LEA powers to guide the allocation process are much diminished. There is evidence from interviews with LEA officers that there is a developing competitive spirit between headteachers. Initially, head teachers in the county have held on to a 'gentlemen's agreement' not to compete too fiercely against one another, and not to poach from each other's 'area of prime responsibility'. However, this agreement was soon broken, with the resulting widespread impact on the variation in admissions patterns already reported, indicating the real impact of these new competitive pressures within the school system in the county.

Information

The provision of adequate information is specially important in the education setting because it is difficult and costly for parents to detect the quality of education provision before the pupil has spent some time at a school. In a technical sense, education is an 'experience good' (see Nelson, 1970). The so-called 'pre-costs' of discerning quality before admission to a school are high relative to the 'post-costs' which are incurred after admission has taken place.

At the same time it is relatively difficult and costly for pupils to switch schools if the quality of educational provision does not meet up to expectations (not necessarily costly in a monetary sense but in terms of adjusting to new routines, both for pupils and teachers). Klemperer (1987) argues that the presence of switching costs in a general market setting may reduce the welfare gains associated with the use of market-like methods of resource allocation. Policy intervention and regulation may then be required to reduce switching costs and improve the efficiency of such a market. The quasi-market mechanism will not work well where imperfectly informed consumers base their choice of school on non-educational characteristics such as the predominant social class or racial composition of the school intake. A "bandwagon effect" may develop with some schools becoming increasingly popular and desired whilst other schools develop a poor reputation even though they may be capable of providing effective levels of educational quality. As a result, a minority of relatively privileged schools may be able to reduce costs and increase incomes, while other schools may suffer financial instability. Should such effects occur as a consequence of a lack of adequate information, the quasi-market system will tend to generate increasing inequality in levels of educational provision.

In practice, the county LEA has attempted to direct the process of choice, rather than increase the amount of information provided to parents, in an attempt to limit the extent to which the allocations of pupils to schools vary from one year to the next. The LEA has established an area of prime responsibility for each secondary school, and has tried to guide parents to choose the secondary school in whose APR they live. In addition, schools have been encouraged by the LEA to give priority to pupils who live within their APR. The main source of information provided to parents is a letter from the LEA sent to parents towards the end of a child's time at primary school listing three local schools in whose APR they live, to which the LEA recommends that parents should send their children. Parents are invited to state an order of preference for these schools. The LEA makes an allocation decision, and if a parent does not agree to it he or she can lodge an appeal. In addition the LEA can use its extensive control over busing routes to guide parents choice of schools. In general the amount of documentary information available about the various schools in the case study area was limited to school brochures and reports in the local newspapers. Other sources of information included school visits by parents', and schools' reputations spread by word of mouth among parents' social networks. It is likely that in future, as the powers of the LEA to control and guide the admissions process is progressively diminished, the dissemination of information will become a more important part of its functions.

Transactions Costs and Uncertainty

To the extent that the operation of open enrolment and formula funding leads to a more responsive allocation process, it is also likely to lead to a large increase in the number of appeals, and accordingly to a more costly appeals service. In the case study area, for example, open enrolment has brought about a marked increase in the number of schools which were oversubscribed in 1991. In the 1990/91 school year, for example, only 10 secondary schools were oversubscribed, but by 1991/92, as many as 20 out of the 60 secondary schools in the area were oversubscribed. This led to an increase in the time taken to allocate pupils, and for appeals and decisions to be made. To deal with the increased allocation activity, the LEA funded 600 hours of extra overtime to deal with the excess applications for oversubscribed schools. Appeals continued to be heard right up until the beginning of the school term in early September. Pressure on appeals boards brought about a situation in which many panels were reduced from the full five members to the minimum number of three members. There was a marked increase in complaints about the conduct of appeals to the local government ombudsman. This situation arose as parents became increasingly aware of their right to apply for places for their children in schools outside their local area, that is which were not their designated schools.

There was a special pressure on primary schools for which school rolls had been increasing since 1986. Headteachers and governing bodies expressed concern about the resulting pressure on class sizes and on teaching resources. Parents were also dissatisfied that it took over six months to complete the initial allocation of places. In some cases, parents were not informed of the placing of their children until the beginning of the summer term, and the orderly arrangement of pre-school visits was disrupted.

Between 1990 and 1991, the number of appeals for year 7 entry increased from 81 in 1990 to 175 in 1991, and the number actually heard increased from 68 to 146, an increase of over 100 per cent. Of these 68 were upheld (compared to 26 in 1990) and 78 were dismissed (compared to 42 in 1990). Five schools in the county were the subject of an excess of ten appeals each against the LEA allocation decision. These data indicate that the enrolment system was far from being completely open: 78 parents were refused permission to send their children to the school of their choice.

The increase in admissions appeals between 1990 and 1991 has led to an increased need for the LEA to devote substantial extra resources to this stage of the admissions process. The number of LEA officers presenting appeals in 1991 rose by 100 per cent compared with 1990 (from five to ten officers). In addition the number of administrative staff had to be increased from seven to ten. This pressure on resources is likely to increase with the streamlining of the admissions process, and an increasing parental perception of their rights to exercise choice in the selection of school for their children.

Opposite types of effects on costs may occur where schools which operate delegated budgets are highly risk-averse in the face of uncertainty. Although governors are not personally liable for any losses (the LEA retains ultimate financial responsibility), any overspend would be deducted from the following year's budget. Equally, any underspend can be carried forward, although it is likely that in the event of significant underspending, the central government would reduce its grant funding of local educational services. This could have a ratchet effect, progressively reducing public expenditure on education. Despite this danger, in practice there was significant underspending in the county by schools operating delegated budgets. In 1990/91, the first year of operation of the new system, locally managed schools underspent by £7 million. The underspending came about because headteachers and governing bodies adopted a cautious approach to spending and created numerous contingency funds at school level. This contrasts with the consistent pattern of overspending which characterised the previous system of centralised administrative budgeting. Under that system, head teachers tended to overspend their budgets, aware that the LEA was ultimately accountable for the expenditure which they incurred.

The system of delegated management also involves an increase in the administrative costs of school management. Many governors have found themselves faced with an unexpected and unwelcome increase in their responsibilities and in the amount of time which they are required to devote to school affairs. Some schools have found difficulty in recruiting sufficient numbers of willing candidates for positions on the governing body, and in some cases the governing body has become inquorate. This is not surprising since governors are not entitled to any form of financial compensation for expenses incurred, or for time spent on the activity of the governing body. Nor are schools compensated for the extra time spent by teacher governors, or for the extra temporary staff cover involved. In addition, these effects are likely to be uneven across school groups, since schools located in prosperous areas may find it easier to attract a sufficient number of willing governors than those in poorer areas.

Although teachers in locally managed schools are still within the county pay-roll, the responsibility for personnel management resides with the school. Governors in locally managed schools have the responsibility to hire and fire teaching staff. They deal directly with the labour unions rather than the LEA over personnel matters, although the LEA is spending a significant amount of time and resources in providing advice to schools and to governors on this issue, particularly in managing redundancies (in fact redundancy pay is still managed by the LEA). Since the pay-roll is still funded by the LEA, it is likely that local management will not produce significant upward pressure on labour costs in the new system. However, the loss of the LEA central role in managing labour redeployment within the school service as a whole is likely to increase the use of redundancy as a means of teacher redeployment and increase the costs of adjustment as a consequence.

Motivation

In the absence of more detailed survey research little can be established about the motivations of the various organisations involved in the provision of education services. However, impressions gained from the case studies suggest that the principal actor (the LEA purchaser) is concerned to maximise the educational welfare of all the children in its locality. The individual school (the education provider) is concerned both to generate the best final overall results for the children which graduate from that particular school, and to maximise its budget, which in the context of the formula implies maximising the level of admissions. Given this motivation structure, individual schools' responses to the differential age-weighting basis of the formula have been varied. A drawback of the scheme is that schools may, in order to increase their budget, begin to adopt opportunistic strategies (a concept introduced by Williamson, 1975, to describe welfare reducing aspects of managerial discretion in markets characterised by asymmetrical information flows). Such opportunistic strategies of provider units operating on a quasi-market derive from differences in the aims and objectives of purchasers and providers. Opportunistic behaviour would characterise a school which, for example, admitted sixth-form students with low chances of successful graduation, but with high expected drop-out rates, for the sake of enhanced income generation through the formula. Examples of such behaviour were reported in interviews carried out in the course of the research, although there is no firm evidence to substantiate such claims.

Cream Skimming

A key characteristic of the pricing structure created by formula funding is that each school faces the same level of funding per pupil, so that 'fairness' between schools is achieved. It discriminates only on the basis of age. The basis of the discrimination is partly to do with the way in which the weights for each age group within the separate subjective headings have been determined, and partly to do with the way in which the budget has been allocated across the headings. The former is based on an informed assessment of the differences in costs of providing the various inputs to each age group, the latter on an administrative allocation of the budget based on historical patterns.

However, the advantage of 'fairness' is only achieved in a contingent sense, namely, on the assumption that all schools face the same average costs of educating children of a given age. In practice, the cost of educating children differs according to educational needs. And it is likely that children's educational needs differ according to the initial level of ability and characteristics of the home background such as family income. In order to deal with the latter aspect of this problem, the funding formula is adjusted on the basis of the take-up of free school meals. However this is not really satisfactory, since children with the greatest educational need due to low family incomes are often reluctant to attend for school meals at all (due to a preference for local fast food retail outlets, or to a religious objection to some meat products). In addition, the link between entitlement to free school meals and poverty is tenuous since the basis of entitlement is that a parent should be in receipt of Income Support payments from the Department of Social Security. Parents on low incomes who are receiving Family Credit, on the other hand, are not entitled to free school meals for their children. Moreover, many poor parents who would be entitled to free school meals for their children do not claim them because of stigma. Some schools therefore find themselves adopting a social work role, trying to persuade reluctant parents to apply for free school meals on their child's behalf. Moreover, the full effect of these changes has not yet been felt, as the system of transitional protection has operated to reduce the full impact of the scheme for schools which would otherwise face a much reduced budget.

In addition, the formula has failed to make any allowance for special educational needs based upon initial levels of attainment. The LEA is seeking ways to improve the formula so that it bears a closer relation to real educational need. It has begun a pilot study in six primary schools in the county designed to measure the degree of educational attainment at the age of four when a child first enters the primary school. The scheme involves assessment interviews with parents, who are asked about their child's abilities in basic areas of achievement, such as speech, colour recognition and so on. The formula can, however, only be changed with an 18-month lag, and so even if the pilot study were to be completed quickly, no changes could be introduced until Autumn 1995, long after the transitional protection has been withdrawn.

An advantage of the previous system of central administrative funding of schools was the way it could be adapted to address the differential impact of special educational needs between schools. By basing the funding mechanism on the pupil–teacher ratio, schools with special needs could be staffed more favourably than other schools. However, once the formula system was introduced, it became impossible to maintain this type of reverse discrimination in favour of schools with a higher proportion of children with special educational needs. In consequence the schools which faced financial losses under the formula funding system tended to be schools which drew the greatest proportion of pupils from the most disadvantaged section of the community.

Some school groups lost or gained quite substantial shares of their budget following the introduction of formula funding, in one case exceeding 6 per cent of the aggregated group budget. Four individual schools stood to lose over 10 per cent of their budget. The system of transitional protection ensured that they would not lose more than 5 per cent in the first year of operation of the scheme, although this protection is designed to be progressively withdrawn. Average forecast losses across school groups also differed, though not as widely as between individual schools. The greatest losses were predicted to occur in school groups 12 (down 6.33 per cent), 13 (down 3.09 per cent) and 5 (down 2.5 per cent) (calculated from the LEA's projections for individual schools). These groups are all located mainly in inner-city areas, and areas containing peripheral council housing estates, both of which are likely to be areas of the greatest educational need.

Increasingly, parents are becoming more aware of their new opportunities to express a preference for the school of their choice, and queues are developing for the schools with the best reputations. Although, officially, schools are not allowed to introduce selective entrance procedures, in the face of queues it is only to be expected that they will in fact do so. Indeed, the circumstantial evidence is that the more popular schools are becoming increasingly selective. For example, interviews are held, and parents can be invited to bring along examples of their child's work. Invitations may be sent out for both parents to attend, so as to filter out children of single-parent families.

It would appear, therefore, that 'open enrolment' is very far from being a wide-open door. The door is firmly closed once a school's standard number is reached. And by encouraging an increasingly selective admissions policy in such schools, open enrolment may be having the effect of bringing about increased opportunity for cream-skimming and hence increased inequality.

Conclusions

The reforms of the education system in the case study area have been carried out in three key areas: funding, management and admissions policy. The introduction of formula-based funding has replaced a system based upon the administrative allocation of budgets, by a quasi-market system in which a school's budget reflects the number of pupils it is able to attract. In practice this reform has so far only been achieved to a limited extent: only just over one half of the schools' budgets in the county have been determined by actual admissions. The introduction of formula funding brought about fairly large shifts in the distribution of resources between schools, due primarily to changes in the way special educational needs have been treated in the formula funding system. Some schools have lost out from this process, others have gained, although the losers have been offered some degree of protection by a phasing in of the changes and through the operation of a 'safety net' to limit the losses faced by any individual school. The direction of the impact of the changes, however, has been to reduce the funding available to schools in the poorest inner-city areas, and to increase the funding of schools in the more prosperous areas of the county. This change may, in principle, lead to more 'fairness' and openness in the system of budget allocations, but in practice has led to greater inequality of provision and to discrimination against schools with the greatest need.

Formula funding has been accompanied by a process of delegation of management to individual schools, as the direct managerial responsibility of the LEA has been transferred to the headteachers and the governing bodies of schools. This change has generally been welcomed by both head teachers and by LEA officers. The main perceived advantage is that resources which a school receives can be managed more efficiently at a local level, since the direct involvement of the governors and teachers in the educational process means that they have far more information available about the best ways to spend the budget than was ever available to the LEA. At the same time they have a strong incentive to use the budget effectively. In addition, the system may lead to increased levels of local community involvement in school management. These changes have led to improvements in the efficiency of resource administration, but these improvements have been gained at the expense of large hidden costs in terms of extra burdens of time and expense being placed upon governing bodies. In the initial stages of implementation, the system has relied upon the enthusiasm and goodwill of governors to meet these extra responsibilities. There are, however, already signs that this fund of goodwill is depreciating, and that some schools are experiencing difficulty in recruiting enough governors to operate delegated management effectively. In order to realise the full potential efficiency advantages of delegated management, it is likely that in the future school governors would need to be paid expenses and disturbance allowances to reflect the time and effort devoted to their increased managerial responsibilities.

Linked to the reforms in the areas of funding and management, reforms in the area of admissions policy have been introduced through the system of open enrolment. The principal change has been the removal of the power of the LEA to set admissions limits in order to plan for an even distribution of pupils across schools. Under the new system, admissions limits are set by the central government which establishes a capacity benchmark for each individual school. This has led to significant changes in the distribution of pupils across schools reflecting an increased responsiveness of the system to parental choices. This effect is reflected in observable shifts in the variance of admissions rates between different schools in the county: some popular schools have been able to attract pupils, other less popular schools have experienced a drop in pupil numbers with an associated drop in funding. This situation contrasts with the situation in previous years when all schools experienced similar changes in admissions rates which essentially followed the lines set by the LEA's admissions policy. The net result has been that despite the assertion that a system of open enrolment has been introduced, access to education in oversubscribed schools remains rationed, and subject to more or less arbitrary admissions policies which include examples of back-door selectivity, or 'cream-skimming'. The quasi-market is 'fixed', to the advantage of such schools, by the way in which admissions limits are set by the central government.

Overall, the study has revealed that the new system has brought about a number of improvements in the provision of education services in the areas of efficiency and responsiveness through the mechanisms of delegated management and open enrolment, which are welcomed by the key decision-makers. The main problem areas are associated with the way in which formula funding generates inequality, and the way in which centrally established admissions limits restrict the degree to which open enrolment can work to provide a genuinely free choice of school.

The solution to the first problem would involve changes to the formula funding system so that the implicit prices established by the formula discriminated on the dimension of educational need as well as on the dimension of pupil age, so as to reflect children's different initial educational abilities. A solution to the second problem could involve implementing a genuinely 'open door' policy through removing (essentially arbitrary) admissions limits altogether. This, if combined with a requirement that a school should accept all applicants, would remove the opportunities for cream-skimming. In the short run, more popular schools would experience an increase in their pupil–teacher ratio, and less popular schools would experience a decrease. To the extent that quality of provision is inversely related to the pupil–teacher ratio, the quality differential between different schools would eventually be eliminated as increased admissions to popular schools reduced the pupil–teacher ratio. In the long run however, as funding followed pupils, inequalities would re-emerge. There is therefore a case for maintaining admissions limits. Given this, it would seem preferable that such limits should be determined by the LEA in line with the capacity of the local education system as a whole, rather than by the remote decisions of central government. This would ensure that rationing takes place on an explicitly community-wide basis, rather than through the development of a two-tier system of favoured and less favoured schools which is the likely outcome of the existing quasi-market arrangements.

Quasi-Markets and Social Housing

7

Glen Bramley

The main thrust of this chapter is to argue that the general concept of a quasi-market fits quite well as a description of the emerging pattern of social housing provision in Britain following the reforms of the late 1980s. Many of the preconditions for the existence and, in some senses, 'success' of the quasi-market are potentially met by the new models for social housing provision, possibly more clearly so than in the cases of health or education. At the same time, there are significant differences in the nature of the beast that make direct comparisons with these other major welfare services a little problematic; these relate to the residual role of the social housing sector, the capital investment focus, and the important role of user-charging.

These preliminary conclusions emerge not so much from local case studies, as in the other service areas, as from a general appraisal of the evolution of policy nationally and a broad scan of local responses to this new framework. Some of the impacts of the new regimes can be readily discerned from published data and reports. Other kinds of impact we can only speculate upon at this stage. The quasi-market concept provides a convenient framework of questions which can both channel our speculations and provide an agenda for future research.

The new framework for social housing is not the outcome of a single piece of legislation conceived in a coherent and comprehensive review, unlike the situation in health and education, although the 1987 White Paper (Department of the Environment, 1987) had some pretensions to providing such a radical reform agenda for rented housing. The reforms of the late 1980s came in the form of several separate pieces of legislation which together form some sort of jigsaw, albeit one which does not fit together without problems. However, it is argued here that the most important element, the emergence of the housing association sector, was actually the gradual outcome of much earlier legislation and policy preoccupations.

Because the way in which the framework relates to legislation and policy mechanisms is complex, the chapter opens with a description of the principal policy developments so as to clarify their main features. The main part of the chapter then examines how far the 'conditions for success of quasi-markets', identified in Chapter 2, are met in the case of social housing. The likely outcomes of the quasi-market process, in terms of efficiency, responsiveness, choice and equity are then discussed.

This chapter is about the provision of 'social' housing services, rather than housing as a whole. 'Social' housing is housing provided for rent (or part-rent/part-buy) at less than full market cost by a socially responsible agency conforming to some form of tenants' charter or guarantee and allocating accommodation on a basis related to need. The main institutional vehicles involved are local authorities (that is, council housing) and housing associations; some social housing is also provided by other types of body (for example, development corporations, local trusts, cooperatives) but these are relatively unimportant. In 1990 local authorities owned 22.4 per cent of the British housing stock while housing associations owned 3.0 per cent. Social housing is essentially a residual sector catering for that part of the population (about a quarter) who, because of low income, wealth, or special-need factors, cannot or choose not to be housed in either the mainstream tenure of owner occupation (67 per cent) or the small private rented market (7.5 per cent of dwellings).

In considering the provision of social housing, it is useful to distinguish three distinct sets of decisions, to each of which quasi-market models might be applied, but in differing ways and with differing implications. These three sets of decisions are:

1. *Investment* in new social housing schemes;
2. *Allocation* of households to social housing vacancies;
3. *Management* of existing stocks of social housing.

This chapter focuses mainly on the first and second of these. The quasi-market concept fits these most closely. The third is increasingly subject to compulsory competitive tendering for contracts, and is also affected by stock transfers. The line between contracting-out of this kind and quasi-markets may be a fuzzy one, but insofar as we can draw it our focus is on the latter rather than the former.

The Policy Framework

Table 7.1 attempts to summarise the main features of British housing policy in the 1990s, drawing out (in the left-hand column) the main outcomes that have a bearing on the framework for social housing provision and the potential development of a quasi-market. The middle column of the table shows the principal mechanisms that contribute to each outcome, and the right-hand column identifies the main relevant piece of legislation.

The predominant role of owner occupation has already been noted, and it should be recognised that this reflects a strong general policy stance which has applied over a long period and, with differing intensity, to all the main political party programmes. In the 1980s, the growth of owner occupation was given a substantial boost by the Right to Buy, under which about a quarter of the 1980 council stock (over a million dwellings) changed ownership. The existence of the Right to Buy is an important factor in the trend towards a more residual role for social housing (Forrest and Murie, 1983, 1989); it also conditions local policy responses and stances, for example by encouraging more use of housing associations rather than direct provision by LAs so as to avoid or reduce the impact of sales. Owner occupation continues to be fiscally privileged, as it has been for many years, which in turn helps to explain much of the apparent preference for this tenure and the failure of the private rented sector, on the whole, to thrive (Kemp, 1988).

The shift of local authorities from a mainstream provider role to that of a residual provider is one which has been emerging over a decade or more (Forrest and Murie, 1983). However, the 1987 White Paper (Department of the Environment, 1987) was much more explicit in stating that this was a desirable outcome.

TABLE 7.1

Key Features of British Housing Policy after 1987

Main outcomes	Key mechanisms	Relevant legislation
Owner occupation predominant	Right to Buy	1980 Housing Act
	Tax reliefs	(Finance Acts)
LA residual enabling role	Capital controls	1989 L G & Hsg Act
	Stock transfers	1985 & 1988 Hsg Acts
	Homelessness	1985 Housing Act
	Planning	Circ 7/91 & Planning Policy Guidance (PPG3)
	Housing Investment Programmes (HIPs)	Circular letters
Tenant choice accountability	Tenants' Choice	1988 Housing Act
	Hsg Action Trusts	"
	Voluntary transfer	1985 Housing Act
	Performance Indics	1989 L G & Hsg Act Citizens Charter
	Competitive Tendering (CCT)	1988 Local Govt Act
	Estate Mgt Boards	
Hsg assocs as main providers	Hsg Corp Devel Prog	Public Exp Plans
	Stock transfers	see above
	LA funding & land	1985, 1988 & 1989 Acts
	Planning	see above
	Tenants' Guarantee	1988 Housing Act
Hsg assocs with risk/autonomy	Mixed public/private finance	1988 Housing Act Hsg Corpn Circulars
	Lower Grant (HAG)	
	Rent-setting	
	Major repairs funding	
Private renting revival	Deregulation of rents	1988 Housing Act
	Assured (non-secure) tenancies	"
	LA subsidies	1988 Local Govt Act
	Tax reliefs (BES)	1988 Finance Act
	Housing Benefit	1986 Social Sec Act
	Leasing	
Target subsidies (poor people, worst housing)	New regime LA Accounts & subsidies	1989 L G & Housing Act
	Higher LA rents	"
	Reliance on Housing Benefit (HB)	ditto plus 1986 Act
	HA financial regime	see above
	Renovation grants	1989 L G & Hsg Act

> *Provision of housing by local authorities as landlords should gradually be diminished, and alternative forms of tenure and tenant choice should increase. . . . Local authorities should increasingly see themselves as enablers who ensure that everyone in their area is adequately housed; but not necessarily by them.* (Department of the Environment, 1987, Cm 214, p. 3).

In the political rhetoric council housing was portrayed as a failed social experiment (Coleman, 1985, provides one example of this genre) and as an inefficient, bureaucratic and paternalistic monopoly (Henney, 1984). Tenants were to be given more choice and independence. Much of housing policy since 1987 has been driven by the essentially negative goal of reducing the role of local councils. Mechanisms like the annual approval of capital programmes have been used increasingly to steer authorities in the desired direction, for example away from new building.

However, there is a positive side, even for the local authorities, in the expansion of their 'enabling' role (Bramley, 1992). Greater powers to use land-use planning to facilitate affordable social housing provision provide a good example (Bishop and Hooper, 1991; Barlow and Chambers, 1992). The annual Housing Investment Programme (HIP) system is being adapted to reinforce this altered role, in the process giving more emphasis and legitimacy to evidence of local needs (Department of the Environment, 1989; Institute of Housing, 1990). Local authorities retain the primary responsibility for aiding the homeless, whether or not they continue as landlords, and priority groups (particularly families) continue to have a right of access to social housing (Department of the Environment 1988). But to the extent that the homeless are disproportionately drawn from the poorest section of society, this tends to reinforce the socially 'residual' role of local authorities in housing.

The high-profile policy innovations of 1987 were the idea of giving council tenants a choice of alternative landlord ('Tenants' Choice'), and the mechanism of Housing Action Trusts which could take over problem estates and undertake improvements as well as creating tenure diversification. These mechanisms were intended simultaneously to open up choice and make landlords more accountable as well as to effect tenure transfers and reduce the scale of municipal landlordism dramatically. In practice, these mechanisms have scarcely been used at all in the form originally envisaged. The main reason for this has been tenant reluctance to agree to changes of landlord, particularly any involvement of private landlords. In addition, few private landlords or housing associations were interested in this approach. The main effect seems to have been one of a threat of potential competition galvanising many local authorities into renewed efforts to improve management performance and responsiveness; in this sense, as with compulsory competitive tendering in some other services, the policy could be said to have had some success.

Alternative mechanisms of tenure transfer, in which the local authority voluntarily initiates a transfer (normally to a specially created housing association), securing the approval of tenants in the process, have been more successful. At the time of writing about 20 authorities have disposed of most or all of their stock in this way, which strongly resembles the management buy out, while others are disposing of particular estates or blocks or trying to dispose of individual dwellings on a gradual basis.

A number of other mechanisms are being introduced with the aim of increasing competition, accountability and efficiency/effectiveness in the management of the remaining council stock. These include the compulsory publication of performance indicators, compulsory competitive tendering of major management functions (being phased in during the 1990s), and the encouragement of devolution of management to estates. These initiatives suggest that the Government recognises that a significant council housing sector is likely to remain for the foreseeable future.

Housing associations have now become the main providers of new units of social housing. Associations are regulated by the Housing Corporation which also channels most of the public finance for this investment programme to them, based on the government's expenditure plans. Associations are also increasing their stock through transfers and do undertake some development subsidised by local authorities or through cheap land from other sources (particularly where planning powers are used). While current growth is rapid, the modern housing association movement is mainly derived from developments in the 1970s under the impetus of the 1974 Housing Act.

The 1988 Housing Act introduced a new financial regime for housing associations. Instead of being heavily subsidised and protected by guarantees from the public sector, associations now have to operate more autonomously, interacting more directly with financial and housing markets and taking considerable risk. Associations get fixed up-front capital grants and set their own rents, with regard to vague guidelines on 'affordability', so as to try to maintain financial viability while taking responsibility for cost overruns and major repairs. Grant rates are lower and rents much higher than under the previous regime. Associations borrow directly from the private market, this borrowing not counting as public expenditure.

In 1987 the Government appeared to view a revived private rented sector as a major alternative to the local authorities. Although deregulation of rents and tenancies and one specific tax-subsidy intitiative (Business Expansion Scheme, or BES), have seen some modest revival in some sectors and areas, part of this may be due to the recession in the owner-occupation market. Major institutional investment in long-term private renting remains largely conspicuous by its absence.

The line between a quasi-market and an actual market is not clear-cut here, because Housing Benefit (the means-tested rent allowance or rent element of income support, HB for short) is available to tenants in both the social and private sectors. HB may be likened to a voucher, with individual tenants in theory able to exercise a choice of landlord. In practice, social landlords ration accommodation using waiting-lists and need criteria; private accommodation may not be available, suitable, or of an adequate standard, and may be rationed using financial or other mechanisms. Some landlords are happy to take tenants on HB, but in other cases rents may be beyond the 'reasonable market level' which rent officers must now set as a limit to HB subsidy.

Apart from reinforcing the move towards quasi- or actual markets, by generally pushing up rents, the new financial regimes have the general characteristic of targeting subsidies more specifically on poor people and poor housing. The general shift from subsidising 'bricks and mortar' to subsidising people, which began a decade or so ago, has been reinforced. Public expenditure has shifted away from general subsidies towards HB (Hills, 1991, ch. 3). This kind of shift makes a quasi-market model more of a possibility. At the same time, the remaining subsidies to the social sector are supposed to be increasingly 'targeted', geographically, although the precise target tends to move around with new data, new ministers and new priorities.

The Conditions for Success

Market Structure

On the face of it, competition does exist, actually and potentially, in social housing, and is expanding. In a typical local housing market area, there is a local authority provider together with a number of autonomous housing associations already established and operating. For example, in the city of Bristol there are 50 associations managing about 6000 homes and letting 300–400 per year. In 1992/93 ten associations are undertaking about 25 developments with a total value of about £30 million.

In addition to associations already based in the area, housing associations from other areas may be wishing to expand into this area. Taking the Bristol example again, half of the ten associations currently undertaking development have entered the area relatively recently, including in some cases through the takeover of local associations. The private rented sector also exists as a possible alternative, at least for some clients (particularly single people). The private rented sector also plays a role of providing some housing on short leases and Bed and Breakfast accommodation for the homeless.

In the case of *new investment*, in any locality there will be a number of associations competing for opportunities to undertake developments, which may be likened to contracts. These opportunities may arise in relation to particular sites which the local authority wishes to see developed, as well as in relation to bidding for funds. The main funding agency is the Housing Corporation; it allocates funds mainly scheme by scheme through regional offices on a basis of policy guidelines and target allocations to geographical areas. Some funds are allocated in blocks to large associations (so called 'tariff arrangements'), while others go in blocks through local authorities. In the latter case the LA has a programme agreement with the Corporation, and the funds are set against the authority's own capital spending limit. On the whole the process may be seen as a bidding one, and the number of bids greatly exceeds available funds in most cases so that the purchasers can exercise choice. The rules of the HA subsidy regime are intended to discourage negotiations being about rent levels/affordability (for example, cheap LA land is offset by lower subsidy), and focus attention on the number and quality of units.

There are essentially two purchasers, the Housing Corporation and the local authority; hitherto their programmes have not been formally coordinated, but there is a proposal to bring the annual programme approval process together. This provides an interesting case of the tension between the case for a monopoly purchaser and a fully coordinated plan, on the one hand, and 'competing bureaucracies' which can to some extent promote diversity and compensate for each other's inadequacies, on the other.

In the past, the LA would have had the choice of buying provision from itself or from HAs; political preferences would have had a considerable impact on this decision, but so also would the different subsidy availability. Currently, there is very strong discouragement of new provision by LAs and a presumption in favour of HAs, the private sector, and other possible providers where relevant.

At the level of the *individual household* needing a home, there is either a direct relationship with the provider, typically through applying and joining a waiting-list, or an indirect relationship whereby the LA acts as an intermediary and nominates the household to a housing association (normally 50–75 per cent of HA vacancies are made available to LA nominees). Households in the most urgent need, the homeless, would normally come through the LA route. The LA becomes effectively the third-party intermediary, akin to GP fundholders. The intermediary function of the LA may be increasingly distinguished from its provider role, with the move to Compulsory Competitive Tendering (CCT) of housing management functions and the spread of voluntary transfers.

The products confronting the individual household are relatively standardised, although far from being identical. The biggest difference may well be in the rents; typically HA rents on new lettings are much higher (about £50 per week compared with £30 per week for council lettings; see National Federation of Housing Associations, 1992; Association of District Councils, 1992). It should be remembered that for those on very low incomes the HB subsidy is portable and will offset any rent differences, but this will not assist the large minority of tenants not eligible for HB. HA properties may differ in type of location and style of building; the typical council let will be a flat on a large peripheral council estate built in the 1950s or 1960s, while the typical HA property may be a 1980s flat in a small infill scheme in a more central area. The amount of choice the typical client will have will be limited, perhaps to one offer or not more than three offers.

Entry and Exit. Entry to the market is quite possible, particularly for existing HAs wishing to move into new districts, although this is not costless in terms of setting up a local organisational presence. It is also necessary for the purchasers to approve, or not disapprove of, such a move. Exit may simply be the reverse of this process; for example, some associations have transferred, sold or swopped stock in order to consolidate their management responsibilities in particular areas. Another common form of exit from the new investment part of the quasi-market is simply to cease development; a very high proportion of all HAs are not active developers at any one time. Mention has been made of the much greater risks incurred by HAs under the post-1988 regime; the corollary of this is that bankruptcy is a possibility. Associations may get into financial difficulty with an adverse cash flow, but they always have a major asset base, and one response to this situation may be to sell vacant units on the market (this does not look good, in terms of the association's social mission, but may deal with the financial difficulty). Another response is to raise rents, much of which will be met by HB subsidy. Where associations are in serious difficulty which cannot easily be resolved in these ways, the normal practice is for another association to be asked to take them over and rationalise the two organisations.

It is important to qualify this picture of a rather competitive market structure by identifying a number of factors which may in practice *limit competition*. First, one major provider normally continues to dominate this quasi-market, namely the local authority or (in the case of large scale voluntary transfer) the transfer association. In the Bristol example quoted earlier, the City Council has six times the stock of all the 50 associations; nationally, the ratio is similar. While the local authority still dominates in terms of stock and the supply of lettings, it is actually more or less prevented from competing in the supply of new units of accommodation. This is a very significant restriction on competition, especially since LAs would have been able, given the structure of their finances, to provide new housing relatively cheaply.

Second, the resources available for new investment are limited by public expenditure constraints, which limits activity and new entry in the market for new investment contracts. New entry is also potentially limited by the regulatory control exerted by the Housing Corporation. The Corporation may be reluctant to register new associations or to support operations out of areas of origin, although its current policy appears to be one of encouraging competition at the expense, if necessary, of using associations without local roots.

Economies of scale are a classic source of non-competitiveness in normal markets, and may also operate in this quasi-market. First, there are bound to be some economies in relation to the scale of a local management organisation. In their formative years in the 1970s and 1980s housing associations were small and relatively costly in their management, although often producing a higher-quality (more personal) service (MacLennan, 1989). In the more cost-conscious nineties the need to streamline management is more apparent, and associations are becoming more concentrated partly for this reason. As in other social services the relevant market area is a local one, and management and maintenance services have to be locally based to be effective. Indeed, other strands of policy (decentralisation, estate-level management) reinforce this point. Thus, the gains from competition may quickly be offset by the higher costs of small scale, and competition may not remain a viable, stable state. Specialisation of role among associations, which is in any case an important feature of the sector, would also militate against competition (for example, as with 'regional specialties' in the health service). Finally, the higher risks of the post-1988 financial regime are encouraging associations to merge in order to pool risks, and the future of the smaller association is seen as problematic (National Federation of Housing Associations, 1992).

Competition may also be deliberately avoided, either by the way the LA operates or by the behaviour of the HAs. The ethos of the HA movement may be seen, by many of its key actors, as being more in tune with collaboration than competition. This may operate inform-ally, although reinforced by local forums and networks, or it may be more formalised in agreements set up between groups of associations in a locality, possibly involving the local authority as well. In many areas there was also a practice developed in the 1970s of zoning associations by sub-area, to avoid problems of 'pepperpotting' and of competition for sites/properties between associations driving up prices. In some urban areas large sites are being developed by consortia of associations linked by formal agreements. None of this necessarily invalidates the argument that the structure of the system now requires associations effectively to be in competition, although it may affect the style in which competition expresses itself and limit its effects in certain respects.

Information and Transactions Costs

At the level of new investment decisions, the capital costs are likely to be reasonably well-known to all parties, and the purchasers would have some independent expertise and data to draw on in evaluating the proposals of providers. Initial recurrent costs and rents would also be known, but future rent and management cost levels would be more difficult to judge. This is obviously a key problem for individual households, who would in any case have less access to information or comparative standards against which to set it.

As in other social services, information about quality may be more of a problem, although not perhaps as severe as in the case of health. The quality of the design itself is often likely to be the subject of comparison in a formal tender situation, and in any case building standards are fairly uniform and well-documented. Management quality is less easy to monitor from the purchaser's point of view, because the relationship with the client and the scheme tends to be lost once it is completed and occupied. Individual tenants in the social sector have relatively limited opportunities to apply the 'exit' option, and excess demand is endemic. This is one area where autonomous providers could act opportunistically, by economising on the delivery of management quality and instead maximising some other organisational goals. The Government and the Corporation have seen it as necessary to complement other reforms by introducing regimes of compulsory reporting of performance indicators and other mechanisms to bolster tenant consultation and accountability. The Corporation does periodically undertake 'monitoring' inspections of associations, and the Audit Commission performs a similar function for local authorities albeit with perhaps more emphasis at times on cost than quality. Many local authorities, if they are concerned about quality management, are likely to favour continuing relationships over time with particular associations, in whom they have some confidence over quality issues, at the expense of competition in the form of a series of 'one-night stands' with mobile providers.

These problems are of an altogether different magnitude with the potential alternative type of provider, the private landlord. Because of their different ethos and for-profit motivation, discussed further below, private providers are much more likely to act opportunistically in this regard. It is not necessary to argue that all landlords act in this way; merely sufficient for the purchasers to lack trust in the sector as a whole, which lacks for example the peer pressure that probably operates in the voluntary housing movement. The Government as funder also has a major problem of an open-ended financial commitment through Housing Benefit, which can easily be exploited by unscrupulous landlords and only imperfectly regulated by the mechanism of regulation of subsidy by the Rent Officer. Direct regulation of quality in the private rented sector runs directly into conflicts with other goals and constraints for the LAs which might attempt regulation: the more unsatisfactory multiply-occupied or unfit properties are acted against, the less low cost accommodation is available, the more homeless people present themselves to the authority, and the more funds for improvement work are preempted.

Quality of management and support services are much more crucial issues in the housing of various groups with special needs or vulnerabilities – frail elderly people, ex-offenders, young people leaving care, battered women, ex-mental patients. The housing association movement has played an increasing role in housing these groups, forming an important component of the strategy of Care in the Community. Often very specialised associations are involved. As in the social housing world generally, much of the quality assurance rests on assumptions about the motivation, commitment and ethos of the groups and individuals running these services. These services are very similar to the personal social care services discussed in Chapter 5.

Risk and Uncertainty

There are considerable *risks for providers* in the social housing quasi-market. Even near the outset of the scheme the project can overrun on time or cost, the so-called 'development risk'. Interest rates can and do fluctuate rapidly and by large amounts, and housing providers tend to use finance which contains an element of variable interest rate (Pryke and Whitehead, 1991). Future major repairs and renewals have been recognised as a major issue for housing associations, which now have to fund these themselves rather than get access to further grants from the Government (Hills, 1991). However, it can be argued that the 'sinking funds' set up for this purpose are an inappropriate, 'overkill' response (National Federation of Housing Associations, 1992).

All social housing providers share the inherent risks of landlordism. Properties may be empty and not generating rents, for example because at the rent asked and in current market conditions they are unlettable. Some tenants get into arrears with rent and, if unwilling to pay these back, are difficult to remove through court actions. Some tenants are 'difficult' and create disproportionate problems for their neighbours, caretakers, estate managers and others.

Significant risks also arise out of the uncertain future behaviour of governments. The funding programme may suffer public expenditure cuts or be diverted, leaving associations stranded without ongoing work to support a local development team (this has frequently happened in the past). The subsidy regime may change again, or discretionary levers within it may be operated in a different way (the LA subsidy regime is particularly vulnerable to this). The Housing Benefit regime may also be changed, as it has been frequently over the years. Rents which looked affordable to the target client group when the scheme was conceived might not be later on.

Housing Benefit is important in a different way, though, which very much eases the problems caused by risk. It can be argued that housing organisations, while they may be exposed to many risks, can generally shift them to tenants in the form of rents; for example, the effect of the risk premia in private lending to HAs and other conservative financing practices is to raise rents (Pryke and Whitehead, 1991; Hills, 1991). Tenants can in turn, in a majority of cases, shift the extra cost in full to the Government through the HB system. HB currently provides a 100 per cent marginal subsidy on rent increases for eligible tenants. In the longer run, this imbalance in the bearing of costs and risks, as well as the rising cost of HB, may lead to a re-think of this aspect of the system.

One feature of the current social housing scene in Britain is the growing role of low-cost home ownership initiatives, particularly shared ownership schemes (Department of the Environment, 1992b;

Bramley, 1991; Barlow and Chambers, 1992; Shephard Associates, 1991). Another feature, particularly under planning agreements on larger sites with mixed developments, is the use of cross-subsidy from private sale housing to assist provision of social housing. In both of these cases there is a substantial risk factor relating to the state of the (very volatile) house purchase market; houses intended for part or outright sale may not attract buyers when they are completed, or may have to be further discounted in price. These risks may be borne directly by the providers or shared by the various partners involved in the scheme; social housing provision may be delayed by the delay in realising sales. This illustrates the general point that quasi-markets are not wholly insulated from the private market, and in the case of housing, where the market is particularly unstable, this may have serious implications.

For housing associations the initial cushion for financial risks are the organisation's reserves. Some HAs are much better placed in terms of amount of reserves than others. Many have been using reserves to cross-subsidise rents on new schemes in the name of affordability (National Federation of Housing Associations, 1992). Thus there may well be a trade off between expansion and the maintenance or building of adequate reserves for an uncertain climate. Housing Corporation rules on the old system subsidies mean that only limited contributions can be made to reserves from raising rents on pre-1988 schemes. Local authorities are also, since 1990, in a position where most risks or cost increases fall on the tenant, thanks to the so-called 'ring-fencing' of their Housing Revenue Accounts (Hills 1991; Association of District Councils, 1992).

Motivation

Local authorities are complex beasts about which it is dangerous to generalise. They may be seen as a branch of 'the state', as autonomous and alternative centres of political power and influence, or as a multiple service-providing industry. There is a general view of them as rather typical bureaucratic organisations, with all that entails about motivation and behaviour: hierarchical; driven by formal procedures; unresponsive; cautious/risk-averse; lacking in individual financial incentives. It should also be remembered that local authorities are strongly dominated by key professional groups, for example lawyers, accountants and architects, as opposed to an administrative Civil Service on the Whitehall model, which conditions their behaviour in particular ways (Dunleavy, 1981; Stewart, 1983). This has to be balanced against the recognition of them as politically governed, with party politics and ideology as a factor, along with the pluralist influences of pressure groups and the traditional politics of local patches. Finally, the strong local accountability of local government (much more open than central government) and its permanent commitment to the locality, are important to remember.

For reasons to do with size, political control/priorities, and the dominance of particular professions/individuals, local authorities vary a great deal in their approach to housing. Some, for example, have favoured a low-rent, low service quality approach, while others have gone for higher rents; some have subsidised housing from local taxes, while others have transferred cash surpluses the other way (since 1990, such subsidies/transfers are disallowed in most cases). Some local authorities stopped building new council houses, apart from certain special-needs accommodation, in the 1970s; others continued to try to build into the late 1980s. In some cases housing is a low-status, low-priority service; in others it may be the most important strategic concern and the largest, most powerful department. In the 1970s and 1980s there was a move to raise the status and influence of the housing profession and of housing departments, often linked to the notion of a comprehensive housing service. The introduction of more of a quasi-market and the increased purchaser/provider split, reinforced by CCT for housing management, could be seen to undermine this, by splitting the housing department and potentially weakening it. This may be particularly likely where stock transfers take place (Institute of Housing, 1990).

One implicit tension for local authorities in their investment programme has been the relative priority given to three distinct types of problem affecting three distinct groups of people: (a) the need for new/additional affordable social housing provision to house the homeless and others without suitable long-term accommodation; (b) the need to make good backlogs of disrepair and upgrade the standards and amenities of the existing council stock; (c) the need to ensure adequate standards and to reduce the incidence of unfitness, disrepair and disamenity in the private housing stock. The recent Audit Commission (1992) report on local housing strategies makes particularly effective use of this distinction. A purchaser provider split may help to make this choice more explicit, and may even help to shift priorities. In particular, many authorities had given increasing emphasis to type (b) needs; this could be seen as a response both to the perspectives and interests of the provider-dominated organisation and to the political lobbying power of tenants' groups.

However, strategies towards the future of the council's own stock may continue to dominate LA thinking for some time. The option of voluntary transfer may be the expression of an anti-public sector ideology or of an uninterested/inactive authority; equally, it may be an attempt to meet category (b) needs more quickly, by overcoming capital control restrictions and giving managers more autonomy, while releasing some cash which could be ploughed back into category (a) and (c) needs. Alternative models for arm's-length local housing companies are intended to capture some of the same kinds of benefits. The phased introduction of CCT will, as in other LA services, dominate the thinking of many managers over several years.

The local authority as purchaser is discussed further below. The LA provider will be mainly concerned with trying to provide a good management service and to upgrade the standard of the stock, within a budget constraint which is considerably harder than under previous financial regimes because of ring fencing and shortage of capital. However, the bottom line is the rents that must be set to balance the Housing Revenue Account, and with 60 per cent or more of tenants on HB, and with LA rents still well below HA or market levels, the temptation is to raise rents further. It is noticeable that the general tendency of LAs in the first three years of the new financial regime has been to raise rents further than Government Guidelines (Association of District Councils, 1992). This process is limited to some extent by tenant consultation processes.

Perhaps the most interesting questions about the social housing quasi-market concern the motivations and behaviour of the *housing associations*, but pending more detailed research we can only really speculate about this. HAs are very diverse (Hills, 1991; Housing Corporation, 1991; National Federation of Housing Associations, 1992), especially in scale and scope, but they still have quite a lot in common. They are formally and effectively non-profit organisations. Although they are currently divided into 'charitable' and other categories, it is not clear that this distinction is very important other than as a device to circumvent the Right to Buy legislation.

They are normally registered with the Housing Corporation and as such are expected to adhere to elaborate codes of practice and are subject to periodic monitoring. The origins of individual associations vary but on the whole they come out of the voluntary action and charity traditions: churches; local community associations; voluntary organisations concerned about particular social problems and groups; pressure groups. Many people work for associations in a voluntary capacity. It is significant that the sector as a whole is still generally referred to as 'the movement'.

Generalising heroically on the basis of a general knowledge of HAs, one might tentatively suggest some differing strategies that they might pursue.

(a) *expansion* of the size of the organisation, measured by stock and staff, subject to budget constraints (including provision of reserves against risk factors) and a broad set of parameters about the sort of people to be housed, rental affordability, normal standards of design and management;

(b) *development* as the primary activity, with a large/growing programme of development work, including diverse types/tenures (for example, shared ownership) and possibly development on behalf of other associations and a leading role in partnerships or consortia;

(c) *social mission* in the form of providing for a particular type of client or local area, perhaps with special needs, and a strong concern about affordability and support services;

(d) *sticking to its roots*, that is, trying to remain a small, friendly, locally based organisation providing affordable housing, and not entertaining expansion and development which threatens these priorities.

If this type of classification, albeit simplified, has any truth in it, then clearly not all associations are behaving in the same way or effectively competing in the quasi-market. If an LA (or the Corporation) is choosing an association to do a general-needs development, it may find its choice confined to those in categories (a) and (b), and there may be very few of these that have a recognisable base in its locality. Category (d) might be common in all areas, but may not wish to tender, particularly on the financial terms available under the post-1989 regime; alternatively, it may tender with a naive appraisal of the risks to which it is exposed.

Category (b) may tender recklessly, from the risk point of view, in order to maintain its development team's workload. If the LA or the Corporation are seeking an association to do special needs work, it may find that it has effectively only one category (c) choice in a particular area, and this association may want different terms than those on offer.

Will providers compete on price? There is a problem of multi-dimensionality here, since 'price' may mean subsidy (per unit) or it may mean outturn rent levels. However, the Government has tried to set the subsidy rules to avoid competition developing in relation to rents, as noted earlier. The recent Audit Commission (1992) report explicitly encourages LAs to evaluate new provision options in terms of a 'cost per letting' criterion. A degree of price competition may occur, at least for general needs housing, in that category (a) and (b) associations will be structurally able to and possibly motivated to put in bids at competitive prices in terms of subsidy per unit; in this competition they will tend to win out over category (d) associations, unless these are strongly supported on quality or local accountability grounds by the purchasers.

However, it can be argued that most associations, including category (a) as well as (c) and (d), will be reluctant to compete on price. The priorities of a good housing manager are to have stock which is of a good standard and economical to maintain, easy to supervise, and satisfactory from the users' point of view. Voids and rent arrears must be avoided at all costs; this argues not only for the above, in order to minimise turnover and refusals, but also for rent levels that are not too high and unaffordable. In addition, future contracts depend on the general reputation of the HA as a good, responsible landlord; such a reputation could be tarnished by one problem scheme. These arguments will tend to lead to an approach to tendering and negotiation which emphasises the quality of design and of the management service back-up, and treats the grant level as a given parameter based on government norms. The minority of associations (for example, category (b)) which try to compete on price could be labelled as risky in financial and quality terms.

What more can be said about the *motivations of the purchaser*? The LAs as purchasers can be assumed to be motivated by a concern about meeting local needs, although the precise balance between the three types of need mentioned earlier may vary. They are likely to have a particular concern about homeless families, because of their statutory responsibilities in this area. Unitary authorities may have an additional concern about special-needs provision which would complement their social services responsibilities. The biggest constraint on their activities is the capital control system, so the Audit Commission is probably right in suggesting that the crucial thing to maximise is new lettings per pound of capital. In allocating households to lettings, LAs will be concerned that the most urgent needs (for example, the homeless) get access.

The motives of the *Housing Corporation* will be in part similar, although set in a wider geographical framework. In addition, the Corporation will have some goals relating to the creation of a particular structure of HA providers. This seems to include the creation of a degree of competition in many localities. At the same time, there are various pressures leading to the encouragement of a structure of fewer, larger HAs; these pressures include the desire to minimise the risk of collapse and scandal, and the desire to reduce the number of separate organisations that have to be dealt with and monitored.

Cream-Skimming

The final condition for success identified in Chapter 2 is that there should not be serious opportunities and incentives for 'cream-skimming', that is the selection of clients by providers on some discriminatory basis so as to exclude high-cost problem cases. It would seem that this is potentially quite a serious problem in the case of social housing. There is a real danger that HAs (and other providers like local community trusts or cooperatives, if they emerge) will not accept and rehouse a balanced cross-section of those seeking and in need of social housing. For example, HAs may not rehouse a 'fair' proportion of the statutorily homeless, and indeed there was clear evidence in the late 1980s that few did so (Bramley, 1989). Applicants who look likely to create problems as bad payers or bad neighbours may also be subtly discouraged.

Why does this kind of cream-skimming occur? In Chapter 2 it was suggested that the main reason was the lack of a price-discrimination mechanism. This may indeed be part of the reason in this case, because nominations do not carry individual price tags (although groups of nominations on schemes are valued and paid for, indirectly, in partnership schemes). But equally important are other factors. First, the urgency of the need for rehousing is crucial in the case of the homeless; except in some large cities where the regular supply of HA lettings may be considerable, there may be no obvious vacancy available on the right day or week. Only the LA has a large enough stock to have a steady supply of vacancies, and also only the LA has the incentive and opportunity to provide temporary accommodation. Other factors include the specialisation of HAs, which may enable them to say that the homeless or other household being nominated does not fit their particular view of whom they are there to help, and the type of stock they have. LAs as the landlords of last resort cannot be so fussy; they often end up having to put families in unsuitable high-rise blocks as the least of several evils. It is difficult to monitor lettings by HAs, particularly of casual relets, although recent developments like the CORE monitoring system do help in this respect. There has also been considerable attention recently to codes of good practice and training in relation to equal opportunities in allocations, and it would be fair to say that the situation has changed considerably in the past few years.

There are other examples of this kind of process, this time at the level of choices about investment. HAs have not been very keen to come forward and manage the worst problem blocks and estates in the council stock, for example. Since the 1988 Act regime came in, there has been a striking move of HAs out of the rehabilitation field, from 50 per cent to 20 per cent of activity (National Federation of Housing Associations, 1992). This seems to be mainly a consequence of the higher risks and costs associated with this kind of activity, which now have to be borne by the HA. If this is perceived as a problem, in terms of the wider strategy for urban renewal, then there would seem to be a pricing solution to it in terms of the grant system, together perhaps with some greater element of risk-sharing.

The Likely Impact of Quasi-Markets

Efficiency

How is the emerging quasi-market in social housing likely to perform in relation to our first key criterion, efficiency? It is rather difficult to judge at this stage, and the *a priori* arguments are mixed. The ultimate test will be empirical, in the light of research which has yet to be carried out.

We may take *productive efficiency* first. Competition is supposed to stimulate efficiency, and the new system does introduce a degree of competition. However, this has to overcome two countervailing costs, those of small scale and those of the processes of organising competition (tendering, and so on) and of monitoring performance. The new competing providers, the HAs, have to overcome an initial cost disadvantage associated with small scale. The evidence of major studies in the 1980s (MacLennan, 1989) was that HAs had significantly higher average unit costs; this appeared to produce higher quality in the sense of higher tenant satisfaction ratings, but how much this benefit was worth was difficult to quantify (and is in any case an allocative efficiency question). Furthermore, HAs have to pay a risk premium for their private borrowing which increases their debt service costs, relative to traditional LA provision (Pryke and Whitehead, 1991). If one believed in the 'small is beautiful' view of organisations, in other words that any very large organisation is inherently inefficient, then it could be argued that a quasi-market structure would be bound to be more efficient than the large city housing authorities, although probably not more than the smaller district councils only employing a few dozen staff. However, there are more direct solutions to the problem, including possibly decentralisation or, as is now coming, CCT (CCT had already been applied to construction and maintenance Direct Labour Organisations since 1981).

Inefficiency may arise both in the capital investment programme itself and subsequently in the ongoing management and maintenance of the stock. The quasi-market is better geared to producing efficiency in the first of these stages; as mentioned earlier, the purchaser has only limited opportunities to monitor the second, and the client does not have easy exit or voice options. Efficiency in the capital programme is not to be dismissed as unimportant; this was one of the main points of criticism of LAs in the 1970s, that capital programmes were poorly managed with endemic slippage and cost overruns, and of course that the products were often inappropriate (Department of the Environment 1978; Henney 1984).

There are some costs involved in processes like tendering and monitoring. It is difficult to argue that these are excessive enough to invalidate the whole exercise, although practitioners argue that the new enabling style of provision through outside agencies is costly in staff time relative to the number of units produced. This feature is not necessarily inherent in a quasi-market approach; it has a good deal to do with the small average size of schemes and attempts to navigate through or circumvent complex and changing government rules (Bramley, 1992). It should also be remembered that even with in-house provision tendering for contracts or evaluation of scheme costs may well be necessary, as would arrangements for monitoring the adherence to LA policies in management, lettings, and so forth.

There is another aspect to productive efficiency, which is the 'choice of technique' and the associated mix of capital, labour, land and other factors of production, which is generally distinguished from pure managerial efficiency. Some aspects of this are not much affected by the quasi-market: the ratio of capital to land, that is, density, is determined mainly by planning control, for example. It could be argued that the HA financial regime is rather better in the incentives it gives for balancing capital costs against future recurrent main-tenance, management and user costs, than the current LA regime (Hills, 1991). In addition, the very much higher post-1989 rents have made HAs much more aware of user costs (for example, fuel). But these are comments about particular features of financial regimes rather than the inherent merits of quasi-markets. Indeed, it could be argued that in this respect a purchaser provider split might lessen efficiency, by focusing too much attention on the up-front capital cost.

What bearing do quasi-markets have on the broader issue of *allocative efficiency* (that is, the amount of resources devoted to housing of different kinds, and its pricing)? Both the level of investment in social housing and the rents prevailing are largely determined by the Government, and feedback mechanisms from direct consumers or interested third parties are largely suppressed. Reducing the average rate of subsidy and having rents closer to cost and market levels is in general a move towards more allocative efficiency (for example, by discouraging underoccupancy). However, the benefits of this are substantially negated by the present form of HB subsidy (100 per cent at the margin for the majority of social tenants) and by the rigidity of many administered allocation systems. The lower grants and higher rents in the HA sector, together with the greater financial autonomy of HAs, have enabled private finance to be used in a way which increases the social housing output of a given public sector budget (the increase was about 15 per cent in the first two years, but may now be higher).

Output has also been increased by measures to stimulate the release of surplus public sector land at less than full market value and by the use of planning agreements to bring in subsidy from privately owned land (Bramley, 1992; Barlow and Chambers, 1992). On reasonable assumptions about the social welfare function this increase in output could be described as a gain in allocative efficiency. These measures certainly seem to represent a gain in cost-effectiveness from the public sector perspective.

Responsiveness

There are reasons for believing that the quasi-market will promote a more responsive service. First, most HAs are inherently less bureaucratic in style than most LAs. Second, they are single-purpose organisations and thus may be expected to be more single minded in their attention to housing services. Third, given the origins of HAs and recruitment patterns, it is plausible to argue that their staff are on average more highly motivated. The recent history of central–local relations have not of course helped to motivate LA staff. Fourth, there is no doubt that the threat of competition unleashed by the 1987 Conservative policy programme for housing galvanised many LAs, especially some larger cities, to improve both their act and their image. Better communications with tenants, decentralisation initiatives, and more responsive services in key areas like repairs featured strongly in the responses of these LAs, which were quite clear that such measures were necessary if tenants were to remain loyal and not vote for alternative landlords.

There are some counter arguments to consider, thinking especially about the future. First, the archetypal small, informal, locally based housing association is in decline, hastened by the new regime and competition. Instead, the typical HA tenant will have a rather large landlord operating in many districts with quite a large staff. Some will in fact be tenants of former LA housing departments which have undertaken 'management buy-outs'. The differences will then be less sharp.

Second, the HA tenant does not have the mechanism of accountability and redress provided by elected local councillors. That this mechanism is imperfect is testified by the need to decentralise as perceived by many LAs. But it is still a valuable check in the system. The mechanisms of accountability of HAs are by comparison much more opaque, particularly to the individual consumer. The benign qualities of HAs rely essentially on the goodwill of the people running them.

Choice

The quasi-market in social housing does provide some modest gains in choice, but these should not be exaggerated. At the level of investment decisions, the LA as purchaser can choose among several HAs which may well offer different styles of design solution, process and management. At present, however, the choice of direct in-house provision or procurement from a contractor is effectively not allowed. Neither can the purchaser do much to change the rent levels significantly. In the past, in the typical LA, the in-house solution might have effectively been the only choice, although this was less true by the 1980s. There were HAs active which the LA could fund. There were also housebuilders offering design-and-build package solutions and partnership arrangements.

At the level of the individual client, some widening of choice may be experienced. In particular, clients who are not in very urgent need may apply directly to one or more HAs, if there are appropriate ones, if they know about them and if the HAs have currently open lists. In addition, greater availability of shared ownership may widen choices for moderate-income households. Otherwise, the point that social housing clients have relatively little choice remains true, especially for those in urgent need like the homeless. Typically only between one and three offers of accommodation are made. Furthermore, the number of suitable or relevant vacancies available at the time of offer may be very small.

Equity

At least three kinds of equity problems seem to be potential problems with the quasi-market in social housing: cream-skimming; the rent–income relationship; and geographical inequalities.

The selection of tenants by HAs may well be such as to lead to a further concentration in the diminishing LA sector of households on the lowest incomes, those whose needs are most pressing, and possibly those who have or cause greater problems. If the relatively low take-up of homeless families by HAs that was characteristic of the 1980s continues, then this might indirectly discriminate against black and other ethnic minority households, and female-headed lone-parent households, with regard to access to the better, newer housing stock with the more responsive management and lower user costs. Along with other factors like higher rents and the Right to Buy, this pattern would reinforce the already strongly 'residual' character of council housing. This in turn could have both efficiency costs, in the sense that highly concentrated social problems may be more unmanageable, and further inequity.

The higher rent regime causes a particularly high-rent burden for moderately low-income households, those typically low-paid working households just off or only slightly on HB. This group also experience very steep marginal tax rates creating a virtual poverty-trap situation. Arguably these problems result as much from particular features of the design of the HB 'voucher' as from the general quasi-market approach. In other major social services (education, health) these problems do not arise because the voucher is universal and the service is free at the point of delivery.

The new regime has led to a shift of HA investment and activity from north to south, from cities to more rural areas, and (as already noted) from rehabilitation to new-build (National Federation of Housing Associations, 1992). To some extent these shifts were warranted by changes in the balance of needs, notably the crisis of homelessness in the south of England and the relatively limited supply of social housing outside the urban centres (Bramley, 1989). But perhaps the shifts have gone further and faster than intended, as an indirect effect of the new funding regime, particularly risk factors, and new methods of generating social housing using land subsidy. These imbalances again are not inherent in quasi-markets; they could be corrected by appropriate adjustments in grant rates and risk-sharing arrangements.

Conclusions

Housing is a case where the introduction of a quasi-market is taking place, but in a context where an actual private market predominates and where social housing provision is a residual sector. Major legislative and national policy change since 1987 has hastened this process, but the roots of the quasi-market structure go back to the early 1970s. The local authority role is shifting from that of direct provider of housing on a large scale to more that of enabler and intermediary, while autonomous housing associations have become the main providers of new social housing. At the same time financial and other regimes have changed significantly, reinforcing the quasi-market model significantly in some respects while, arguably, hampering it in other respects. The policies with the highest political profile have not necessarily been the ones with the largest effect, although psychological effects (the threat of competition) have been quite potent.

In this chapter the quasi-market model has been examined at two levels, that is, new investment and the allocation of housing to individual households; the management of existing housing stocks has received only passing attention.

There is no question that a quasi-market is developing in social housing, and many of the conditions for its existence and effective functioning are met at least in part. Competition between providers (housing associations) exists and is expanding, although there are some limitations both from scale economies and artificial restrictions. Potential competition is also highly significant. Currently there are two purchasers, the local authority and the Housing Corporation, whose relationship is an uneasy mixture of cooperation, complementarity and competition. The local authority is the intermediary rationing agency for most individual households, and competition is not translated into much wider choice for individual clients.

The information and transactions costs seem to be less severe problems than in the health care case, particularly in relation to the investment decision. The main problem area concerns quality of future management, into which both purchaser and client become locked and which is less easy to monitor. Management quality is critical in special-needs housing. This problem tends to lead to the practice of using a limited number of trusted providers, which negates competition; it is also the principal objection to the use of for-profit private landlords for social housing.

Providers face a range of risks relating to the development process, finance, the housing market, and the nature of landlordism, plus political risk from changing government policies and regimes. The two main responses are to go for larger scale (also limiting competition, choice, responsiveness and so on) and higher rents, which shift the risk to tenants and the government (through the Housing Benefit system).

Local authorities face tensions between different motivating forces, particularly between supporting their provider function and existing tenants and supporting new investment and new clients; the purchaser provider split which is gradually developing may help to balance these in a more satisfactory way. Associations are very varied and their motivations can only be speculated about. A broad typology of different strategies is suggested, which leads to the view that associations are not all in competition and will not all behave or respond in the same way. The more active associations will tend to maximise output subject to budget and quality constraints. How far price dominates the competition depends on the behaviour of the purchasers.

Cream-skimming is potentially a serious problem, based on the past performance of associations, and must be countered by monitoring and codes of practice. Like management quality, much depends on the goodwill of association staff and management.

The competitive structure is likely to bring some gains in productive efficiency, although there are offsetting costs. The likely tendency at the moment is to lower cost and lower quality; similar outcomes could have been achieved by other mechanisms, for example decentralisation or CCT. Areas of inefficiency include the current arrangements for obtaining private finance and the promotion of small scattered stocks of dwellings to be managed. The allocative efficiency gains are limited by central control over capital programmes and the current form of Housing Benefit.

While the greater use of assocations is likely to improve responsiveness, associations are changing in ways which will lessen their distinctiveness. The alternative accountability mechanism of elected councillors is greatly weakened. The gains in choice for individual clients must be seen as very limited; this is especially true for those in most urgent need.

Three equity problems are raised by the new quasi-market structure. Cream-skimming could well lead to a further residualisation of the diminishing council sector, with more acute problem estates developing and less opportunities for some of the poorest and most vulnerable households. High-rent burdens and poverty traps are a characteristic of the new system, although arguably this relates more to the design of the HB system than to the quasi-market *per se*. There has also been a pronounced shift of investment from the north, the cities and rehabilitation in favour of new building in the less urban parts of the south; if this is considered a problem, grant systems could be modified accordingly.

The overall picture is one where a quasi-market is both feasible and happening. It is still too early to reach firm conclusions on its impact. Some modest gains in efficiency, responsiveness and choice have to be balanced against some concerns about equity. The conditions for success are more favourable than in health, and perhaps quite similar to the social care case. One striking paradox emerges: in many ways a successful outcome, in terms of management quality, equity, and responsiveness, depends on the goodwill of HA staff and management and the survival of some of the qualities that stem from their voluntaristic origins. This of course is the opposite of the famous dictum of Adam Smith, about the motivations of butchers and bakers; the fear in the housing 'movement' is that 'marketisation' will destroy the motivational qualities that make the sector work effectively.

Quasi-Markets and Regulation

8

Carol Propper

Prior to the current reforms in health care, education and social care, local government agencies were delegated by central government to act as both purchasers and providers of services. Under the new quasi-market arrangements the functions of service provision and purchase have been split. Designated purchasers now enter into contracts with providers for services to meet the needs of the population for which they are responsible. The services provided, the level of output and the quality of that output are determined by contracts between the purchaser–provider pair. In the development of these markets, there have been calls for greater monitoring of the behaviour of purchasers and providers, and for greater control over the behaviour of certain types of purchaser and provider. In this chapter I examine whether further regulatory action on the part of government would improve the allocation of resources in the markets for education, health and social care. I use the term 'further' as even after the introduction of quasi-markets, government regulation of these markets remains high. First, central government sets the budgets of purchasers in all the markets. Second, in some or all of the markets, central government sets the form of the contracts between provider and purchaser, quality standards for entrants, terms of access to capital markets, rates of return on capital and some pricing rules. In this context, increased regulation means further actions of central government (or a delegated body) to control the details of the relationship between the purchaser and provider and to control various dimensions of process and performance. These actions could include control over the length and form of contracts, the regulation of provider prices and profits, regulation of entry and of the establishment of national quality standards.

The case for increased regulation depends, first, upon the nature and extent of departures from efficiency and equity in these newly formed markets and, second, on the distortions that increased regulation may itself bring. Evidence on the first is taken from the case studies presented in this book. Evidence on the second is drawn from the general economics literature and the experience of regulation in the newly privatised UK utility industries. On the basis of this evidence, this chapter seeks to determine whether there are any forms of increased regulation which are likely to improve efficiency or equity.

Efficiency and Equity in Quasi-Markets for Social Welfare

In a general review of the economics of regulation, Sappington and Stiglitz (1988) argue that the efficiency benefits of decentralised production relative to direct government provision are likely to be largest if certain conditions are met. These include competition between suppliers either in or for the market, an output which is easy to define and for which consumer valuation can be easily derived, and low transactions costs in determining what has been produced. Where these conditions are met, decentralised production will be more efficient than public (government-directed) production. Where these conditions do not hold, private provision will not necessarily be more efficient than direct public provision. These conditions are general to a variety of markets. In Chapter 2, Bartlett and Le Grand, argue that in the case of the production of welfare services, the motivation of the producers is a further important determinant of the gains from separation of provision and purchase. If providers do not hold the same equity goals as purchasers, the distribution of the final good may not meet society's equity goals, even if production is efficient.

Using these four criteria of motivation, information, transactions costs, and market structure to analyse the developments of quasi-markets of health care, education and social care, the case study evidence presented in ealier chapters suggests that the efficiency and equity gains from the introduction of quasi-markets are not equal across the different markets. In health care, there is evidence of the emergence of bilateral monopoly between the district health authority (DHA) as purchaser and the local provider of hospital care. Entry into the market has been limited; for example there has been relatively little use of private sector hospitals. Purchasers appear to have little information on the nature of production, process and output other than that supplied by the provider. The results are interim ones, for the imposition of a steady-state in the first year of operation of this market restricted the purchaser's choice of provider. At this stage, it is not possible to identify separately the effect of steady state requirements from the workings of the market according to the set 'rules of the game'. However, with or without a steady state, the current 'rules of the game' limit the extent of competition. These rules include the requirement that competition is limited to those services not associated with accident and emergency treatment, that providers earn a 6 per cent rate of return on capital and that providers may not cross-subsidise in their pricing strategy. In addition, evidence from the USA suggests that competition in the market may not be widespread. Hospitals tend to be local monopolies. This, coupled with the informational asymmetry between purchaser and provider, suggests that in the longer term competition for contracts may be limited. Purchasers and providers will seek long-term contracts, which will give the providers rent because of their superior information advantage. While there may be a one-off gain in productive efficiency, the long-term gains may be more limited.

In the case of the GP fundholders, there is evidence that GPs as purchasers are using the power given by having budgets for secondary care to improve the quality of the service provided to patients (Glennester, Matsaganis and Owens, 1992). The information of GPs is better than that of the DHAs, as they see patients both before and after care is received. However, while productive efficiency in the treatment of existing patients may be increased by the creation of fundholders, there are possible equity problems in the distribution of resources. Prices for different types of patient are to be set within broad bands. GPs may not have the objective of maximising the utility of each of their patients as their sole objective. If GPs seek to maximise their own profits, they have an incentive both to under-supply care to high-cost patients and to reject others who are high-risk. Thus certain types of patient might get better treatment than others.

In social care, the extent of contracting-out has been limited, and the evidence indicates that bilateral monopoly between purchaser and provider may emerge. If this is to occur, the evidence from the USA (see Chapter 3) suggests the development of long-term relationships between purchaser and provider, lack of competition for the market and possible lack of innovation in production.

In education, the freedom given to schools to manage their own budgets and the increases in parental choice of school appear to have been accompanied by an increase in productive efficiency (see Chapter 6). However, problems in the distribution of resources could emerge, as unpopular schools lose resources and popular schools are forced to ration places as a result of constraints on capital expansion. There is a danger that those pupils who remain in low-resourced schools will receive a poorer education than those in high-resourced schools.

In summary, there appear to be limits to the efficiency gains in health and social care, and problems of equity in GP-funded care and education. Could these failures be rectified by means of greater and/or different regulatory activity by central government?

The Nature of Regulation

Evidence that the establishment of quasi-markets may not increase either efficiency or equity does not necessarily justify greater regulatory intervention. Early analyses of regulation implicitly assumed that government intervention could, if properly designed, overcome problems of market failure. Recent research has emphasised that, in general, regulation cannot achieve social objectives without efficiency and/or distributional cost (Vickers and Yarrow, 1988). Regulation, like competition, requires information. If full information was available the regulator could simply direct the regulated firm to implement whatever production plan maximised social welfare. However, in practice, those being regulated have better knowledge of the production and/or demand conditions facing them. The regulator generally cannot either observe or infer this information from the behaviour of the firm. This informational asymmetry means that the regulator will not be able to control all aspects of the firm's behaviour. Further, in order to make the firm behave in a manner which meets social objectives, the regulator will have to ensure that the regulated firm gets greater rewards for production than if the regulator had full information. Essentially, the regulated firm derives rent from its information advantage.

The information of the regulator determines which regulatory strategies are most likely to be successful. In the context of the UK utilities, which were generally privatised as monopolies, Beesley and Littlechild (1989) have argued that if the regulator has access to good information about costs and demand, price regulation is likely to be possible without too many distortions. However, where information is low, efficiency is more likely to be increased by encouraging entry and so using competition as a mechanism to reduce monopoly rents.

The extent of information available to the regulator and the structure of the market being regulated are linked. In markets with only one producer, the transactions costs of getting information for the regulator may be considerable. In markets in which there are many producers, the costs of acquiring information will be lower. In addition, information is not static but dynamic, and deteriorates over time. If the rate of deterioration is rapid, say if there are rapid technological developments in production, information gathered in the past will be of less use to a regulator than in a market in which change is slow. If information deteriorates rapidly, Beesley and Littlechild (1989) argue that it is more efficient for regulators to encourage entry than to impose price regulation.

The extent to which regulation is able to meet social goals depends crucially upon the information available to the regulator. This in turn depends on the structure of the market being regulated. In turn, the presence of regulation will affect the development of the market. For example, the activities of the regulator may discourage firms from investing or may cause them to overinvest, depending on the actions of the regulator. Regulated firms will respond to the regulator, perhaps engaging in activity that will cause the regulator to take actions in their favour (so called 'regulator capture').

Finally, regulation is likely to have distributional consequences. Frequently, regulation is undertaken for distributional reasons (an example would be the regulation of UK utilities to prevent the monopoly supplier exploiting their customers). However, literature on the political economy of regulation has argued that regulation is likely to be endogenous to the industry (Peltzman, 1976; Becker, 1983). Regulation occurs because it serves particular interest groups. The introduction of regulation, the form it takes and its operation over time reflect a complex interaction between interest groups that stand to gain or lose from different types of regulation. Thus, for example, regulation introduced to protect the consumer may, over time, come to protect the interests of the producer.

Will Regulation in UK Quasi-Markets Increase Welfare?

It is clear that the impact of the introduction of greater regulation in UK markets for health care, social care and education will depend on what is regulated, the existing market structure and the information available to the regulator and the regulated. The research findings outlined above indicate that there are similarities in market structure between the quasi-markets in health and social care. Common to both are the emergence of bilateral monopoly and informational asymmetry between purchaser and provider. GP fundholding arrangements and changes in education, while taking place in different market structures, both appear to have associated distributional problems. These differences suggest that the different sectors will require different regulatory strategies. Given this, would greater central control over entry, price and quality in the emerging quasi-markets increase either the efficiency of production and/or the equity of the distribution of the service?

Regulation of Entry

Regulation of entry has been widespread in the American hospital and the nursing home markets. Certificate of Need (CON) regulations limit the expansion of capacity, both by restricting the growth of existing suppliers and by preventing entry of new suppliers. These regulations were enacted to limit cost escalation. It was argued that in a market in which funding was provided under third party reimbursement insurance, and where consumers of care had low price elasticities of demand (because premiums were generally paid by employers), moral hazard would result in overconsumption of medical care and cost escalation. One method of controlling this overconsumption was to limit capacity in the market. (In a competitive market suppliers would not seek to expand output beyond the efficient level. Lack of a budget constraint, because providers do not also insure patients and consumers have low price elasticity of demand, means output is expanded beyond the efficient level.)

Such restrictions on entry would be expected to increase the monopoly power of incumbents. If suppliers of health or nursing home care had profit maximisation as their objective, CON regulations would be expected to raise the prices of the producers already in the market. The effect on the whole market is less clear. If unnecessary duplication of facilities was prevented, then the effect on expenditure in the whole market would be ambiguous. The prices of existing suppliers would rise, but the growth in the market and so the increase in costs from this effect would be checked. The results from empirical studies of the effects of CON regulations are mixed. If CON regulations are treated as exogenous, the empirical evidence appears to show that entry regulation has little effect, or decreases costs by limiting plant size (Mayo and McFarlane, 1989). However, if CON regulations are treated as endogenous, the evidence appears to show that entry regulations increase costs (Lanning, Morrissey and Ohsfeldt, 1991). As entry regulation benefits existing suppliers, while harming potential entrants, the evidence that CON regulation may be endogenous is unsurprising.

In all the UK quasi-markets, central government acts as if it is a third-party reimbursement insurer. It provides funding but does not itself deliver care. However, the UK central government as a funder probably imposes a harder budget constraint than third party reimbursement insurers in the USA. Given this relatively hard budget constraint, the likelihood of excess capacity in the market appears small, and so there seems little case for further restriction on entry (subject to providers being of a certain minimum quality standard).

In fact, the evidence suggests that what may be needed are measures to promote entry. While the quasi-market reforms sought to promote competition on the supply side, this appears slow to emerge where the DHA is purchaser in the health care market and in the market for social care services. The informational asymmetry between provider and purchaser, fears of *ex post* poor quality and perhaps risk aversion on the part of the purchaser, and economies of scale or scope in production, mean that competition in the market is unlikely to be high. However, this does not mean that competition for the market would not be efficiency-enhancing. Nevertheless, regulation may not be the only, or the most efficient, way of promoting this type of entry. Franchising and contract design could be used. Possible methods to do this within a contracting framework, such as asset-leasing, 'operating-only' contracts and breaking up contracts into smaller components are discussed in Chapter 3. Removal of restrictions on access to credit for existing provider units may also encourage entry. At present, for example, NHS Trust hospitals are not allowed to borrow on the open market. However, if providers have local monopolies because of informational asymmetry and/or geographical location, restrictions on borrowing may limit the size of each individual provider. Credit restrictions may thus limit the monopoly power of each individual provider. In this case, they may prevent monopoly pricing and so operate to improve the distribution of resources between purchaser (and so the tax-payer) and the provider, but at the cost of a distortion in capital–labour ratios and so a decrease in productive efficiency.

If long-term contracts between provider and purchaser develop in these markets because of lack of observability of outcome and its quality, it is not certain whether encouragement of entry will necessarily increase actual entry. In the absence of better information about quality, encouragement of entry may be fairly ineffective. I return to this point below.

In the education market, consumers (or their parents) directly choose their provider. Equity concerns focus on the development of unpopular schools, with access to resources declining as their intake of pupils declines. Restrictions on new entry into the market, or on the growth of schools which are currently in high demand, may improve the flow of pupils to the low-demand schools. However, such restrictions would limit choice and so defeat the purpose of the present reforms. Such restrictions, implemented in the form of location-based quotas, say, would not appear to enhance efficiency. Another way to tackle this problem is to lift the restrictions on access to capital which currently limits the expansion of schools which are in high demand. Removal of such restrictions would promote choice and may thus reduce inequality in the distribution of schooling. The costs of this capital expansion would have to be met from increases in taxation and/or the use of fees unless low-demand schools could be closed and the funds from their closure were sufficient to meet the costs of expansion elsewhere in the school system.

Entry into the GP fundholding market is currently controlled by central government through the decision to allow a GP practice fundholder status. The criteria on which fundholding status is allowed tends to be financial, rather than on grounds of care provided. The equity concerns in this market stem from the incentives fundholders have to undertreat certain types of patient relative to others. Such incentives are the outcome of relative prices. Thus it would seem more efficient to deal with this source of market failure by means of price, rather than by entry regulation. This is discussed below.

Regulation of Price

The aim of price regulation may be to control the growth of public expenditure on a service and/or to protect consumers against the pricing actions of monopoly suppliers of this service. The intention of the price regulation of hospitals in the USA under the federally funded Medicaid and Medicare programmes has been to achieve the first objective; the intention of price regulation of recently privatised public utilities in the UK has been the second.

In the absence of complete verifiability of the quality of output, price regulation gives producers incentives to manipulate output in order to cut quality. It has been argued that the regulation of hospital prices under the US Medicaid programme has resulted in a change in the production methods by providers. Culyer and Posnett (1990) have argued that changes in the method of treatment (leading to decreases in length of stay) and changes in the type of patient admitted have meant a decrease in the quality of care, though the empirical evidence is mixed. Fixed-price schedules have also given providers incentives to manipulate inputs so as to maximise revenue. The precise form of price regulation in the US health and social care markets, and provider responses to it, are discussed in greater length in Chapter 3. The reduction of quality in response to price regulation is not only a problem in markets for social welfare goods and services. The realisation that regulation of price may be at the expense of quality has led regulators in the more recent utility privatisations in the UK to pay greater attention to the quality of services provided. For example, in the water industry, the quality of water is monitored by three regulatory bodies: OFWAT, the European Commission and the National Rivers Authority.

The UK quasi-markets differ in significant ways from either the UK regulated utilities or the US hospital and nursing home sector. In the case of the US hospital sector, the total Medicaid budget was open-ended prior to price regulation. In contrast, the UK quasi-market reforms have maintained the hard global budget constraint on purchaser authorities. In the US system prior to regulation, incentives operated to overproduce quality. In this case, a squeeze on quality is not necessarily welfare-reducing. In contrast, in the UK, quality was argued to be too low prior to the introduction of the reforms. The introduction of competition is intended to promote efficiency and so increase quantity and/or quality for a given budget. However, where quality cannot be easily observed, it gives suppliers interested in maximising profits an incentive for quality reduction, particularly if contracts are short-term. The adoption of price regulation of specific services where quality is not fully verifiable, in conjunction with a hard global budget constraint, may simply increase downward pressures on quality.

The possible emergence of local monopoly on the supply side in parts of the health care market and in social services could provide a similar justification for price regulation to that used in the UK utility industries. Price regulation might be introduced to limit the monopoly profits of the suppliers. Whether this would be welfare-increasing depends on the extent to which such regulation could be avoided by providers, its impact on the quality of services provided, and the effect on incentives for providers to engage in efficiency-increasing innovation over time. This, in turn, depends on the regulatory instruments chosen. The extent to which providers can avoid the impact of price regulation depends on the precise form of the price regulations. Under the Diagnostic Related Group (DRG) system widely used in US price regulation of hospitals, services are grouped into a relatively large number of homogeneous categories. A maximum price is set for each diagnostic category. Providers receive this price for each patient falling into this category. If there is any uncertainty about exactly which treatment a patient requires, this type of regulation gives incentives to providers to classify the patient as requiring a higher-price service than the patient actually requires. This is termed 'DRG creep'. To limit this type of behaviour, the regulatory body must collect information on the true severity of a patient's illness. This obviously has a transaction cost.

An alternative form of price regulation would specify a limit on the average price that the provider can charge, and then review this average at regular intervals. This is essentially the RPI-X method adopted for many privatised firms in Britain. In principle this method could encourage an efficient price structure if the parameters of the pricing formula were set correctly, but in practice the regulator is unlikely to have sufficient information to make this possible. Providers may negotiate contracts with a number of suppliers, making it easy to circumvent average price regulations. Contracts for different procedures may be of different lengths, which requires that the regulator is able to separate out payment for a service from the payment needed to maintain a long-term relationship. Different procedures may be subject to different degrees of risk, so that the regulator must be able to identify the average risk borne by a supplier. The average pricing constraint allows firms to undercut rivals in the competitive parts of their market, while recouping the costs of doing so in non-competitive parts of their markets.

Of the two methods, the DRG type would appear most useful for regulation of prices charged by providers in the health and social care markets. But the transactions costs of gathering information about providers' costs are high. To get information from providers, the regulator will have to develop close relationships with the regulated providers. 'Gaming' between regulator and regulated may develop and the possibility of regulator capture seems quite high. In addition, much of the information held by providers may be of poor quality, so of little use in implementing regulations which minimise the negative efficiency consequences of regulation.

In the short run, price-capping might also further prevent competition between providers. In the longer run, limiting the profits of providers might deter innovation. If prices are reviewed frequently by the regulatory authorities, the gains to a provider from engaging in cost-reducing or efficiency-increasing actions are only kept for a short time. Thus in the short run the purchaser (and so the consumer or the tax-payer) benefits. But if the provider gains little by improving efficiency because prices are frequently reset in line with costs, it will have no incentive to engage in such activities. Incentives to innovate are thus reduced. In some cases, providers may even have incentives to increase costs just prior to the regulatory review. (Vickers and Yarrow, 1988, among others, discuss the issue of optimal regulatory lag). Lack of innovation appears to be a feature of US markets in social care where contracting is used. It therefore does not seem desirable to build in further incentives to reduce innovation.

The current rules of the game already embody some degree of output price regulation which may inhibit competition. For example, the requirement in the health care sector that all provider prices must reflect a 6 per cent cost of capital prevents a provider from cross-subsidisation within a set of outputs and running loss leaders in order to attract contracts. While such a strategy would not be a long-run equilibrium, it might stimulate competition in the short run.

Relative to many other industries, technological change is not rapid in public sector services. So the decay rate of any information the regulator might acquire would be low. Price regulation cannot be dismissed on this account. However, the quality of the information available in the market is poor. This is both because providers are only now, as part of the quasi-market process, learning about their costs, and because the nature of the output is difficult to measure. Problems in identifying exactly the quality of output mean that costs alone cannot be used as an accurate signal of efficiency. Thus although information does not deteriorate fast, it is likely to be of poor quality and therefore of little use in a regulatory process that seeks to minimise the negative costs of regulation.

This discussion suggests that until better information about outputs and outcomes exists, specification of output prices by a regulatory body is unlikely to improve either productive or allocative efficiency in these markets. There are, however, two other sets of prices in these markets which could be regulated. The first are factor prices; in particular, the price of labour. Prior to the reforms, the health and education services were dominant, if not totally monopsonistic, buyers of labour in these markets. The separation of provider from purchaser in health care and the greater freedom given to NHS Trusts and to schools under the local management of schools system (LMS) to determine pay and employment conditions weakens the monopsony purchasing power of providers of services. Mayston (1990) and Le Grand (1991b) have argued that this weakening of monopsony power will lead to higher factor prices. If factor prices rise, the short-run effect will be an increase in costs with no increase in output. While there may be temptations to curb such cost increases for political reasons, such regulation of price would seem to have little efficiency justification. It would reintroduce a distortion in the price of labour. (If the price of capital is also distorted, a first best analysis does not apply and two small distortions may be preferable to one. However, it would seem preferable to attempt to remove or reduce distortions in the price of capital.) Moreover, given the political power of some of the labour employed in these sectors (for example, the medical professions), such regulation of factor prices would probably be open to regulator capture. The end effect of such regulation could simply be to transfer rent to existing suppliers of labour in these markets.

The second set of prices are those embodied in the budgets allocated to purchasers. Purchaser budgets are based on the population for which the purchaser unit is responsible. In the budget-setting process, central government implicitly or explicitly sets a price for each type of client for whom the purchaser is responsible, and for whom the purchaser has to contract to buy services. Any given budget will therefore embody a particular set of relative prices. Each set of relative prices will give purchasers certain incentives; changing these relative prices will change these incentives. One possible way of overcoming equity concerns in the education and GP fundholder markets is to change these relative prices in order to give purchasers an incentive to finance service provision for certain client groups.

In the case of education, certain children may be viewed as more costly to bring up to a given level of educational attainment. At a price per child which is equal across all children of a given age, providers wishing to attain certain average standards of output (for example, a certain average number of GCSEs per pupil) will be less willing to take these children, as they are more expensive to teach. Let it be assumed that these pupils are those who currently live in the inner city. If prices were altered to make the relative price of a child from the inner city higher, schools would have an incentive to take on these pupils. Since education for these children is to a large extent a joint product with education for other children in the school, the school would not be able to offer a lower service to these pupils. Thus the measure would result in greater equality of access.

Such a change in relative prices would only increase quality of provision for inner-city children if they, or their parents, were concerned with quality of output. If this was not a concern, an increase in the reimbursement rate for inner-city pupils would encourage schools to take on pupils, but the lack of a binding quality constraint would allow schools to drop quality and so to increase their profits. (A similar argument has been advanced by Nyman, 1986, to explain why an increase in the price paid for Medicaid patients in US nursing homes has not lead to an increase in the quality of care for these patients. For further discussion, see Chapter 3.) In addition, the success of the measure requires that schools do not face binding capacity constraints. If constraints are binding (assuming all efficiency improvements have been exploited) the improvement of the quality of education of one group of pupils can only be at the cost of reducing it for another group.

In the health care field, a similar measure would be to increase the capitation payment to GP fundholders for high-risk patients. However, unlike education, the service provided to one patient in health care is not generally joint with the service provided to another patient. Thus, unless the amount of care provided to each patient can be monitored, GP fundholders would have an incentive to take on these patients, but not to provide them with a higher-quality service. This moral hazard problem would mean such a change in relative prices would not guarantee higher treatment for these patients. In order to achieve the equity goal of equal treatment for equal need, any change in prices would have to be coupled with monitoring of fundholder behaviour. One way the regulator could derive information would be to examine specific cases or specific GP fundholders. An alternative monitoring arrangement, which may have lower transactions costs, would be to undertake some kind of yardstick competition in outcomes. The monitoring agency could undertake comparison of simple outcome measures across fundholders and non-fundholders, holding constant for type of patient and other factors known to affect outcomes (a comparison can be made within fundholders alone only if it is assumed that not all fundholders will seek to minimise the care provided to high-risk patients, perhaps because different fundholders have different objective functions). Those practices with below average outcomes for a given structure of clients could then be identified and, if these differences persisted over time, could then be subject to financial penalties. Nevertheless, it may be that the transactions costs of such monitoring outweigh the benefits of improved resource allocation.

Regulation of Quality

I have argued that many of the emerging features of quasi-markets are due to informational asymmetry between provider and purchaser over the quality of output, and that regulation of price is unlikely to rectify this. Is there a case for direct regulation of quality?

In fact, regulation of quality is already widespread in the health care, education and social care markets. It takes a number of forms and includes self-regulation by professional bodies, accreditation and inspection by government watchdogs, such as the Social Services Inspectorate and the Audit Commission. There may be some case for reducing the extent of overlap between the functions of some of these bodies. On the other hand, the existence of a number of regulatory bodies which operate in one market may reduce the extent to which regulator capture may occur. On top of these arrangements, a regulator could seek to define the production technology to be used by providers. This measure might reduce the transactions costs that are incurred in contract specification, as purchasers and providers would no longer have to negotiate contracts in which the production process was specified in detail. However, it is not clear that negotiation of detailed contingent contracts is a feature of an equilibrium in these markets. The high transaction costs that these negotiations impose mean that detailed short-term contracts are likely to be replaced by long-term relationships between purchaser and provider (see Chapter 3). Thus the gain of decreased transactions costs from the imposition of externally imposed quality standards may be short-lived. In addition, detailed specification of the technology of production would reimpose the constraints on choice of technology. The evidence presented for schools in Chapter 6, and by Glennester, Matsaganis and Owens (1992) for fundholding, indicates that relaxation of these constraints may have resulted in gains (at least in a once-off) in productive efficiency. Detailed specification of technology may also perhaps further reduce the incentive to innovate, so having dynamic as well as static efficiency consequences. Finally, such a measure would remove any flexibility of the purchaser to respond to local tastes.

In summary, gains from further regulation of price, entry and quality seem limited. In the case of education, a change in the relative prices in certain purchaser budgets may help reduce the extent of inequity in access. It may possibly prevent increases in inequity in the GP fundholding market, if the problem of moral hazard in this market can be overcome. However, in general, it does not appear that the efficiency of these markets would be increased by greater central control over price, entry or quality.

The problem of poor information and informational asymmetry therefore remains, particularly in those markets where the purchaser is large and not easily able to obtain information from its clients. There may therefore be a case for government intervention to increase the amount of information.

Government Provision of Information

Culyer and Posnett (1990) have argued that greater market-wide information on prices, volumes and quality will encourage competition and will decrease the informational asymmetry between purchasers and providers. In general, information is likely to be undersupplied in the present quasi-markets. Providers have access to better information than purchasers. This informational asymmetry can be used by the provider to extract rent from a purchaser. Thus providers have no incentive to share this information, as greater information would only mean purchasers were better able to choose between competing suppliers. This would lead to a reduction in the provider's monopoly rent. If purchasers are able to collect information, they have no incentive to share it if they compete with other purchasers. Sharing information would deprive them of their advantage relative to other purchasers in contract negotiations, and so would remove their relative attractiveness to potential clients. In social care and education, purchasers only compete to the extent that individuals may relocate to a geographical area where a better purchaser operates. However, in health care, there is competition between GP fundholders and the DHA.

If there is any competition in the market, the fact that the purchaser of services cannot fully observe the actions of a provider may also lead to provider overinvestment in certain activities. The reason a provider would do this is because these actions provide information. For example, let it be assumed that the quality of a hospital was judged only by the number of intensive care beds in that hospital. In order to signal its quality the hospital would have to invest in intensive care beds. At the margin, as none of its other activities could be used to signal quality, the hospital wishing to signal quality would overinvest in intensive care beds. If all hospitals behaved in the same way, the value of the information signal would decrease. All hospitals would have similar levels of the quality signal and the purchaser could not then distinguish between them. Each hospital would then have an incentive to further overinvest in intensive care beds (this argument is an application of an idea initially advanced by Shapiro, 1982). Such overprovision of a quality signal is inefficient, though rational behaviour for each individual provider.

Improvement of the quality of information may therefore improve efficiency and allocation in these markets. A role for a collector and disseminator of information implies that the body responsible for collection and dissemination should be separate from any single purchaser. This would avoid the duplication of resources that would arise if each purchaser sought to acquire information from a number of suppliers. The information would have to be made available in a form which minimised the possibility of identification of individual purchaser–provider pairs. Identification of specific purchaser–provider pairs may make these pairs unwilling to provide information. The argument for a super-purchaser body (that is, a body over and above purchasers) which collects information is strengthened by the research from the US human services markets. This evidence indicates that the establishment of contractual relations between provider and purchaser reduces the number and influence of independent advocates for end-users (for a review see Chapter 3). A regulatory authority whose aim is the collection and dissemination of information may counteract this tendency to the reduction/removal of the consumer advocate in the market.

Should the regulatory authority replace the various (overlapping) sets of quality regulators that already operate in the health or social care markets? The answer would seem to be negative, both because of the costs of replacement and because overlapping bodies may circumvent problems of regulator capture. By not becoming allied with one particular group in the market (provider, professional or purchaser) the likelihood and the extent of regulator capture may be reduced.

What type of information should be collected? Information on costs is not useful unless accompanied by information on the quantity and quality of services supplied. If costs are used to compare providers there is a danger that such activity will simply lead to a decrease in quality, unless good proxies for quality can be found. Information on prices must be accompanied by information on quality, for otherwise buyers will not be able to distinguish low cost from efficient production.

Conclusions

The evidence from the emerging UK quasi-markets indicates that there is considerable variation across these markets. Key differences exist in the technology of production, the relative size of provider and purchaser, information, extent of risk aversion and objectives of provider and purchaser. Thus the efficiency gains and the equity consequences of the introduction of competition in provision differ across markets. In the social and health care markets, there is evidence of informational asymmetry between purchaser and provider. This appears to result in lack of competition, in or for the market. In GP fundholding and in education, the informational asymmetry appears to be less severe, but the allocation of resources may not meet equity goals.

This chapter has investigated whether greater regulatory control of these markets would improve resource allocation. The general literature on regulation stresses the importance of the quality of information to the achievement of regulatory goals. The poorer the regulator's information, the less able will the regulator be to compel firms to achieve its goals. Further, the activities of the regulator influence the dynamic evolution of the market.

Given these considerations the chapter has examined whether greater control of entry, price or quality of output would overcome obstacles to efficiency improvements, and equitable distributions in welfare. The conclusions of this examination are that entry regulation would only transfer rents to existing suppliers and reduce incentives for efficiency. Regulation of output prices would have high transactions costs and would (further) reduce competition. A change in the relative prices implicit in the budgets given to education providers and GP fundholders may overcome some equity problems in both these markets. However, the nature of production of health care means that while a change in relative prices provides an incentive for GP fundholders to take on certain patients, it does not guarantee that these patients will receive higher-quality treatment. Direct regulation of quality already exists. There is an overlap between regulatory bodies responsible for quality regulation, but this probably acts to limit regulator capture.

In most cases increased regulation would probably not be effective in the promotion of either efficiency or equity. However, there would appear to be a role for central government in increasing the flow of information in these markets. An increase in information would allow greater competition, provide better protection for consumers and make it more likely that regulatory activity achieved its goals.

Quasi-Markets and Social Policy: The Way Forward?

9

Julian Le Grand
and Will Bartlett

Chapter 2 laid out the conditions which quasi-markets will have to meet if they are to succeed as instruments of social policy. Subsequent chapters discussed the application of those conditions to specific areas of policy, using particular case studies as a base. In this chapter, we pull some of the material together in an attempt to make a preliminary assessment of the likely impact of quasi-markets in welfare provision and to discuss possible policy implications.

The assessment is preliminary because the quasi-market reforms have not been in place long enough to permit the work necessary to make more definitive statements. However, as the quasi-market 'dawn' breaks, it is possible to discern some of the salient features of the landscape emerging from the mist. For those travelling towards the goal of a better social policy, some of those features seem to offer an easy route; but others appear to be more daunting. If only to facilitate the journey, it seems important to try to distinguish the easy from the difficult, and to offer suggestions as to how the latter might be overcome.

Chapter 2 set out four basic criteria against which the quasi-market policy record could be assessed: efficiency, responsiveness, choice and equity. In the same chapter some of the conditions required for quasi-markets to achieve improvements with respect to those criteria were specified. They related to market structure, information, transactions costs, uncertainty, motivation and cream-skimming. In what follows we summarise the evidence from our case-studies and elsewhere concerning the extent to which each of these conditions are being met, and, for situations where they are not being met, discuss some of the possible policy responses.

Market Structure

This condition requires that, to avoid monopoly, there should be many providers unable to influence bidding processes, the value of budgets, or contract enforcement. Entry by new providers should be relatively costless; and it should be possible for unsuccessful providers to 'fail'. Also, to avoid monopoly purchasing power, there should be many purchasing agents.

Of the areas investigated, health care purchased by district health authorities is perhaps the furthest from meeting this requirement. In the case study by Harrison and Bartlett described in Chapter 4, there were few providers and no sign of any potential competitor entering the market. There was just one major purchaser: one that was about to become even larger (and more monopolistic) due to merger with two other purchasing authorities.

As with any case study there is an issue over representativeness. The situation may be more competitive in other authorities. So, for instance, a King's Fund NAHAT study of the extent of potential competition among hospital providers in the West Midlands suggested that only one-quarter of them operated in areas where there was a significant degree of monopoly or oligopoly power, although these hospitals accounted for 38 per cent of patient episodes (Appleby *et al.*, 1991a; Robinson, 1991). However, this study did not consider the actual extent of competitive referrals, and therefore, as with our case study, any conclusions have to be speculative.

The extent of actual competition will depend in part on the willingness of patients to use alternative, perhaps more distant providers. A King's Fund Sheffield project is exploring the views of a sample of patients with respect to choice of hospital for referrals (Mahon, Whitehouse and Wilkin, 1992b). The results suggest considerable reluctance on the part of patients to travel, with 38 per cent of the sample not prepared to travel at all, and 36 per cent prepared to travel no further than ten miles.

Perhaps the best hope for a more competitive market to emerge in health care lies with the GP fundholding scheme. As the number of fundholders increases, the quasi-market has the potential for being competitive on both sides. Preliminary investigations by a King's Fund LSE study have shown that there is already a significant use of market power, with fundholders 'exercising the power of exit, exerting competitive pressure on hospitals and providing some erstwhile hospital services themselves' (Glennerster, Matsaganis and Owens, 1992, p. 5). This may be in part a function of the type of practices that were selected for inclusion in the first wave of fundholding; arguably these were among the more dynamic of GP practices and the ones most open to the idea of changing their referral patterns. Also, the problem, if it is one, of patients being unwilling to travel still exists. But at least it appears as if the potential for competition is there, and, in some cases at least, it is a potential that is being realised.

At first sight, social care comes a little closer to meeting the market structure condition than health care with the district health authority as purchaser. The case studies of community care by Hoyes and Means reported in Chapter 5 found the market structure to be in general fairly competitive on the provider side, with a combination of profit, non-profit and public providers. If the case studies are representative, they suggest that most areas are likely to have a number of competitive providers of residential care; and in domiciliary care there are national providers who can bid for local authority contracts (although these are few and not well placed to provide an individualised service). However, a tendency, also illustrated in the case studies, of social services departments to rely on familiar providers, means that in practice actual competitive pressures are likely to be rather less than a simple head-count of the number of actual and potential providers would indicate. Nor does it seem likely that, even if they wished to do so, social services departments will have the resources to encourage the growth of new providers, or, more generally, to stimulate the market in more competitive directions.

These conclusions are supported by a study of twenty four social services departments by Wistow, Knapp, Hardy and Allen (1992). They found that most of the authorities investigated were making very slow progress towards implementing the purchaser/provider split and hence towards encouraging provider competition. Also, while there was some interest in encouraging the setting-up of semi-independent providers, such as not-for-profit trusts for residential care, this was driven more by a desire to maintain eligibility for Department of Social Security funding than by a genuine interest in the development of a market. Indeed, most departments found the market model quite alien, and were interpreting their new 'enabling' role in ways that were quite different from that intended by central government.

On the purchasing side, there is likely to be some competition between social services departments and private individuals, purchasing on their own behalf or on that of their families; and there may also be competition between social services departments themselves, at least for departments in geographical proximity to one another. However, at the time of our interviews the studied social services departments seemed unlikely to allow competition to spread much further than this. In particular, there was little sign of the emergence of competitive purchasing by care-managers, and no sign of purchasing being pushed down to the clients themselves. However, subsequent research in a wider range of authorities has indicated that some departments are keen to move in this direction as quickly as possible (Hoyes, Means and Le Grand, 1992).

The possibility that competition in this area may nonetheless remain limited is supported by US experience of contracting in human services, as discussed by Propper in Chapter 3. There competition for contracts has been restricted, contractual relationships have been lengthened, provider and purchaser have developed close relationships and the incumbent has come to dominate the supply side of the market.

Chapter 6 by Bartlett on education and Chapter 7 by Bramley on housing suggest that these are the areas that perhaps come closest to meeting the market structure requirement. In education, there are both many purchasers (parents through the open enrolment scheme) and many providers (locally managed schools, competing with one another for funds). Moreover, at least in the case study, the purchasers appear to be exercising their choices and hence giving rise to considerable shifts in the application rates for different schools. That this in turn may be effective in terms of increasing the responsiveness of schools to parents' wishes is supported by the results of an Open University case study of three schools (Woods, 1992); this found that in each school a number of substantive changes had been made that were directly related to parental choice pressures. However, even here the competitive pressure is limited, most notably by the absence of appropriate mechanisms for entry and exit.

In social housing in terms of new investment in any one area there are two purchasers, the local authority and the Housing Corporation, although there are proposals to bring them together in a unified planning process. On the provider side, although new provision by local authorities is being actively discouraged, there is the potential for competition between housing associations themselves and between housing associations and private providers. At the level of the individual household, Housing Benefit helps to ensure competition among purchasers (the households themselves), and the provision by housing associations and local authorities is again competitive. Entry and exit also seems readily feasible.

What are the policy implications of this? On the purchaser side, it would seem desirable to encourage the types of reform that offer either the reality or the prospect of decentralised purchasers, such as GP fundholding for health care and care-manager budget-holding in the case of social care. This would imply a reduced purchasing role for large-scale purchasers such as district health authorities or local social services departments. This may restrict opportunities for economies of scale from bulk purchasing; but the efficiency gains that would flow from increasing the number of purchasers may make this a price worth paying. It may also create difficulties for good service planning; but a multitude of decisions made closer to users is more likely to reflect accurately their wants and needs than some overall view from a district planning office. Moreover, even with decentralised systems, central authorities would still have control over the funding formulae used to determine budget-holders' budgets, and strategic priorities could be built into these.

On the provider side, measures appear to be needed to improve the mechanisms of entry and exit, and to remove the restrictions on competition that presently exist. For instance, entry could be encouraged through government-subsidised schemes for providing training and start-up capital. More specifically, there could be 'incubator' schemes to allow for the managed birth of new enterprises; for instance, state sector managers could have a leave entitlement to start a new business with their job back if they fail.

Another method of encouraging entry is through franchising and asset-leasing schemes as discussed by Propper in Chapter 8. Franchising and asset-leasing would also facilitate exit, in that a provider failure resulting from management inefficiency need only require replacement of the management team by other managers, instead of the complete closing-down of the unit and the sale of its assets. Propper also notes that the principal restriction on existing competition in most quasi-market areas concerns the limits on capital investment for provider units; removal of these would go a long way to allowing successful units to compete more effectively.

Information

The importance of information for market efficiency was emphasised in earlier chapters. Providers must be able to price and to cost their activities properly. Purchasers must have accurate and independent information about the quantity and particularly the quality of the service being provided, so as to prevent opportunistic behaviour (moral hazard and adverse selection) by providers.

For all the areas explored, the information available to all parties – purchasers and providers – is currently in a highly imperfect state. Throughout the welfare area, providers are only just beginning to come to grips with the problems of costing. But the problems are probably most acute on the purchasing side.

In the case study of the DHA as purchaser of health care, the purchaser seemed to be heavily dependent on the providers for information; in particular, it had no independent mechanisms for monitoring quality. Although this has not been investigated systematically, this situation does not seem unrepresentative of the UK as a whole. Moreover, information problems do not seem to be confined to health authorities; the Sheffield study mentioned above has also been exploring the views of GPs on patient referrals and found a surprising lack of information on such basics as waiting times for different providers (Mahon, Whitehouse and Wilkin, 1992a).

Again, GP fundholding seems to offer better prospects in this respect. GPs have access to the best possible information concerning the quality of care: they can assess a patient's health before he or she goes into hospital and they can assess it when he or she comes out. Moreover, being medically qualified they are able to assess the quality of the treatment given (Glennerster, Matsaganis and Owens, 1992).

Our case studies suggested that social services departments acting as purchasers had little information concerning costs and even less on outcomes; they also lacked the necessary technology to process information and had little by way of resources to improve that technology. The extent of this problem has been confirmed by subsequent research in a wider range of authorities (Hoyes, Means and Le Grand, 1992). Wistow *et al.* (1992) found that most authorities had very little information about supply by either voluntary or private providers. However, there is some evidence that imbalances of information of this kind will not necessarily lead to opportunistic behaviour by providers. Common and Flynn (1992) found that several of the small providers they were investigating in the community care would prefer more contact with purchasers than they are actually getting. Part of the motivation for this is a need for reassurance that they are meeting the terms of their contract, and hence that they will be likely to obtain a renewal of the contract and/ or further contracts. Under those kind of circumstances, therefore, providers may have an incentive to supply appropriate information to purchasers which may in part offset the latter's relative disadvantage in this respect.

In education, the information gap between purchasers and providers is perhaps less than in other areas. Parents do have access to some independent information about schools; and they are better placed to use that information than, for instance, some patients are with respect to information concerning their medical condition. However, an information imbalance is still likely to persist, with parents being less knowledgeable than professionals concerning educational developments (and hence often excessively suspicious of those developments), and at the same time being possibly subject to promotional advertising of a misleading kind by schools. In consequence, parental choice may be based on bandwagon effects and changes in admissions patterns may not reflect the real educational quality of the services provided.

In housing, information about quality is a problem, although perhaps not as severe as in some other areas. Difficulties for potential purchasers are probably most acute in the assessment of quality of management, especially when the purchasers themselves have special needs or vulnerabilities.

The consequences of these information deficits may be serious. How are the purchasers to guard against opportunistic behaviour by providers if they do not have adequate information about the quality and costs of various sources of provision? How can they write appropriate state-contingent contracts, when they know little about the possible 'states of the world' against which they are insuring, or what should happen if they did occur?

The difficulty for purchasers of obtaining information on quality means that purchasers may become dependent on providers for information of their own. This was apparent in the health authority case study; but something similar was happening in social services, where adverse selection was avoided by purchasing only from well-known providers. However, as noted above, this undermines the otherwise competitive nature of those markets.

There is also a problem on information asymmetry in relation to purchasers' knowledge about new entrants as compared with that about incumbents. The quality of the provision by new entrants is less well-known than that of tried and tested incumbents and this may be one of the biggest barriers to entry (Mueller, 1991).

What are the policy implications of these information gaps? It is commonplace to argue that one solution to the kinds of problems created by imbalances of information in a market is increased government regulation: of entry, of price, or of quality. However, Propper in Chapter 8 has argued that this would be misplaced in a quasi-market context. Regulation of entry would simply reduce further the already attenuated competition within the relevant quasi-markets. Regulation of price, in conjunction with an overall budget limit, would probably increase downward pressures on quality and innovation. And, in the absence of good outcome measures, regulation of quality tends to concentrate on inputs or production technology, both of which discourage flexibility and innovation.

But if not regulation, then what? One possibility is simply to leave it to purchasers and providers to remedy the information gap themselves. However, this is likely to take a good deal of time and to require considerable financial investment in information technology; not an option open to all potential providers, and one which would put severe pressures on the budgets of purchasers. It may also lead to monopoly as purchasers get together to pool information.

In Chapter 8, Propper suggests that an alternative is to set up a kind of 'super-purchaser': an authority whose principal role is to obtain independent information and to disseminate it to the actual purchasers. This could be done by converting existing centralised purchasing agencies, whose role as a purchaser is to be diminished if the recommendations of the previous section are followed, into information-providing authorities. So, for example, the local education authority could concentrate on assembling and providing information to parents on the costs and quality of the education provided by different schools within its area; similarly, social service departments could provide cost and quality information to care-managers, as could health authorities to GP fundholders.

Transactions Costs and Uncertainty

Here the condition for quasi-markets to succeed requires that the institutional framework be designed to achieve as low a level of transactions costs as possible, taking account of the degree of uncertainty which surrounds those transactions. Purchasing by the district health authorities and by social services departments appears to be heavily reliant on the block contract in health or the 'generalised service agreement' in social services, thus reducing the level of *ex ante* transactions costs, but increasing the potential for *ex post* ones. The problems involved in drawing up such contracts in conditions of uncertainty over costs and activity levels are likely to increase as the system moves away from its inital 'steady state' pattern over the next few years. Purchasing by GP fundholders appears to be more varied, with all three kinds of contract (block, cost-and-volume and cost-per-case) being used (Glennerster, Matsaganis and Owens, 1992, ch. 5). However, transactions costs for providers of negotiating with a large number of fundholders may well be high.

In education, the increased opportunities for parents to express a choice of school in the face of continuing capacity limits resulted in a twofold increase in the number of appeals made against the allocation decisions of the local education authority in the case study area, with a proportionate increase in the transactions costs of operating the admissions system. In education, but also in other areas, further transactions costs are involved where providers engage in costly overinvestment for the purpose of signalling the quality of their services in a market with imperfect information (see Chapter 8). In social services and secondary health care, the transactions costs involved in encouraging the entry of new competitive providers are likely to inhibit the further development of a competitive market structure.

In general, the development of quasi-markets invariably results in an increase in the transactions costs of delivering welfare services, if only because of the increased amount of information required to coordinate the transactions between the now separate decision-making centres of purchaser and provider organisations. In addition, extensive new monitoring costs are incurred wherever the monitoring of quality of service provision is required to avoid the problems associated with information asymmetries between separated purchasers and providers. Such transactions costs, magnified where information is imperfect and activity flows are uncertain, will offset to some extent the potential efficiency gains associated with the introduction of decentralised budgeting, and enhanced incentives for providers to achieve productive efficiency. Although the quantitative impact of this trade-off is difficult to measure, the case studies have revealed that in many instances the transactions costs of operating quasi-markets can be substantial.

Transaction costs may therefore be a significant problem, and one which needs to be addressed by policy-makers. Possible directions to pursue include the provision to purchasers of expert skills and advice on contracting, and the provision of a similar service to providers, particularly small ones. Also, it would seem desirable to place a great reliance on decentralised purchasers, backed up by the suggested support service. The first part of these should reduce *ex ante* transactions costs, through disseminating good practice and avoiding the necessity to re-invent the wheel every time a new contract is constructed; the last should reduce *ex post* transactions costs, since decentralised purchasers are in closer touch with their clients than centralised ones and are therefore better placed to monitor contract compliance, otherwise appropriate policy actions will reflect the varying circumstances in each area of activity. In the study of health services in Chapters 3 and 4, for example, it was suggested that the degree of cost-sharing between purchasers and risk-averse providers will be a key element in the design of an institutional framework which will be capable of minimising transactions costs in conditions of uncertainty over future activity levels which can only be imperfectly contracted for. In education the elimination of artificial admissions limits would remove the need for costly appeals procedures, but may have adverse consequences for the diversity of provision and reduce the extent of competition between providers. Overall, the issue of appropriate institutional design to minimise transactions costs is one which will undoubtedly require a long period of experimentation and disruption in the evolving quasi-market system.

Motivation

On the purchaser side it is important that purchasers are motivated to fulfil the needs and wants of users. It would appear that this is more likely to be the case the closer purchasers are to users. In housing, for new investment there are only two purchasers, one elected, the local authority, one unelected, the Housing Corporation. However, so far as 'purchasing' existing housing services are concerned, the purchasers are the households themselves. In education, purchasers (parents) are probably about as close to users (children) as it is possible to be without actually being those users. In health and social care again GP fundholders and care-managers would seem to dominate district health authorities and social services departments in terms of meeting this condition – although care-managers, as employees of their departments, may face a conflict of loyalties of a kind that would not face GPs (as independent contractors).

On the provider side, as with normal markets, it would seem that for quasi-markets to be efficient, providers would have to be profit-maximisers. Otherwise they would have little reason to respond to market incentives for efficiency. A key characteristic of all the observed quasi-markets is the presence of suppliers who are not necessarily profit-maximisers. These include voluntary organisations, such as housing associations, semi-independent public bodies, such as NHS Trusts and LMS schools); and public bodies, such as local authorities in the case of housing. In these cases it would appear on the face of it that this condition is not fulfilled.

However, this would be somewhat misleading. In the case studies, most of the organisations concerned appear to be have an interest, if not in making a profit, at least in not making a deficit, in part as a direct result of the introduction of quasi-markets. Indeed it could be argued that to introduce a quasi-market in provision is a way of confronting bureaucratic suppliers (such as a teaching hospital) that were previously known to be loss-makers, but who were subsidised for political reasons, with a 'hard' budget constraint.

Moreover, there may be an efficiency advantage in the fact that profit maximisation is not the only motivation of many purchasers or providers in quasi-markets. For this might operate partly to offset the potential for inefficiency generated by the failure of the quasi-market to meet one of the earlier conditions: a competitive market structure. If neither purchaser nor provider are motivated by profit, they are less likely to exploit their monopoly position. This is an example of what economists term 'the theory of the second best': if one condition for efficiency cannot be fulfilled, efficiency may be better served by moving away from the fulfilment of other conditions, rather than trying to ensure that they are fulfilled. In this case, if the relevant markets remain uncompetitive, it would not be desirable to encourage profit-maximising behaviour on the part of the agents concerned; rather, if possible, it would be better to encourage their commitment to the public weal.

This argument is similar to one discussed in some of the American literature on non-profit organisations, such as Hansmann (1987). There it is argued that purchasers worried about quality may prefer to contract with a non-profit organisation, on the grounds that those who control the organisation either are directly motivated to provide a high quality service, or are constrained in their ability to benefit personally from providing low quality services by the organisation's rules concerning the disposal of surpluses. Our case studies provide evidence to support this view.

In short, other things being equal, in a situation where purchasers have less information about quality than providers, non-profit organisations may be more efficient than profit-maximisers, and purchasers may recognise this. However, it is also true that non-profit organisations have less incentive to minimise costs than profit-maximising ones, even if the latter are in a monopolistic situation; and it is possible that the cost-minimising gains from employing a profit-maximising provider may outweigh the allocative efficiency gains from employing a non-profit one. A highly wasteful non-profit organisation, however publicly motivated, may do a worse job of meeting purchaser wants than a highly efficient profit-maximiser, even if those in control of the latter make 'excessive' personal gains from the project.

What policy implications are relevant to this condition? On the provider side, most of the relevant provider organisations seem so far to be sufficiently financially sensitive for the quasi-markets to 'work' and there may be dangers in encouraging those organisations to be more profit-oriented. On the purchaser side, again the balance of the arguments would seem to favour encouraging the decentralised purchasers, such as GP fundholders and care-managers. Where such decentralisation is not possible, it will be important to have user participation on the relevant purchaser boards so as to ensure a better convergence between agents' motivations and user preferences. Such participation would need to be properly funded so as to allow the participation of disadvantaged users, for example, single parents, and to cover the opportunity cost of time. A similar argument applies to the funding of parent governor participation in the local management of schools.

Cream-Skimming

At first sight the problem of cream-skimming does not appear to arise in the case of health authorities or social service departments since their potential clients are determined by the geographical area in which they operate. However, in practice both health authorities and social services departments have to ration the services they will purchase and, as such any rationing system, this clearly creates the opportunity for cream-skimming. Also, in both health and social care, providers may cream-skim, particularly since, as we have seen, in both cases there is a heavy reliance on the block contract or on the generalised service agreement, both of which allow providers considerable freedom in how they deliver their services.

Cream-skimming is potentially a serious problem for social housing, with housing associations being reluctant to accept certain categories of possible tenant. There is an obvious danger of cream-skimming by GP fundholders in their selection of patients for their lists; a fear to some extent supported by US experience of Health Maintenance Organisations which have a number of similarities to fundholders (Weiner, 1990) – although as yet there appears to be little sign of this actually happening in the UK (Glennerster, Matsaganis and Owens, 1992, p. 33). For similar reasons, care-managers would also have an incentive to cream-skim.

In education, there are preliminary signs of cream-skimming in our case study, with successful schools reportedly setting up informal means of selection. This is consistent with Scottish experience, where parents have had stronger rights to choose schools than their English counterparts for several years. A study of admissions into Edinburgh and Dundee secondary schools (Adler and Raab, 1988) found that parents appeared to be choosing more effective schools, but also that there was a growth in inequalities among secondary schools of formerly equal status.

What are the policy implications? In practice it may be possible to rely in part on the ethos of service purchasers and providers to limit cream-skimming. However, there is likely to be a contradiction between this and the fulfilment of the financial objectives that they may have, whether these are profit-maximisation or simply breaking even. It would be preferable to try to offset the incentives to cream-skim, if this were possible.

There are in fact a number of ways of dealing with cream-skimming. One is to offer some kind of insurance to the purchaser or the provider, so that if they offer a service to a user that is likely to be expensive, they can shift the extra costs on to the insurer. The insurance could be provided privately, or could be offered by the government. An example of the latter already exists with the GP fundholding scheme, whereby if the cost for the treatment for any one patient exceeds £5000, the district will meet the excess.

The problem with this is that it undermines the incentive structure for the agents (purchaser or provider) concerned. If providers know that if they exceed their budget, there will be no penalty because the insurance system will pick up the bill, then they have little incentive to remain within their budget. Any incentive for economy, or, more generally, for efficient resource allocation within the budget, is reduced or, if the insurance system is comprehensive enough, eliminated altogether. The cream-skimming problem is replaced by one of moral hazard.

Now there are a number of ways of adjusting insurance systems so as to cope with moral hazard problems of this type, including the provision of a 'deductible' or of co-payment. Deductible provisions would require the agent to meet the full costs of expensive users up to a certain limit, after which any excess is met by the insurer. The £5000 limit for GP fundholders is an example of this. However, while this preserves the incentive to economise below the limit, there is no incentive once the limit has been exceeded. A co-payment system would require the agent to meet a percentage of the costs of any excess, while the insurer met the rest; this would preserve some incentive for economy, but would not completely eliminate the temptation to reduce the extent of co-payment by cream-skimming.

A second way to deal with the problem is to require agents to accept any users who present themselves for service. So GP fundholders could be compelled to accept patients; schools could be compelled to accept pupils. If the number of potential users for any one agent exceeded the capacity of that agent, then users would have to be selected randomly, or at least in such a way as not to favour the less expensive. There might also be some kind of appeals procedure by which both users and providers could appeal against a particular allocation.

The difficulty here would be to prevent agents from trying to set up informal or concealed selection procedures to bypass the allocation mechanisms. Agents could make access by potentially expensive users inconvenient; they could make the actual use of the service by such users uncomfortable, or indeed could simply skimp on the services provided to them. To prevent such occurences it would be necessary to engage in extensive monitoring of agents, which could be very costly.

Another possibility in the case of education would be to combine an open access policy with the removal of admissions limits altogether. This would remove the possibilities for cream-skimming, but in the long run it could further increase inequalities between providers due to the link between funding and the level of admissions.

A more promising alternative than either of these routes, discussed by Propper in Chapter 8, is to adjust the funding mechanism so as to eliminate, or even reverse, the incentives for cream-skimming. The GP fundholding formula could give an extra weight for patients on the fundholders' lists that fall into categories that might lead to a need for expensive treatment. Similarly, the formula for determining the allocation of funds to care-managers could be weighted so as to give more resources for potentially expensive clients; and that for schools could be weighted so as to attach more resources to pupils with greater educational needs. This latter idea underlies the Positively Discriminating Voucher or PDV (Le Grand, 1989), whereby education vouchers of a higher value would be given to pupils from poorer backgrounds so as to encourage schools to accept them.

There are two practical difficulties with this approach. First, it must be possible to differentiate potentially expensive users from less expensive ones, so that the formula may be applied appropriately. Second, it would be necessary to get the weights right. The extra resources attached in the funding formula to potentially more expensive users must be sufficient to meet the extra costs, but not so large as to reverse the incentive structure, thus penalising less expensive users.

One way of overcoming both these problems is to base the formula on a detailed model that predicts service expenditures on the basis of a number of identifiable characteristics of a potential user, such as age, gender, place of residence, socio-economic factors, past use of the service, and so on. The possibilities for doing this in the health care case have been explored in The Netherlands (van de Ven and van Vliet, 1990; van Vliet and van de Ven, 1990), which found that, among other things, current health status and past use of health services were good predictors of health expenditures. Reviewing this evidence and applying it in the fundholding context, Glennerster, Matsaganis and Owens concluded that: 'the "right" formula can only be derived with greater effort and care. However, it seems possible that the wealth of health-status information contained in the medical records which practices possess could be used in order to identify the parameters that predict future expenditure more accurately (perhaps just enough to be a disincentive to cream-skimming)' (1992, p. 33).

However, the construction of such models would take time and, in the short run at least, it might be necessary to use simpler identifying factors. For example, the value of an education voucher allocated to households could vary inversely with the average property values in the area of residence (Le Grand, 1989). This would have the advantage that it could not be easily manipulated by the better-off; if they moved into an area so as to take advantage of the preferential voucher, they would drive up house prices, thus lowering the voucher's value and defeating the purpose of the exercise.

A final, methodological point before we conclude this section. For reasons already explained, we have not been able to assess directly whether the quasi-market changes have actually improved efficiency, choice and responsiveness and equity. Proper research into that question will have to wait until the quasi-market reforms have been in place for some time. However, when that research is undertaken, some care will be necessary over any interpretation of its results – particularly over the question of attributing any changes observed to the reforms themselves. An illustration of the kind of problems that might arise is provided by the preliminary work on a SAUS King's Fund study of hospital Trusts (Bartlett and Le Grand, 1992). This suggests that the hospitals that were to become opted-out Trusts were already more efficient, in the sense of having lower operating costs, than their directly managed counterparts, even before the reform process started.

More generally, there may be a Hawthorne effect from the reforms, with any improvement in efficiency, choice or responsiveness resulting from the process of change itself rather than from the specific form the changes have taken. With respect to this it is worth noting that, although the hostility of medical practitioners to the NHS reforms has been widely noted, there has often been a positive attitude among NHS managers towards them. For instance, a King's Fund NAHAT survey of Unit General Managers (Appleby *et al.*, 1991b) found that 84 per cent approved of the changes, with 13 per cent having no reservations at all about their implications.

Conclusions

In so far as it is possible to make an assessment at this stage, the evidence so far suggests that social housing, school education, GP fundholding and community care at the level of care-management seem to be closer to meeting the market structure and information conditions for quasi-market success than community care, at the level of the social services department, and health authority purchasing. However, even here there are problems; and there is cause for concern in education, fundholding and social housing with respect to the other conditions, particularly those of transactions costs and cream-skimming.

The quasi-market reforms are in their infancy and it is too early to predict their long-term consequences. However, we have seen that it is possible to combine theoretical considerations with some of the evidence that is now beginning to emerge on the process of implementation to make some preliminary assessments – or at least to point to areas where there might be possible sources of concern. It is perhaps oversimplistic, but we could summarise the argument so far as saying the reforms that involve the district health authority as a purchaser of health care and the social service department as a purchaser of social care do not seem to hold out much prospect of gains in terms of efficiency, choice and responsiveness, but may not have much adverse impact on equity either; whereas the housing, education, GP fundholding and care-management reforms seem to hold out the prospects of real improvements in efficiency, responsiveness and choice, but, unless the incentives for cream-skimming are reduced, may have a detrimental effect on equity.

None of the above discussion is intended to suggest that any of these quasi-market changes have failed. They certainly have the potential for failing to promote efficiency and/or equity; but there are ways in which this potential may be reduced. As outlined above, these include:

- *An increased reliance on decentralised purchasers, such as GP fundholders or care-managers.* This would improve the quasi-markets' ability to meet the market structure, information, transactions costs and purchaser motivation conditions.

- *As a corollary, a reduced role for centralised state authorities as direct purchasers, but an increase in their role as information and skill providers.*

- *Adjustments to the funding formulae for decentralised purchasers so as to reduce the possibilities for cream-skimming and to provide incentives for the meeting of strategic objectives.*

There are two final points that should be made. First, an issue that has not been extensively explored in this book concerns the considerable transition costs of the introduction of quasi-markets. Any final reckoning of the overall impact of these reforms will have to take account of the organisational disruptions that they have caused and the costs, both financial and human, that those disruptions have created.

Second, on a more positive note, it is essential to remember that the systems the quasi-markets are intended to replace also had their inefficiencies and inequities. It would be unfair to judge the new systems purely on their own; their performance needs to be compared with that of the old. As is always the case in the analysis of social policy, the task of evaluation is finding the 'least worst' system: to compare not perfect systems but imperfect ones. After the reforms have been given time to work their way through, we will be able to assess them properly and to compare the new systems with those they replaced. Perhaps then we shall discover whether quasi-markets are the way forward, or a step back, in the development of an efficient, responsive and equitable social policy.

References

Adler, M. and Raab, G. M. (1988) 'Exit, choice and loyalty: the impact of parental choice on admissions to secondary schools in Edinburgh and Dundee', *Education Policy*, 3, 2, 155–79.

Appleby, J., Little, V., Ranade, W., Robinson, R. and Salter, J. (1991a) *How do We Measure Competition?* Monitoring Managed Competition, Project Paper No. 2, National Association of Health Authorities and Trusts)

Appleby, J., Little, V., Ranade, W., Robinson, R. and McCracken, M. (1991b) *Implementing the Reforms: A Survey of Unit General Managers in the West Midlands Region*, Monitoring Managed Competition, Project Paper No. 5, National Association of Health Authorities and Trusts.

Association of Directors of Social Services (1986) *Who Goes Where?*, ADSS.

Association of District Councils (1992) *ADC–AMA Housing Finance Survey 1992–3* (London: ADC and AMA).

Audit Commission (1986) *Making a Reality of Community Care* (London: HMSO).

Audit Commission (1992) *Community Care: Monitoring the Cascade of Change* (London: HMSO).

Audit Commission (1992) *The Enabling Role of the Local Authority: The Strategic Framework* (London: HMSO).

Barlow, J. and Chambers, D. (1992) *Planning Agreements and Social Housing Quotas* (York: Joseph Rowntree Foundation).

Barr, N. (1989) *Student Loans: The Next Step.* David Hume Paper No. 15. (Aberdeen: Aberdeen University Press)

Barr, N. and Barnes, A. (1988) *Strategies for Higher Education* David Hume Paper No. 10, Aberdeen: Aberdeen University Press.

Barr, N., Glennerster, H., and Le Grand, J. (1989) 'Working for patients? The right approach?' *Social Science and Administration*, 23, 117–127.

Barr, N., Glennerster, H., and Le Grand, J. (1988) *Reform and the National Health Service*, Discussion Paper No. 32 (London: LSE Welfare State Programme).

Bartlett, W. (1991b), *Privatization and Quasi-Markets*, Studies in Decentralisation and Quasi-Markets No. 7 (Bristol: SAUS Publications, University of Bristol).

Bartlett, W. (1991a) 'Quasi-markets and contracts: a markets and hierarchies perspective on NHS reforms', *Public Money and Management*, 11, 3 (Autumn 1991), 53–61.

Bartlett, W. (1992) *Quasi-Markets and Educational Reforms* Studies in Decentralisation and Quasi-Markets No. 12 (Bristol: SAUS Publications, University of Bristol)

221

Bartlett, W. and Le Grand, J. (1992) *The Impact of NHS Reforms on Hospital Costs*, Studies in Decentralisation and Quasi-Markets No. 8 (Bristol: SAUS Publications, University of Bristol).

Becker, G. (1983) 'A theory of competition among interest groups for political influence', *Quarterly Journal of Economics*, 98, 371–400.

Beesley, M. and Littlechild, S. (1989) 'The regulation of privatised monopolies in the UK', *RAND Journal of Economics*, 20, 4554–72.

Bishop, K. and Hooper, A. (1991) *Planning for Social Housing*, report prepared for the National Housing Forum, London, Association of District Councils.

Booth, T. and Phillips, D. (1990) *Contracting Arrangements in Domiciliary Care*, A Report of a National Survey by the Joint Unit for Social Services Research, University of Sheffield, National Council for Domiciliary Care Services.

Bradshaw, J. and Gibbs, I. (1988) *Public Support for Private Residential Care* (Aldershot: Avebury).

Bramley, G. (1989) *Meeting Housing Needs* (London: Association of District Councils).

Bramley, G. (1991) *Bridging the Affordability Gap in 1990: update of research on housing access and affordability* (Birmingham: BEC Publications).

Bramley, G. (1992) 'The enabling role for local housing authorities: a preliminary evaluation', in P. Malpass and R. Means (eds) *Implementing Housing Policy* (Milton Keynes: Open University Press).

Bristol and Weston Health Authority (1990) *Health of Bristol and Weston 1990*, Department of Public Health Medicine, Bristol: Bristol and Weston Health Authority.

British Medical Association (BMA) (1989) *Supplementary Report to a Special Conference of Representatives of Local Medical Committees on 27 April 1989* (London: General Medical Services Committee of the British Medical Association).

Coase, R. (1952) 'The nature of the firm' *Economica*, 4 (1937), 386–405, reprinted in: G. Stigler and K. E. Boulding (eds) *Readings in Price Theory* (Homewood, Ill: Richard D. Irwin).

Coleman, A. (1985) *Utopia on Trial: vision and reality in planned housing* (London: Shipman).

Common, R. and Flynn, N. (1992) 'Contracting for Community Care: Report on the Third Round of Interviews', London School of Economics, unpublished.

Coyte, Peter C. (1987) 'Alternative Methods of reimbursing hospitals and the impact of certificate-of-need and rate regulation for the hospital sector', *Southern Economic Journal* (April 1987), 858–73.

Craig, G. (forthcoming) *Cash or Care: A Question of Choice?* (York: Social Policy Research Unit, University of York).

Culyer, A. and Posnett, J. (1990) 'Hospital behaviour and competition', in A. Culyer, A. Maynard and J. Posnett (eds) *Competition in Health Care: Reforming the NHS*, (London: Macmillan).

Culyer, A., Maynard, A. and Posnett, J. (eds) (1990) *Competition in Health Care: Reforming the NHS* (London: Macmillan).

Davies, A. and Willman, J. (1991) *What Next? Agencies, Departments and the Civil Service*, Constitution Paper No. 5 (London: Institute for Public Policy Research).

Davies, B. and Braund, C., (1989) *The Local Management of Schools* (Plymouth: Northcote House).

Day, P. and Klein, R. (1987) 'The regulation of nursing homes: a comparative perspective', *The Milbank Quarterly* 65, 3.

DeHoog, R. Hooland (1985) 'Human services contracting, environmental, behavioural, and organizational conditions', *Administration & Society*, 16, 4 (February), 427–454.

Department of Education and Science (1988) *Top-up Loans for Students*, Cm 520 (London: HMSO).

Department of Education and Science (1991) *Local Management of Schools: Further Guidance*, Circular 7/91 (London: DES).

Department of the Environment (1978) *Value for Money in Local Authority Housebuilding Programmes*, Second Report of the Development Management Working Group (London: Department of the Environment).

Department of the Environment (1987) *Housing: The Government's Proposals*, Cm 214 (London: HMSO).

Department of the Environment (1988) *The Government's Review of the Homelessness Legislation* (London: HMSO).

Department of the Environment (1989) *Local Authorities Housing Role: 1989 HIP Round*, Appendix to letter from Department to Local Authorities inviting annual submission of Housing Strategy and Investment Programme (London: Department of the Environment).

Department of the Environment (1991) *Circular 7/91: Planning and Affordable Housing* (London: HMSO).

Department of the Environment (1992a) *Planning Policy Guidance Note 3* (London: Department of the Environment).

Department of the Environment (1992b) *Annual Report 1992: The Government's Expenditure Plans 1992–93 to 1994–95* (London: HMSO).

Department of Health (1989a) *Caring for People: Community Care in the Next Decade and Beyond* Cm 849 (London: HMSO).

Department of Health (1989b) *Working for Patients*, Cm 855 (London: HMSO).

Department of Health/Social Services Inspectorate (1989) *Homes are for Living In* (London: HMSO).

Dixon, R. (1991) 'Local management of schools', *Public Money and Management*, 11, 3, 47–52.

Dnes, A. (1991) 'Franchising, natural monopoly and privatisation' in C. Velanjovski (ed) *Regulators and the Market* (London: IEA).

Dreze, J. (1985) 'Labor management and general equilibrium', in D. Jones and J. Svejnar (eds), *Advances in the Economic Analysis of Participatory and Labor-managed Firms* (Greenwich: JAI Press) 1: 3–20.

Dunleavy, P. (1981) *The Politics of Mass Housing in Britain 1945–75* (Oxford: Clarendon).

Ellis, R. and McGuire, T. (1986) 'Provider behaviour under prospective reimbursement', *Journal of Health Economics*, 5, 129–151.

Evandrou, M., Falkingham, J. and Glennerster, H. (1990) 'The personal social services: everyone's poor relation but nobody's baby', in Hills (1990).

Feldman, R. and Scheffler, R. (1982) 'The union impact on hospital wages and fringe benefits', *Industrial and Labor Relations Review*, 35, 196–206.

Ferguson, B. and Posnett, J. (1990) *Pricing and Openness in Contracts for Health Care Services*, Centre for Health Economics, University of York, Occasional Paper on the NHS Reforms 11.

Flynn, N. (1990a) 'Maintaining the monopoly', *Insight*, 11 April 1990.

Flynn, N. (1990b) 'Stirring up supply' *Insight*, 23 May 1990.

Flynn, N. and Common, R. (1990) *Contracts for Community Care*, Caring for People Implementation Document (London: HMSO).

Forrest, R. and Murie, A. (1983) 'Residualization and council housing: aspects of the changing social relations of housing tenure', *Journal of Social Policy*, 12, 4, 453–68.

Forrest, R. and Murie, A. (1989) *Selling the Welfare State: the privatisation of public housing* (London: Routledge).

Forrest, R. and Murie, A. (1991) *Selling the Welfare State*, revised ed (London: Routledge).

Gaumer, G., Poggio, E. L., Coelen, C. *et al.* (1989) 'Effects of state prospective payment systems on hospital mortality', *Medical Care*, 27, 724–36

Gertler, P. J. (1989) 'Subsidies, quality and the regulation of nursing Homes', *Journal of Public Economics*, 38, 33–52.

Glennerster, H. (1991) 'Quasi-markets for education?' *Economic Journal*, 101, 1268–1276.

Glennerster, H. and Low, W. (1990) 'Education: does it add up?', in Hills (1990).

Glennerster, H., Matsaganis, M. and Owens, P. (1992) *A Foothold for Fund-Holding*, Research Report 12 (London: King's Fund Institute.

Glennester, H., Merret, S. and Wilson, G. (1968) 'A graduate tax', *Higher Education Review*, 1, 26–38.

Griffiths, Sir Roy (1988) *Community Care: Agenda for Action* (London: HMSO).

Gutch, R. (1990) 'The contract culture: The challenge for voluntary organisations' in *Contracting: In or Out?*, 4 (National Council for Voluntary Organisations).

Hansmann, H. (1987) 'Economic theories of non-profit organisations', in W. Powell (ed.) *The Non-Profit Sector* (New Haven, Conn. and London: Yale University Press).

Harrison, L. (1991) *Implementing the White Paper: Working for Patients*, Studies in Decentralisation and Quasi-Markets No. 6 (Bristol: SAUS Publications, University of Bristol).

Harrison, S. and Whistow, G. (1991), *The purchaser–provider split in health care: towards explicit rationing*, paper presented at 22nd Annual Conference of the Regional Science Association, Oxford, Sept. 1991.

Henney, A. (1984) *Inside Local Government: the case for radical reform* (London: Sinclair Brown).

Hewitt, P. (1989) 'A way to cope with the world as it is', *Samizdat*, 6, 3–4.
Hill, D. (1988) *Local Management of Schools* (London: Industrial Society Press).
Hill, D., Smith, B. O. and Spinks, J. (1990) *Local Management of Schools* (London: Paul Chapman).
Hills, J. (1991) *Unravelling Housing Finance: subsidies, benefits and taxation* (Oxford: Clarendon Press).
Hills, J. (ed.) (1990) *The State of Welfare: the Welfare State in Britain Since 1974* (Oxford: Oxford University Press).
Hills, J. and Mullings, B. (1990) 'Housing: a decent home for all at a price within their means?', in Hills (1990).
HMSO (1990), *NHS Trusts: a Working Guide* (London: HMSO).
Hirschmann, A. (1970) *Exit, Voice and Loyalty* (Cambridge, Mass.: Cambridge University Press).
Hoggett, P (1990) *Modernisation, Political Strategy and the Welfare State: an organisational perspective*, Studies in Decentralisation and Quasi-Markets No. 2 (Bristol: SAUS Publications, University of Bristol).
Holahan, J. and Cohen, J. (1987) 'Nursing home reimbursement: implications for cost containment, access, and quality', *The Milbank Quarterly*, 65, 1, 112–147.
Housing Corporation (1991). *Housing Associations in 1991* (London: The Housing Corporation).
Hoyes, L. (1990) *Promoting an Ordinary Life* (University of Bristol, SAUS Specialised Publication).
Hoyes, L. and Harrison, L. (1987) 'An ordinary life – or an imitation?', *Community Care*, 12 February 1987.
Hoyes, L. and Le Grand, J. (1990) *Markets in Social Care Services Resource Pack* (Bristol: SAUS Publications, University of Bristol).
Hoyes, L. and Means, R. (1991) *Implementing the White Paper on Community Care*, SAUS Studies in Decentralisation and Quasi-Markets No. 4 (Bristol: SAUS Publications, University of Bristol).
Hoyes, L., Means, R. and Le Grand, J. (1992) *Made to Measure? Performance Measurement and Community Care* SAUS Occasional Paper No. 39 (Bristol: SAUS Publications, University of Bristol).
Hurst, J. (1991) 'Reforming health care in seven European nations', *Health Affairs*, 10, 7–21.
Institute of Housing (1990) *Social Housing in the 1990s: challenges, choices and change* (Coventry: Institute of Housing).
Kemp, P. (ed.) (1988) *The Private Provision of Rented Housing* (Aldershot, Avebury).
Kestenbaum, A. (1990) *Cash for Care* (Nottingham: Independent Living Fund).
King's Fund Institute (1988) *Health Finance: Assessing the Options*, Briefing Paper No. 4 (London: King's Fund Institute).
King's Fund Institute (1989) *Managed Competition: a new approach to health care in Britain*, Briefing Paper No. 9 (London: King's Fund Institute).
Klein, R. and Day, P. (1991) 'Britain's health care experiment', *Health Affairs*, 10, 39–59.

Klemperer, P. (1987) 'Markets with consumers switching costs', *Quarterly Journal of Economics*, 376–94.

Knapp, M. (1989) 'Private and voluntary welfare' in M. McCarthy (ed.), *The New Politics of Welfare* (London: Macmillan).

Kramer, R. and Grossman, B. (1987) 'Contracting for social services: process management and resource dependencies', *Social Service Review*, 61, 32–55.

Kreps, D. (1990) *A Course in Microeconomic Theory* (London: Harvester Wheatsheaf).

Laffont, J.-J. and Tirole, J. (1991) *Cost Padding, Auditing and Collusion*, Institut D'Economie Industrielle, Document de Travail, 01.

Lanning, J., Morrissey, M. and Ohsfeldt, R. (1991) 'Endogenous hospital regulation and its effects on hospital and non-hospital expenditures', *Journal of Regulatory Economics*, 3, 137–54.

Le Grand, J. (1982) *The Strategy of Equality* (London: Allen & Unwin).

Le Grand, J. (1987) 'The middle class use of the British social services', in Goodin and Le Grand (1987).

Le Grand, J. (1989) 'Markets, welfare and equality', in J. Le Grand and S. Estrin (eds) *Market Socialism* (Oxford: Oxford University Press).

Le Grand, J. (1990a) *Quasi-Markets and Social Policy*, SAUS Studies in Decentralisation and Quasi-Markets No. 1 (Bristol: SAUS Publications, University of Bristol).

Le Grand, J. (1990b) 'The state of welfare', in J. Hills (ed.) *The State of Welfare: the welfare state in Britain since 1974* (Oxford: Oxford University Press).

Le Grand, J. (1991a) *Equity and Choice: An Essay in Economics and Applied Philosophy* (London: HarperCollins).

Le Grand, J. (1991b) 'Quasi-markets and social policy', *Economic Journal*, 101, 1256–1267.

Le Grand, J. (1991c) 'The theory of government failure', *British Journal of Political Science*, 21, 423–442.

Le Grand, J. and Winter, D. (1987) 'The middle classes and the welfare state under Conservative and Labour Governments', *Journal of Public Policy*, 6, 399–430. (Also Goodin and Le Grand (1987) ch. 8).

Le Grand, J., Propper, C. and Robinson, R. (1992) *The Economics of Social Problems*, 3rd edn (London: Macmillan).

Le Grand, J., Winter, D. and Woolley. F. (1990) 'The National Health Service: safe in whose hands?', in Hills (1990).

Loveman, G. and Sengenberger W. (1991) 'The re-emergence of small-scale production: an international companion', *Small Business Economics*, 1, 1–38.

McAfee, R. P. and McMillan, J. (1987) 'Competition for agency contracts', *Rand Journal of Economics*, 18, 296–307.

McAfee, R. P. and McMillan, J. (1988) *Incentives in Government Contracting*, (Toronto: University of Toronto Press).

McCall, N. Henton, D., Haber, S., Paringer, L., Crane, M. Wrightson, W. and Freund, D. (1987) 'Evaluation of the Arizona health care cost containment system 1984–85', *Health Care Financial Review*, 9, 79–90.

McGuire, A., Fenn, P. and Mayhew, K. (1991), 'The economics of health care', in: A. McGuire, P. Fenn and K. Mayhew (eds), *Providing Health*

Care: The Economics of Alternative Systems of Finance and Delivery (Oxford: Oxford University Press).

MacLennan, D. (1989) *The Nature and Effectiveness of Housing Management in England*, Centre for Housing Research (London: HMSO).

Mahon, A., Whitehouse, C. and Wilkin, D. (1992a) 'Patient choice and changes to the referral system – general practitioners views' Centre for Primary Care Research, Department of General Practice, University of Manchester, unpublished.

Mahon, A., Whitehouse, C. and Wilkin, D. (1992b) 'Patient choice and changes to the referral system – NHS patients' views', Centre for Primary Care Research, Department of General Practice, University of Manchester, unpublished.

Maynard, A. (1991) 'Developing the health care market', *Economic Journal*, 101, 1277–86.

Mayo, J. and McFarland, D. (1989) 'Regulation, market structure, and hospital costs', *Southern Economic Journal*, 55, 3, 559–69.

Mayston, D. (1990) 'NHS resourcing: a financial and economic analysis', in A. Culyer, A. Maynard and J. Posnett (eds) *Competition in Health Care: Reforming the NHS* (London: MacMillan).

Means, R. (1992) 'The future of community care and older people in the 1990s', *Local Government Policy Making*, 18, 11–16.

Means, R. and Harrison, L. (1988) *Community Care Before and After the Griffiths Report* (Association of London Authorities).

Means, R. and Hoyes, L. (1992) 'Information technology and the reform of community care', *Social Work Today* (forthcoming).

Means, R. and Smith, R. (1985) *The Development of Welfare Services for Elderly People* (London: Croom Helm).

Morrissey M., Conrad, D., Shortell, S. and Cook, K. (1984) 'Hospital rate review: a theory and an empirical review', *Journal of Health Economics*, 3, 25–47.

Mueller, D. C. (1991), 'Entry, exit and competitive processes', in P. Geroski, and J. Schwalbach (eds), *Entry and Market Contestability: an International Comparison* (Oxford: Basil Blackwell).

National Federation of Housing Associations (1992) *Housing Associations After the Act*, Research Report 16 (London: NFHA).

Nelson, P. (1970) 'Information and consumer behaviour', *Journal of Political Economy*, 78, 311–29.

Newchurch (1990) *The Newchurch Guide to NHS Trust Applications* (London: Newchurch).

NHSME (1990) *NHS Trusts: a Working Guide* (London: HMSO).

Nyman, J. (1986) 'Improving the quality of nursing homes: regulation or competition?', *Journal of Policy Analysis and Management*, 6, 247–51.

Nyman, J. (1988) 'Excess demand, the percentage of medicaid patients, and the quality of nursing home care', *Journal of Human Resources*, 23, 1, 76–92.

Peltzman, S. (1976) 'Towards a more general theory of regulation', *Journal of Law and Economics*, 19, 211–40.

Price Waterhouse (1991) *Executive Agencies Facts and Trends: Survey Report* (London: Price Waterhouse).

Propper, C. (1992) *Quasi-Markets, Contracts and Quality*, Studies in Decentralisation and Quasi-Markets No. 9 (Bristol: SAUS Publications, University of Bristol).

Pryke, M. and Whitehead, C. (1991) *Private Finance for Social Housing: Enabling or Transforming?*, Monograph 23 (Cambridge: Department of Land Economy).

Robinson, J. (1988) 'Market structure, employment and skill mix in the hospital industry', *Southern Economic Journal*, 55, 315–25.

Robinson, R. (1991) 'Who's playing monopoly?' *The Health Service Journal*, 28 March, 20–22.

Rochaix, L. (1992) 'Joint price–quantity regulation, in the market for physician services: the Quebec experiment' in *Incentives in Health Care Systems* (Springer-Verlag).

Sappington, T. and Stiglitz, J. (1987) 'Information and regulation' in E. Bailey (ed.), *Public Regulation: New Perspectives on Institutions and Policies*, (Cambridge, Mass.: MIT Press).

Schlesinger, M., Dorwart, R. and Pulice, R. (1986) 'Competitive bidding and states' purchase of services', *Journal of Policy Analysis and Management*, 5, 245–263.

Shapiro, C. (1982) 'Consumer information, product quality and seller reputation', *Bell Journal of Economics*, 13, 20–35.

Shavell, S. (1979) 'Risk-sharing and incentives in the principal and agent relationship', *Bell Journal of Economics*, 10, 55–73.

Shephard, Tony, and Associates (1991) *Shared Ownership and the 'Middle Market' in Social Housing* (London: National Federation of Housing Associations).

Shortell, S. and Hughes, E. (1988) 'The effects of regulation, competition and ownership on mortality rates among hospital inpatients', *New England Journal of Medicine*, 318 (28 April), 1100–7.

Sloan, F. and Elnicki, R. (1978) 'Professional nurse wage setting in hospitals' in F. Sloan (ed.) *Equalizing Access to Nursing Services* (Washington, DC: US Department of Health and Social Services).

Social Services Committee of the House of Commons (1985) *Community Care with Special Reference to Adult Mentally Ill and Mentally Handicapped People*, Vol. 1 (London: HMSO).

Stewart, J. (1983) *Local Government: the conditions of local choice* (London: Allen & Unwin).

Stigler, G. (1971) 'The theory of economic regulation', *Bell Journal of Economics*, 2, 3–21.

Taylor, M., Hoyes, L., Hart, R. and Means, R. (1992) *User Empowerment in Community Care: Unravelling the Issues*, Studies in Decentralisation and Quasi-Markets No. 11 (Bristol: SAUS Publications, University of Bristol).

Thomas, G. and Levacic, R. (1991) 'Centralising in order to decentralise? DES scrutiny and approval of LMS schemes', *Education Policy*, 6, 401–16.

Thorpe, K. and Phelps, C. (1990) 'Regulatory intensity and hospital cost growth', *Journal of Health Economics*, 9, 143–166.

Tirole, J. (1988) *The Theory of Industrial Organisation* (Cambridge, Mass.: MIT Press).

van de Ven, W. (1991) 'Perestroika in the Dutch health care system', *European Economic Review*, 35, 430–440.

van de Ven, W. and van Vliet, R. (1992) 'How can we prevent cream skimming in a competitive health insurance market?' in P. Zweifel and H. E. Frech III (eds) *Health Economics Worldwide* (The Netherlands: Kluwer Academic Publishers).

van Vliet, R. and van de Ven, W. (forthcoming) 'Towards a budget formula for competing health insurers', *Social Science and Medicine*.

Vickers, J. and Yarrow, G. (1988) *Privatisation: an economic analysis* (London: MIT Press).

Vita, M. (1990) 'Exploring hospital production relationships with flexible functional forms', *Journal of Health Economics*, 9, 1–21.

Walker, A. (1989) 'Community care', in M. McCarthy (ed.), *The New Politics of Welfare* (London: Macmillan).

Weiner, J., with Ferris, D. (1990) *GP Budget-Holding in the UK: Lessons from America*, Research Report 7 (London: King's Fund Institute).

Williamson, O. (1975) *Markets and Hierarchies: Analysis and Antitrust Implications* (New York: The Free Press).

Williamson, O. (1985) *The Economic Institutions of Capitalism* (New York: The Free Press).

Wistow, G., Knapp, M., Hardy, B. and Allen, C. (1992) 'From providing to enabling: local authorities and the mixed economy of social care', *Public Administration*, 70, 25–45.

Woods, P. (1992) 'Empowerment through choice? Initial findings of a case study investigating parental choice and school responsiveness', paper presented to the International Conference on Accountability and Control in Educational Settings, University of Warwick, April.

Woolley, F. and Le Grand, J. (1990) 'The Ackroyds, the Osbornes and the Welfare State: the impact of the welfare state on two hypothetical families over their lifetimes', *Policy and Politics*, 18, 17–30.

Wright, C. (1990) 'Money is always the problem', *Care Weekly*, 29 October, 10–11.

Young, M. (1989) 'A place for vouchers in the NHS', *Samizdat*, 6, 4–5.

Index